Philosophical Perspectives on Land Reform in Southern Africa

Erasmus Masitera
Editor

Philosophical Perspectives on Land Reform in Southern Africa

palgrave
macmillan

Editor
Erasmus Masitera
University of Johannesburg
Johannesburg, South Africa

ISBN 978-3-030-49704-0 ISBN 978-3-030-49705-7 (eBook)
https://doi.org/10.1007/978-3-030-49705-7

Cover illustration: Maram_shutterstock.com

This Palgrave Macmillan imprint is published by the registered company Springer Nature Switzerland AG.
The registered company address is: Gewerbestrasse 11, 6330 Cham, Switzerland

I dedicate this book to all individuals who are concerned with the cause of a peaceful resolution of land redistribution and reform in Africa. I pray that those efforts will not go for naught.

The book is also a remembrance of my late father, Mr. Martin Masitera, who was always troubled by the unsettled expropriations of land in Zimbabwe and which always made him question the presence of humanity in the land redistribution. In a way, this book acts as a means to responding to his questions, and I hope that the contributions somehow come close to his expectations.

I also dedicate this book to my late mother, Felistas Bwanya Masitera, a women of high moral integrity, who was always committed to the upliftment of humanity.

Through this book I also remember my late younger brother Daniel Masitera and my late daughter Anotidaishe Masitera. You guys left this world in your innocents. May the innocence of the young be the guiding light in enlightening individuals in the search for a lasting resolution to the land redistribution debacle in Africa and the world at large.

Acknowledgements

I am grateful to the support I have received from the University of Johannesburg Philosophy Department for the support they have offered me during my stay as a Postdoctoral Fellow in the department and during the period of working on the book.

In addition, it will be unjust not to express gratitude to the university's Postdoctoral Research Office (and indeed to the officers and administrators in that office) who have managed funds that aided me in carrying out this research. The Fellowship (UJ Global Excellence and Stature –GES) has been of particular assistance to both my upkeep and for facilitating some aspects related to this book project.

To ignore mentioning the role that Professor Thaddeus Metz played during this period will be grossly unfair. Metz was my hosting professor and was responsible for overseeing my academic grooming and growth at UJ for the period 2018–2020. His expert ideas and encouragement have been invaluable to the ultimate realization of the book. Thank you very much Professor; may you continue the good work of grooming future African scholars.

I would also like to express my gratitude to the Great Zimbabwe University authorities, in particular the Department of Philosophy and Religious Studies for granting me the study leave to undertake a Postdoctoral Fellowship at the University of Johannesburg.

My immediate family is worth mentioning as well for they gave me space and time to work on this. Thank you Lindah, Anesu, Anopaishe, and Anashe Masitera for understanding that it was a worthy cause for me to work on this project.

Lastly, my appreciation goes to all those who have contributed to the book through chapter contributions, through reviewing and through the publication of this book. You guys are just wonderful, *Thank you, ngiyabonga, ndatenda chose, merci mes amis*. I cannot mention names since you are too many I hope you forgive me for thanking you in mass!

Contents

Notes on Contributors

Aderonke E. Adegbite is a Lawyer with a PhD in Law (2018) from the University of Ibadan Nigeria. She is presently a Senior Lecturer and the Head of Department, Private and Business Law, Lead City University, Oyo State Nigeria. Her research interest covers Private Law (Children), African International Law, Conflicts in Development Rules and African Customary Law. She is also interested in Yoruba living philosophies, especially those based on conceptions of the divinity and deities. She was a Visiting Fellow at the African Studies Centre Leiden April–June 2019. She has also participated in several other international and domestic conferences on children, minority rights, development and culture among others. She has publications in both local and international journals.

Christopher Allsobrook is the Director of the Centre for Leadership Ethics in Africa (CLEA) at the University of Fort Hare. He also leads the Social Sciences and Humanities Research Niche in 'Democracy, Heritage and Citizenship'" at Fort Hare. He is a founding member of the national African Political Theory Association and an associate editor of the journal *Theoria*. His research background is in African Political Philosophy, Critical Theory and Intellectual History, and his current projects include Justifications for Colonialism, Customary Rights Recognition and Land Reform.

Munamato Chemhuru is an Alexander von Humboldt Fellow in the department of Philosophy and Systematic Pedagogics at the Katholische Universität Eichstätt-Ingolstadt, KU, Eichstätt, Germany (2020–2022); a Senior Lecturer in Philosophy at Great Zimbabwe University; and a Senior Research Associate in Philosophy in the Faculty of Humanities at the University of Johannesburg from 2018–2020. His research interests are in the area of African Environmental Ethics. He has edited a book, *African Environmental Ethics: A Critical Reader* (2019).

Yolandi M. Coetser graduated with a DLitt et Phil in Philosophy from the University of Johannesburg in 2018. Her research focus is largely social philosophy, focusing specifically on ethical approaches to animals and the environment. She is currently a Postdoctoral Research Fellow at the University of South Africa, as well as a Philosophy Lecturer at St John Vianney Seminary.

Ephraim Taurai Gwaravanda is a Senior Lecturer in Philosophy in the Department of Philosophy and Religious Studies at Great Zimbabwe University. He has published articles in *Educational Review* , *Journal of Black Studies* and *Alternation.* He has also published book chapters with *Routledge*, *Springer* and *Palgrave Macmillan.* His research interests are in Logic, Epistemology, African Philosophy and Philosophy of Law.

Joseph Pardon Hungwe is a Postdoctoral Research Fellow at the University of South Africa (Unisa) in the Education Faculty. A PhD holder in Education from the University of Johannesburg, he has interests in researching and publishing on Internationalization and Continentalism of Higher Education in Africa, Contextualization of Critical Thinking, Student Protests and Violence, Land Reform in Africa, Decolonization and Epistemic Justice, Ethnic Imperialism and Social Justice. Hungwe has vast experience in lecturing in higher education institutions in Zimbabwe and South Africa.

Nolubabalo Lulu Magam has an undergraduate degree in Peace Studies, a Master's in International Relations from the North West University (South Africa) and a PhD in International Relations from the University of KwaZulu-Natal (South Africa). Magam is a Political Science and Conflict Transformation and Peace Studies Lecturer at the University of KwaZulu-Natal, South Africa, and has taught Political Science and

International Relations at the University of Pretoria (South Africa) and North West University (South Africa). She has published in the area of alternative energy and climate change adaptation as a means to peace and security; immigration policies in South Africa, and her recent publication is titled 'Frustration-Aggression, Afrophobia and the Psycho-Social Consequences of Corruption in South Africa'. Nolubabalo Lulu Magam is currently interested in exploring the potential of paradiplomacy in Africa's development. Her PhD thesis focused on paradiplomacy in South Africa from a constructivist perspective looking into the role of interest and identity in facilitating paradiplomatic activities.

Dennis Masaka is a holder of a PhD in Philosophy and a Senior Lecturer in Philosophy at Great Zimbabwe University in Zimbabwe. He is also a Research Fellow in the Department of Philosophy at the University of the Free State, Bloemfontein, South Africa. He has published papers in journals that include *South African Journal of Philosophy*, *Philosophical Papers*, *African Identities Journal*, *Journal of Black Studies*, *Education as Change*, *African Study Monographs*, *Journal of Negro Education*, *Theoria: A Journal of Social and Political Theory*, *Alternation Journal*, *Journal on African Philosophy* and *CODESRIA Bulletin*. His areas of interest include Philosophy of Liberation and African Philosophy.

Erasmus Masitera is a postdoctoral research fellow at the University of Johannesburg, South Africa, and is a lecturer in Philosophy at the Great Zimbabwe University, Masvingo, Zimbabwe. His research area oscillates on connections of Ethics, Ubuntu, land reform, social justice and related issues.

Bernard Matolino is an Associate Professor in Philosophy at the University of KwaZulu-Natal. His most recent book is *Afro-Communitarian Democracy*.

Thaddeus Metz is Distinguished Professor of Philosophy at the University of Johannesburg (2020–2024). Author of more than 250 published works, he is particularly known for having analytically articulated an African moral theory, applied it to a variety of ethical and political controversies, compared it to East Asian and Western moral perspectives, and defended it as preferable to them. His next book, *A Relational Moral Theory: African Contributions to Global Ethical Thought*, is to be published soon.

Motsamai Molefe is a Senior Researcher at the Centre for Leadership Ethics in Africa (CLEA) at the University of Fort Hare. He specializes in African Philosophy, Moral Philosophy, Social and Political Philosophy. He is the author of *An African Philosophy of Personhood, Morality and Politics* (2019, Palgrave Macmillan) and *African Personhood and Applied Ethics* (2020, NISC).

Mbhekeni Sabelo Nkosi is in the Department of Philosophy, and is also a Researcher in the School of Public Health at the University of the Western Cape (UWC), South Africa.

Mark Rathbone is an associate professor at the Faculty of Economic Sciences, North-West University, Potchefstroom.

Anné Hendrik Verhoef is Professor of philosophy at the Faculty of Humanities at the North-West University's Potchefstroom Campus. He studied at the University of Stellenbosch and at the Catholic University of Leuven in Belgium. His philosophical interests are in the philosophy of religion, metaphysics, the philosophy of Paul Ricoeur, hermeneutics, ethics, and the philosophy of happiness. His research focuses mainly on transcendence and the transcendent in contemporary culture, and its relation to ethics, politics, meaning of life and happiness. He is the author/co-author of various chapters in books and articles in national and international scientific journals and conference papers. He is the associate editor of the academic journal *Transformation in Higher Education* and he is a rated NRF researcher.

Rodwell Kumbirai Wuta is currently employed on a full-time basis as a high school teacher in Zimbabwe since 1999. Kumbirai is also a Part-Time Lecturer at Great Zimbabwe University teaching modules in Philosophy of Education at both Bachelor's and Master's Levels. He is a PhD candidate in Philosophy of Education at the Great Zimbabwe University. Currently, Kumbirai is working on several book projects and on research articles for possible publication with local, regional and international journal and publishing houses. His research focus is philosophy that addresses issues that are mainly situated within the domain of education and beyond.

1

Thinking about Land Reform in Southern Africa: The Introduction

Erasmus Masitera

Different African states have dealt with the lkand reform issue differently. The same applies to ideas on addressing skewed land reform that have also been proffered by scholars. These perceptions emanate from the different African political, social and economic environments; in fact the different circumstances assisted in the shaping of the different theoretical and practical responses to the land challenges. For note is the fact that land distribution in almost all African states—with the exception of Ethiopia, Eretria (which was part of Ethiopia then) and Liberia[1]—followed the Western distributive pattern. The Western distributive system was established at the colonisation of Africa by Western countries. The Western distributive pattern was skewed in favour of the colonialists (colonial countries, race and individuals). This has not only been unfair and/or unjust on the part of the local inhabitants, but marked the end of the locals' land distributive systems in favour of the colonialists' own. In

[1] These three countries were never colonised.

E. Masitera (✉)
University of Johannesburg, Johannesburg, South Africa

E. Masitera (ed.), *Philosophical Perspectives on Land Reform in Southern Africa*,
https://doi.org/10.1007/978-3-030-49705-7_1

that sense the colonial distributive system was not only foreign but was imposed on the locals. The imposition and disregarding of the locals' land tenure systems constitute the unfairness and injustice that the colonial distributive arrangement brought.

In regard to views on skewed colonial land distributions, there is a general agreement that considers that arrangement as unjust, unfair and out-dated. By out-dated, I mean that is the land arrangement is out of touch with contemporary African interests. The interest of equitable distribution of resources burdens and benefits linked to land ownership and use. Connected to this is that the colonial framework is unjust;[2] unjust in that it disregarded the political, social and economic systems of the locals. In addition, there was the establishment of deprivations, discriminations, social exclusions and violation of the natives' rights (Thomas 2003, 695; Wuriga 2008, 5; Openshaw and Terry 2015, 73). The establishment of unjust land distributions lead to vulnerability of the locals especially abuse, exploitation and manipulation on farms, on mines and in other activities that occurred on land (van Onselen 1976, 91).

In as much as abuse and exploitations directly coming from unjust practices, the two are also connected to unfair treatment of individuals and groups that have suffered at the hands of colonial skewed land distribution. Unfair as a social dimension refers to biases and unequal treatment of people (Boss 2008, 582), in some cases this is manifested in racism or some other form of exclusion related to favouritism. In the context under discussion, my concern is on land distribution, in that sense colonialism produced unequal distribution of land in that it favoured ownership and use that was tilted towards the colonialists. As if that were not enough the colonial administrations always set aside financial funds to support colonialists activities while nothing or very little was reserved for the colonised (Marongwe 2007, 29; Obeng-Odoom 2012, 162–163). All this increased the gap and the exclusion of the natives from the settlers.

In light of the mentioned, there is a general agreement among African populace, particularly in Southern Africa, that there is need to revisit and

[2] Here I use the term unjust in a broader sense to include unfair and unequal distributions.

rework the land distributive framework so as to respond to contemporary African interests.

What are these contemporary African interests? This is a loaded question, which I think cannot be answered in one chapter and in one book like this one. However, I note that what is contemplated by African scholars who contributed to this work is that justice, fairness, stability, inclusivity, prosperity and harmony ought to be achieved. Justice for the scholars is a situation that promotes fair access and use of land, non-discriminatory prosperity for all and maintaining peace. In that sense, thought provoking views are forwarded by the contributors who are adding a voice to the thinking that have already been proffered on land reform Southern Africa.

The views forwarded address pertinent questions to thoughts about and on issues that are related to land reform. The questions are within the ontological and related epistemological realms. These questions are as follows, though not limited to these: What are some philosophical thoughts on land as the very life of Africans? How can philosophy be relevant to the issue of humans and resolving the land question in Africa? What are some of the ethical considerations on land reform in an African context? Which mechanisms should be used in addressing past injustices and promoting justice in the present and in the future in regard to land reform and redistribution? Apart from these questions, I note that the contributors in this book respond to these questions by directing their discussions to themes that address issues that have to do with identity, compensation, rights, justice, restitution, reconciliation, history on and of colonial land distribution and the role of the local community(ies), land distribution as source of empowerment or disempowerment.

In addition, most of the chapters in this book indirectly or directly echo that land reform ought to build communities rather than be a divisive instrument. In that regard, the contributors express concern at land reform practices and/or theories that are limited in particular those that seem to promote the perpetuation of a vicious circle of exclusion, marginalisation, discrimination and dehumanisation. The kind of land reform that perpetuates exclusion and the like is one which limits its practice and thinking to bettering and/or maintaining status quo of one group of people be it racial, social and economic. A strong ethical persuasion underlies the presentations that are portrayed in this book. The ways in which the chapters are written are such that they have a say in, and possibly influence, policy formulation in Africa, in particular Southern Africa. Beyond the confines of influencing policy formulation, the chapters reflect the desire for Africans to be accommodative and that this desire is reflected in community thinking, in practice and in the policies that would govern land reform. I realise that the contributors use philosophical tools—epistemic, hermeneutical and moral among others—to interpret historical, social, political and economic events and issues related to land reform. By bringing in these tools, the chapter authors have departed from descriptive approach of interpreting land reform and have become philosophical (critically analytic) in interpreting land reform in Southern Africa.

Though contributors in this book have their views about land reform and in some instances reflecting upon other people's thinking on land reform, I want to point out that there are other perceptions that have already been advanced by many other philosophers on issues related to land reform in Africa. I now present the reflections of what some Africans have said concerning the land reform.

Chitonge and Mine (2019, ix) concede that the land and agrarian reform (though, agrarian is not a particular focus of this book) has always been tinkered with by governing African systems, though at most the contemporary African states have maintained the colonial frameworks and land-governing systems. In a sense the colonial legacy has persisted, contemporary African states have failed to produce their own land-governing frameworks. In fact decolonising the land framework (tenure system) is still a matter to be resolved. In relation to that, Chitonge (2019) situates the land reform issue within the decolonisation discourse. Chitonge argues that land reform as part of decolonisation is a process that as Africans we still have to go through, in the same sense land decolonisation is not an event but a process that Africans have to embark on. By using the term 'Africans,' Chitonge refers to the inclusive understanding of the term African. In this sense I share his views that the land reform discourse has to be diverse in its nature and inclusive at the same time. The contemporary of African societies requires this and therefore the need to have a multicultural and multiracial approach to African land reform.

Contributing to the debate on land decolonisation, Sam Moyo adds a perspective that says land is the real life of the African people. Moyo thus reasons that land reform ought to enhance this perspective. Moyo (2005) observes that land is central to the life of Africans and that the life of the Africans revolves around the land. For the African, land is crucial despite one's employment status because all activities for living or survival for the African be it in family, religious, agricultural, mining, tourism, housing and industry are anchored on owning, having access to and using land. The underpinning philosophical thinking that Moyo exposes is the social dimension of the connection between land and the African person. For Moyo (2008) land is intricately connected to identity. Moyo clandestinely argues that identity of the Africans is not fully expressed if it fails to be linked to owning and use of land. This is why he urges for land reform. The land reform for Moyo ought to be premised upon repossession and reclamation of land from which the natives were removed from, through Africans' repossession of land. Moyo thinks that this contributes to the decolonisation process, thus fully expressing African identity and reclamation of African inheritance.

Aside the discussion on identity and decolonisation, philosophers such as Shaw (2003a, b) and Scalet and Schmidtz (2010) proffer that land reform ought to be concerned about property rights. In particular Shaw's argument posits that the respect of property rights ought to be prioritised in the land reform. Shaw's position is derived from the Lockean Proviso and closely follows the Nozickian Entitlement Theory. The argument forwarded by Shaw is that, respect and recognition of land titles established since the beginning of the colonial period are critical. Further, he assumes that, it is through the respect of these titles (property rights) that all other rights will be respected in contemporary societies. The same perspective is shared by Scalet and Schmidtz. The two views, Shaw's and Scalet and Schmidtz's, are very persuasive but miss a critical aspect concerning native Africans or the original inhabitants whose rights (property rights included) were abrogated or overlooked at colonisation. In most cases, there has been no attempt to address (compensate) the violated and abuse of the rights of the natives. Thus the views expressed by these philosophers may raise more questions and may be discredited on the basis of this concern.

Apart from the issue of property rights, Scalet and Schmidtz (2010) add another dimension to the thinking on land reform, they add the dimension of human well-being. By human well-being they refer to the emotional, physical and material safety of all individuals. In their perception, human well-being is a requirement for human survival and it is best realised when rule of law exists, that is a situation whereby individuals are agents and agency of their choices (Scalet and Schmidtz 2010, 171). Plausible as this argument is, it ignores the historical imbalances created by the unequal distribution and access of/to resources emanating from the colonial period. Implicitly, the colonial inequalities directly and indirectly contribute to racial, economic, social and political differences that also translate into contemporary racial economic disparities. Again in this way, the argument is found wanting: it fails to cater for the native Africans or those who were displaced at the beginning of colonisation.

A more persuasive argument that has been forwarded is the economic argument. This argument proceeds by noting that economic injustices among the indigenous population were a result of the unequal, unjust and racially skewed land redistribution caused by colonialism (Thomas 2003, 695; Wuriga 2008, 5; Openshaw and Terry 2015, 73). Proponents of the economic argument argue that the inequalities that emanate from the unequal and discriminatory colonial land expropriations led to economic disempowerment (poverty), deprivation, displacement and exploitation of locals (Weiner 1989, 401; Thomas 2003, 695). In light of these views, the locals argue that land expropriation (repossession) is the considered way to decongest overpopulated areas and that redistribution would also empower locals economically. The thinking is that economic benefit would accrue from the fact that the poor and formerly landless would have access to and control of productive land. That is, the possession of land empowers, thus helping to secure adequate food supply and boost agricultural production (Lebert 2006, 45–46; Naldi 1993, 585). Most importantly, land redistribution would be a way of addressing colonial land imbalances and other colonial social injustices (Lebert 2006, 45–46).

The assumption that land redistribution would empower local communities raises other problems. Annexing land from the hands of white farmers and placing it in the hands of black farmers only meant a reversal of the colonial setup favouring one group of people over others, thus recreating discrimination. Discrimination is indirect racism and violates the principles of social justice and social equality. Secondly, the argument misleads the world community to think that African, indeed Southern African economies are only reliant on land activities. The argument fails to note that economies are no longer dependent on land holding and productivity alone, but are also dependent on other productive sectors. Thirdly, the argument presumes that all native Africans are concerned with owning and using land for their economic prosperity. This perspective is misleading, it fails to capture the real aspirations of the Africans, I am of the view that there are many who are not worried about owning and using land. They may be interested in other areas which they think would empower them.

Having reflected on what has been said by other scholars on land reform and noting shortcomings of their views, I am left with no option but present the ideas contained in this book's chapters. The following paragraphs reflect some indirect responses to the thinking that already exists. I now give a summary to the chapters contained in this book.

In Chap. 2, 'Exploring Foundational Principles for Land Redistribution and Management in Africa,' Aderonke Adegbite acknowledges that despite its limited availability, the largest percentage of all human's events can only thrive on land. In her exposé she notes the role played by international laws and national domestic laws in promoting and governing rights over land. This includes entitlements, use, exchange and control of land. However, she notes that in Sub-Saharan Africa conflicts, expropriation and exploitation are on the increase especially emanating from land management rules and structures which are unjust, incoherent, inefficient and ineffective. By drawing ideas from various land tenures examined against sustainable philosophies, Adegbite advocates for government reforms that among other things manage citizens' interests on land through promoting rights for all; in this way she thinks will promote justice. Her discussion largely borders around state control and individual (group rights) in the attainment of justice, equality and fairness.

In Chap. 3, entitled 'Political Economy and the Socio-cultural History of Land Dispossession, Proselytization and Proletarianization of African People in South Africa: 1488–1770 (Part 1),' Mbhekeni Sabelo Nkosi traces the historical philosophical thinking that relates to South African skewed land ownership and use. In the chapter, Nkosi shows the ideas that were behind the European settler expropriation of lands in South Africa. Further, Nkosi notes that the devastating political and economic impact emanating from the skewed land ownership and use indirectly and directly contributes to prevalent poverty amongst the African majority. As a result of European exclusive (colonial) land expropriations and tenures, Africans experienced a number of injustices that range from violence, oppression, racism and discrimination. Subsequently enslavement, subjugation, impoverishment, proselytisation and proletarianisation of African people ensued. Basing on these historical facts and philosophies, Nkosi encourages land expropriate without compensation as a way to achieve equitable resource distribution, access and use.

From exposing the thinking behind expropriation and proletarianisation of the African people, Nkosi goes on to reveal the construction of the Afrikaner ethnic group and its ethic and at the same time reveal the role of the European missionary in land dispossession. By philosophising on the idea of social inculturation which the European settlers used in the dispossessing African people off their land, Nkosi reveals the thinking behind European settler colonialism and imperialism. In Chap. 4, entitled, 'Political Economy and the Socio-cultural History of Land Dispossession, Proselytisation and Proletarianisation of African People in South Africa: 1795–1854 (Part 2),' Nkosi discloses the religio-philosophical thrust or influence in the discourse of African dispossession of land between 1795 and 1854.

Chapter 5, by Joseph Hungwe, discusses land reform in Zimbabwe. Hungwe juxtaposes the Zimbabwe's Fast Track Land Reform Programme (FTLRP) to the Ubuntu philosophy. In this chapter, entitled '*Ivhu Kuvanhu/Umhlabathi Ebantwini*: The 'Violent' Ubuntu in the Fast Track Land Reform Programme in Zimbabwe,' Hungwe notes that by appealing to the notion of Ubuntu, the FTLRP resulted in latent racial exclusivity and xenophobic tendencies. In addition, Hungwe argues that the Zimbabwean post-independence endeavours towards land distribution have been characterised by the dehumanising physical and verbal violence perpetrated by the black 'indigenous' Africans as the supposedly custodians of Ubuntu towards white farmers and 'foreign' farm workers in Zimbabwe. The violation of Ubuntu precepts, which includes respect and recognition of each other, leads the author to three compelling questions that this chapter seeks to conceptually interrogate. Firstly, if Ubuntu connotes the primacy of a common or shared humanity, to what extent does Ubuntu appropriate the notion of humanity to non-black Africans? Secondly, as an evolving concept, does Ubuntu gradually incorporate or assimilate non-black Africans? Thirdly, in instances where foreign farm workers are dehumanised, can Ubuntu not be accused to be xenophobic? Drawing from newspaper articles and scholarly literature, this conceptual chapter lays out the salient exclusivity in Ubuntu and its (un)intended implication on the land reform programme in Zimbabwe.

In Chap. 6, 'A Logical Evaluation of the Fast Track Land Reform Economic Argument in Zimbabwe,' Ephraim Taurai Gwaravanda examines the logical cogency of the fast track land reform economic argument in Zimbabwe and demonstrates that the argument is largely fallacious. The fallacious nature of the argument rests on three problems. First, the assumptions of the argument that include (1) the view that land deprivation is the cause of poverty and (2) the claims that the land is the economy and the economy is the land are both mistaken and grossly problematic. Secondly, the premises used to buttress the argument such as the fast track land reform creates employment, generates foreign currency, promotes industrialisation and economic growth are false. Thirdly, the conclusion arrived at to justify fast track land reform, namely, land reform is good for the overall economic well-being does not follow with probability from the given premises. Given these logical problems, Gwaravanda concludes that the fast track land reform economic argument in Zimbabwe is more emotive than reasonable.

Chapter 7, 'We Acknowledge that We Reside on...: Canadian land acknowledgments and South African Land Reform' written by Yolandi M. Coetser, explores the importance of appreciating the role played by previous land inhabitants. By drawing arguments from the Canadian land acknowledgments, Coetser proposes that the same views may inform, persuade and motivate South Africans to adapt the same philosophy in the South African land reform. She says a land acknowledgement is a written or spoken declaration that responds to the question: Whose land are we on? The declaration, she avers, obligates individuals or groups to acknowledge the land, its previous inhabitants, expropriations that occurred, and mandates humans to the stewardship of Mother Earth and in building relationships with indigenous people and communities. Coetser assumes that by adopting the practice in Africa, there are chances of establishing human relations that capacitate individual and collective duty towards collective responsibility for the world, land and each other.

A way of acknowledgements is restitution. The issue of restitution is tackled by Thaddeus Metz in Chap. 8, entitled 'Must Land Reform Benefit the Victim of Colonialism?' In this chapter, Metz responds to Oritsegbubemi Anthony Oyowe who thinks that land reform ought to be reversal of colonial land expropriation by transferring land *en masse* to the dispossessed African indigenes. For Metz compensation has to be for both those who have suffered dispossessions and those who will lose lands to any form of reform. He reasons that compensating all necessarily improves lives for all and doing so is associated with the Ubuntu values of communion and reconciliation. Moreover, this would reduce (amongst other things) capital flight and food shortages, which would be bad for broader society.

The importance of economic stability and prosperity that Metz forwards is furthered by Dennis Masaka in Chap. 9 entitled 'Reconciling "Title to Land and Productivity" in Land Debates in Africa.' In this chapter, Masaka argues that in most cases African states have prioritised the issue of land ownership over everything else that may be associated with the topic of land reform. In this chapter, he argues that productivity ought to be taken as equally important if countries in Africa are to lessen their levels of dependency on other geopolitical centres in matters of production and provision of economic resources. In arguing thus, he is not implying that countries in Africa do not see merit in the question of productivity. The claim is that they seem to consider reclamation of title as foundational and prerequisite to productivity and thus give it relative importance.

Following from the chapters that support economic prosperity, Chap. 10, 'Is Land Reform the Last Step Towards Africans' Total Emancipation and True Empowerment?,' questions the authenticity of such thinking. In this chapter, Bernard Matolino wonders if land reform will empower Africans economically. He notes that the land question has always featured in the background as a highly contested idea and most visible reality of conquest and disempowerment. Both as an economic tool and as an ideology, the land question is taken as a promise of the turning of the tide in favour of Africans' economic empowerment and the most crucial point at which Africans' dignity is fully restored. It should, therefore, follow that the land issue is tied to matters of self-determination and freedom, which were key to the struggle for independence. In a sceptical manner, Matolino doubts the possibility of attaining the expected economic prosperity; he thus sounds the possible pitfalls of expecting liberty, and empowerment against reality and against the effects of rhetoric, and ideologies of decolonisation. These three, Matolino thinks are part of African ways of hoodwinking each other from the actual goings-on of corruption and other self-inflicted unjust disempowerments within the land reform discourse.

Away from the economic perspectives, Christopher Allsobrook brings in the jurisprudence perspective. In Chap. 11, 'Integrating African Social Tenures through Rights Recognition in Land Reform,' Allsobrook introduces land reform as a complex set of problems around redistribution, restitution and tenure. Allsobrook calls for the integration of different systems of rights recognition, administration and governance in land reform. This he thinks forms a security of social tenures that is acceptable and recognised by the majority of African communities. Allsobrook also avers that expropriations without compensation, be it the colonial and/or as proposed in the post-colonial period creates and reproduces a vicious circle of unrecognised norms of ownership and unrecognised land rights. At most, there are chances of perpetuating segregation, reinventing apartheid (and veiled apartheid in reverse), reproducing poverty, insecurity and disempowerment from dispossession.

Chapter 12, entitled 'Land Reform and Redistribution as Environmental Justice Frameworks for Post-colonial Africa,' by Munamato Chemhuru, brings in the discourse of environmental justice into the land reform debate. This is a dimension that is often ignored in the land reform debate. Chemhuru discusses environmental justice from an African point of view. By environmental justice, Chemhuru means the fair treatment and meaningful involvement of all people regardless of race, colour, national origin, culture, education or income with respect to the development, implementation and enforcement of environmental laws, regulations and policies. This means equal consideration for both the former disadvantaged and those who have been advantaged. He argues that for environmental justice to be achieved there needs to be serious land reform that removes unequal land distributions that were created by colonial systems. Only after robust land redistributions will there be a fair and equal distribution of benefits and burdens related to environmental and climate change.

On a note of justice, Erasmus Masitera brings in the aspect of individual justice in Chap. 13, entitled 'Individual Justice in Land Redistribution: Appropriating Some Ideas from the Capability Approach.' In this chapter, Masitera focuses on the kind of life that individuals ought to live (individuals' well-being or justice) within land reform. Masitera argues that while expanding liberties and rights benefits the formerly disadvantaged communities, it is however important to focus on the individual's well-being which includes the ability to convert those liberties, rights and resources to their advantage. In that endeavour, Masitera suggests and evaluates functionings (beings and doings) that necessarily enhance individuals to realise lives they have reason to value within redistributed land. At the same time, he discusses the possible means of achieving and realisation of individual goals within land reform. For his efforts, he is guided by the Capability Approach's (hereafter, C.A.) conception of justice which promotes individual well-being.

In Chap. 14, entitled 'Towards a Critical Ethic of Land in the Southern African Context,' Mark Rathbone and Anné Hendrik Verhoef contextualise land reform to South Africa. Rathbone and Verhoef develop and propose a critical ethic of land that, they argue, may assist discussion on land reform to move in a more sustainable direction that highlights the complexity of the issue of land. Rathbone and Verhoef analyse Western and African, specifically Xhosa, perspective to develop a land ethic that speaks to the people of South Africa. The land ethic that they have in mind is one that is not reducible to culture, be it Western or African, but rather an ethic that is relevant to all people. In their thinking this is a critical ethic that embraces the diverse and complex views on land.

Chapter 15 reflects on the role that land reform has to play in response to real practical problems associated to it. In this chapter, 'What Can Ubuntu Do? A Reflection on African Moral Theory in Light of Post-colonial Challenges,' Motsamai Molefe and Nolubabalo Magam critique, and, simultaneously, supplement Thad Metz's relational interpretation of Ubuntu that recommends reconciliation as the best response the government could offer to the land question associated with the Marikana massacre. Molefe and Magam argue that Marikana must be understood within the broad narrative of historical injustices with cheap black labour as the core of the issues in the land question. In the chapter the authors argue that there is need to address some of the vestiges of cheap labour that are linked to skewed land ownership and use in South Africa in that way. Ubuntu thus demands, in part, that *inter alia* economic historical injustices be addressed for the sake of making humanity possible for all, particularly victims of oppression.

In a slightly different view on the role of Ubuntu in land reform, Rodwell Kumbirai Wuta in Chap. 16 entitled 'Understanding Unhu/Ubuntu as a Moral Thought on Land Redistribution in Zimbabwe: Ethical Lessons for Future Land Reform in Sub-Saharan Africa,' examines the moral implications of Ubuntu on land reform in Zimbabwe. Kumbirai discusses the biased land distributions and the post-colonial land redistributions in Zimbabwe against the moral expectations of Unhu/Ubuntu. Kumbirai examines the colonial expropriations and the post-colonial restitutions against the Ubuntu ideals of fairness, equity, equality and justice. Hence, on the one hand, the chapter examines land redistribution in Zimbabwe, noting instances where the land redistribution process was in accordance with the dictates of Unhu/Ubuntu. On the other hand, it presents a critique of the land redistribution process, noting cases where the principles of Unhu/Ubuntu were flagrantly contravened.

References

Boss, J. 2008. *Analyzing Moral Issues*. Boston: McGraw-Hill.

Chitonge, H. 2019. The Land Question and the Economy: Cues of an Incomplete Decolonisation Project in Africa. In *Land, the State and the Unfinished Decolonisation Project in Africa: Essays in Honour of Professor Sam Moyo*, ed. H. Chitonge and Y. Mine. Bamenda: Langaa.

Chitonge, H., and Y. Mine. 2019. Preface. In *Land, the State and the Unfinished Decolonisation Project in Africa: Essays in Honour of Professor Sam Moyo*, ed. H. Chitonge and Y. Mine. Bamenda: Langaa.

Lebert, T. 2006. An Introduction to Land and Agrarian Reform in Zimbabwe. In *Promised Land: Competing Vision of Agrarian Reform*, ed. P. Rosset, R. Patel, and M. Courville, 40–56. New York: Food First Books.

Marongwe, N. 2007. *Redistributive Land Reform and Poverty Reduction in Zimbabwe*. www.plaas.org.za/sites/default/files/publications-pdf/Zimbabwe_Marongwe.pdf

Moyo, S. 2005. A Review of Zimbabwean Agricultural Sector following the Implementation of the Land Reform: Overall Impacts of Fast Track Land Reform Programme. archive.kubatana.net/docs/agric/aias_land_reform_040513.pdf

———. 2008. *African Land Questions, Agrarian Transitions and the State: Contradictions of Neo-liberal Land Reforms*. Dakar: CODESRIA.

Naldi, G.J. 1993. Land Reform in Zimbabwe: Some Legal Aspects. *The Journal of Modern African Studies* 31 (4, Dec.): 585–600.

Obeng-Odoom, F. 2012. Land Reform in Africa: Theory, Practice and Outcome. *Habitat International* 36: 161–170.

Openshaw, K.S., and P.C.R. Terry. 2015. Zimbabwe's Odious Inheritance: Debt and Unequal Land Distribution. *McGill International Journal of Sustainable Development* 11 (1): 39–86.

Scalet, S., and D. Schmidtz. 2010. Famine, Poverty, and Property Rights. In *Amartya Sen*, 170–190. Cambridge: Cambridge University Press.

Shaw, W.H. 2003a. 'They Stole Our Land': Debating the Expropriation of White Farms in Zimbabwe. *The Journal of Modern African Studies* 41 (1, Mar.): 75–89.

———. 2003b. Nozick in Zimbabwe. *Journal of Social Philosophy* 34 (2): 215–227.

Thomas, N.H. 2003. Land Reform in Zimbabwe. *Third World Quarterly* 24 (4): 691–712.

Van Onselen, C. 1976. *Chibaro: African Mine Labour in Southern Rhodesia, 1900–1933*. London: Pluto Press.

Weiner, D. 1989. Agricultural Restructuring in Zimbabwe and South Africa. *Development and Change* 20 (3): 401–428.

Wuriga, R. 2008. The Revolutionary Bond and Opposition Politics in Post-Independent Africa: The Case of Zimbabwe. *IKAMVA: International Journal of Social Science and Humanities* 2 (1): 1–36.

Part I

History and Logic on Land

2

Exploring Foundational Principles for Land Redistribution and Management in Africa

Aderonke E. Adegbite

Land in Africa

The term "land" has various legal and proprietary definitions, three of which posit that it;

1. *Is an immovable three dimensional area consisting of a portion of the earth's surface, the space above and below that surface and everything growing on or permanently affixed to it* (Legal-lingo 2020).
2. *Includes the soil which is the surface, the subsoil and any material found underneath the surface such as the soil minerals and natural resources* (Boundless Biology 2019).
3. *Consists or a group of persons who refer to themselves as a nation* (Oxford Advanced Learners Dictionary 2001).

A. E. Adegbite (✉)
Department of Private and Business Law, Lead City University, Ibadan, Nigeria

E. Masitera (ed.), *Philosophical Perspectives on Land Reform in Southern Africa*, https://doi.org/10.1007/978-3-030-49705-7_2

According to Elias T.O. (1972), land and its attachment to indigenous African lives and perpetuity may be succinctly presented through a statement which is credited to a Nigerian chief standing before the West African Lands Committee in 1912. To him:

> *Land belongs to a vast family of which many are dead, few are living and countless members are unborn.*

The above describes the indigenous consideration of land as jointly owned by a set of people who lay claims to same. William Marshall, in reference to Withers (1990) and R. Hofstadter (1955), identifies the unique nature of the Scottish Highlanders attachment to their homelands and the problems that might ensue from a forceful relocation. He gave different rationales for such attachments which to him cannot be formed by strangers. To Hunter J. (1976) and Dodgshon R.A. (1998), the justifying residual element is only explicable by the emotions which the Highlanders strongly feel about their heritage (Duthchas). To Verdier (1964),

> *Land remains the ultimate property, in individuals, of generations dead, living and unborn; hence, the principle of "non exo-alienability" of land in African customary tenure systems.*

Campbell A. (1811) connects the remarkable attachments of people to their homesteads, to the practical necessities that induce people to go to any lengths in order to repossess or validate their right to it. These perspectives suggest that individual or collective attachment of some people to land are often resource or heritage related. To Diaw (1997), African territorial and land tenure rights transit through groups, clan and lineages and are hence founded upon genealogy and the valorization of human labor. Other perspectives border on prominent claims through first occupation of territories, equitable rationales to live from individual labor/sweat/input over land and the rights of unborn generations to inherit useful land. In addition, international interventions have reinstated that land is significant to individual/collective self-determination. This conclusion also covers other issues on citizens' identities and national economic survival particularly for the sustenance of historical, immediate and long-term needs.

Conclusively, the inability to simply forgo autonomous rights to lands, during interferences from perceived non-owners, is invariably the inevitable background to inter/intra conflicts or threats over land. The essence of this chapter is to connect state representatives in high-ranking administrative structures to varying ideas behind land claims. This is done through a review of different theoretical propositions that should guide land reformation processes and influence international calls against land grabbing, unsustainable extractions and other causes of inter/intra land conflicts in Africa.

Government and Land Disputes

Authors such as Charles Darwin (1809–1882), Herbert Spencer (1916) and Truxtun Beale (1916) have explained states as having arisen from that need for persons with different characteristics and aspirations to survive together. Immanuel Kant's and Thomas Hobbes' idea that humans are naturally greedy and that "property" makes people selfish underscores the primary rationale for state interventions in citizens' affairs. In theory, governments are therefore conferred with the monopoly on the use of all measures including violence in order to serve justice to persons, maintain domestic tranquility, defend its territory from external invasion and promote people's welfare. Therefore, all persons within the geographical jurisdiction of a sovereign state are subject to governments powers, laws, policies and institutions.

It is within the above arrangements, that land disputes exist in different forms which include individuals'/communities' conflicts over ownership rights, individuals'/communities' conflicts over land boundaries and easements and also discordances between land users and the states, organizations or institutions. High-value natural resources that generate large revenues have also subsisted as prominent sources of conflicts, since states often hold resource ownership with the rights to award same to commercial companies or utilize it in other ways for state benefits. For example, in the agrarian and life stock sectors of Botswana and Nigeria, the level of success of each government to curtail strives on cattle ranching reveals that engagement in land resolutions is quite dependent on strategic and well principled rules that engage all citizens accordingly.

The volatility of land issues has required that powers of reform, acquisition, management, disposal and control be conferred on public institutions (state establishments). In South Africa, the perennial impact of colonization especially through apartheid systems, that dispossess Black Africans of access and ownership of land, is as reflected in a series of political agenda and innovations to reset equitable land redistribution. In this instant "equitable access" to land under the South African law has been expanded to encompass the property rights for those without properties, lands or homes. These obligations on the state press on the need to provide land and housing to marginalized persons, through efficient and responsive land reform programs. Political motions toward amending the South African Constitutions therefore include those that justify government's discretion to affordably and equitably expropriate and redistribute land without necessarily compensating all claims.

States' discretion to protect citizens' welfare interests within territorial lands is acknowledged by treaties. However, states' power becomes a source of international concern, when governmental actions deprioritize citizens' welfare for other political or neocolonial agenda. On the scale of eventualities, omissions or neglects to abide by standard international prescriptions for land management constitute the constant background to emergencies of splinter groups in repossession, compensatory or secession hostilities.

Human Rights and Land

Existing human rights standards have especially being couched to restrain state powers from indulging in activities that further agenda that have entrenched inequality and apartheid in Africa. An example of such negative potentials is the implication the South African Natives Land Act of 1913 and 1936 Native Trust and Land Act which ensured the forceful displacement of black families from their land irrespective of the resulting socio-economic plights on the country. Till date, the implications of this law in South Africa are landlessness, poverty and inequality. Accordingly international conventions recognize the right to peaceful enjoyment of property, and only allow the deprivation of land entitlements under strict adherence to specific human rights stipulations. For example, Article 17 of the Universal Declaration of Human Rights (UDHR) 1948 enshrines its protective clause as follows:

> *(1) everyone has the right to own property alone as well as in association with others. (2) ….* ***no one shall be arbitrarily deprived of his property.***

Conclusions from statutory perusals, therefore, allow the inevitable, through provisions that mandate a balance between states' powers of acquisition and public interests. Another example in this regard is the *American Convention on Human Rights* (ACHR), which protects the right to property, then equally provides for the right to "just compensation" in cases of deprivations. The treaty also prohibits usury and other forms of exploitation by the state. Article 21 of the ACHR states:

> *(1) Everyone has the right to the use and enjoyment of his property. The law may subordinate such use and enjoyment to the interest of society. (2) No one shall be deprived of his property except upon payment of just compensation, for reasons of public utility or social interest, and in the cases and according to the forms established by law. (3) Usury and any other form of exploitation of man by man shall be prohibited by law.*

Against this backdrop, recent generations of treaties in tandem with the African Commission on Human and Peoples' Rights have, over the years, secured precedents that address issues on land management and reforms. According to Article 6 of the ILO Indigenous and Tribal Peoples Convention (169) these include:

1. The need to sufficiently consult and seek the free, prior and informed consent of affected persons;
2. The willingness of states to provide undertakings and compensations in good faith; and
3. The endurance of reformatory actions that are legal and sustainable actions.

Governments' roles may therefore become more complicated and ineffective where there are no straightforward objectives for achieving these three requirements.

Underlying Principles for State Management Techniques

Utilitarian Agenda: Sovereign Powers and Social Contract

State sovereignty entails the total right of the governing body over its territory, without any interference from outside sources or bodies. The supremacy of state therefore covers its domestic affairs and the formal recognition accorded to it by other sovereign states. In democratic parlance, the term entails a nation's constitutional discretion to control activities, people, institutions and movement within and across its own boundary. This basis of governance is usually as presented in independent constitutions. For example, similar to what obtains under Sections 1, 2 and 9 of the South African 1996 Constitution, the Nigerian 1999 Grundnorm also presents the nation as sovereign, democratic and founded on values toward achieving equality and the advancement of human rights/freedoms. On this note, Sections 6 of the South African Constitution especially affirms that:

> *The state may not unfairly discriminate directly or indirectly against anyone on one or more grounds including race, gender, sex, pregnancy, marital status, ethnic or social origin, color, sexual orientation, age, disability, religion, conscience, belief, culture, language and birth.*

The above frameworks therefore enable the exercise of sovereign discretion and oftentimes brute force toward ensuring that persons, institutions and bodies within a given polity endure the dictates for equal treatment of everyone. In legitimate dispensations, the justification for enforcement of public good, even through force, arises from the agreement of citizens to confer such powers on the government through democratic constitutions.

According to Hobbes, stateless and lawless societies would only live in the "state of war," a way of life that is "solitary, poor, nasty, brutish, and short." The alternative would then be where persons voluntarily enter into implied but mutually beneficial agreements to relegate their individual interests for the larger and encompassing benefits of a social unity. This theory relies mainly on the consent of people and how they freely subject themselves to political authorities. According to the Preambles of the South African, Nigerian and Ghanaian Constitutions:

> *We the people of the South Africa therefore, through our freely elected representatives, adopt this Constitution as the supreme law of the republic.*

This part however does not emphasize the further voluntary interactions between the government and the people. It rather relates from the obligation perspective. That is, a contract connotes that both parties must give and take. Therefore, notwithstanding the status of persons, whether of the minority, local or indigenous population, all persons are bound to subject themselves to authority's agenda; for example, to heal wounds inflicted by histories of segregations, inequality, corruption and absence of rule of law.

On the part of government, all resources notwithstanding their location within a territory constitute the common wealth of all persons within that nation-state. The commonwealth position is to enable actions that maximize happiness and well-being for the majority of a population irrespective of their standings Jeremy Bentham (1789). The above typify governments' designation of vital national resources, especially land as commonwealth best fit to achieve utilitarian values. In Nigeria, Section 1 of Nigerian Land Use Decree of 1979 for example affirms:

> *All lands comprised in the* ***territory of each State*** *in the Federation are hereby vested in the Governor of that State and such land shall be held in trust and administered for the use and common benefit of all Nigerians in accordance with the provisions.*

According to the Government,

All Nigerians are collective owners of all land in the country and the rights of all Nigerians to use and enjoy the land of the country and the natural fruits thereof in sufficient quantity to enable them to provide for the sustenance of themselves and their families should be ensured, protected and preserved.

A popular characteristic of land reform laws is therefore the utilitarian provisions enabling government to revoke or acquire any land within its territory for the benefit of the "nation" notwithstanding the rights of the original users.

On the above demands, other theorists have opined on the complexities of the conditions that states must bear to assert sovereignty and the rule of law on proprietary issues. Most authors assert that the society is constituted by diverse interests and it is often misleading to refer to the capacity of states to "equalize" all. For example, while Raymond J. Michalowski asserts that the society is constituted by persons with core values that are commonly shared, other theorists interpret society as a struggle between groups engaging in conflict for limited resources. Laws should therefore disable circumstances due from social injustices to some/all people or misrepresentations from government that aggravate land crisis rather than resolve them. On this possibility, Karl Marx has opined that the society is usually a reflection of the power in control of material resources, wealth, politics and other decisive institutions. In this instance, inequality strives where the ruling class merely uses the instrumentality of law to allocate resources unevenly distributed between groups. In this instance the capitalist class, male, majority, elite and others are given softer landing, control and access to resources against the relatively powerless citizens.

In South Africa, expropriation without compensation is sought to justify the redistribution of land among all, especially to address the injustice that has been occasioned by existing inequalities. This justification is similar to that expressed by the position of the Nigerian Constitution Drafting Committee, that,

It is revolting to one's sense of justice and equity that one person alone should own about ten or more plots of State lands...when others have none.

These rationales are often insinuated in states' land use laws that allow the deprivation or reallocation of lands on the grounds of misuse, public policy or public use. Nevertheless, states' approbation of communal and private property for common/public good have often been cited as unfair to individual and ancestral thresholds. It is at this juncture the state must endeavor to juxtapose between the entitlement of all persons to common wealth and the right of individuals or communities to enjoy their permanent and historical titles to land.

Pre-empting the implications of the above discretion, the common Article 1(23) of the Covenant on Civil and Political Rights and the Covenant on Economic, Social and Cultural Rights state:

All peoples may, for their own ends, freely dispose of their natural wealth and resources without prejudice to any obligations arising out of international economic co-operation, based upon the principle of mutual benefit, and international law. In no case may a people be deprived of its own means of subsistence.

In addition, Article 47 of the Covenant on Civil and Political Rights and Article 25 of the Covenant on Economic, Social and Cultural Rights further state:

Nothing in the present Covenant shall be interpreted as impairing the inherent right of all peoples to enjoy and utilize fully and freely their natural wealth and resources.

Also Article 21 of the African Charter on Human Peoples Rights provides the rights:

All peoples to freely dispose of their wealth and natural resources and that this right shall be exercised in the exclusive interest of the people. In no case shall a people be deprived of this right.

Accordingly, Article 21 (Chap. 2) emphasized the fact that in case of spoliation the dispossessed people shall have the right to the lawful recovery of its property as well as to adequate compensation".

More expressly, on the procedures for addressing issues that border on the deprivation of some persons of their rights in order to satisfy some utilitarian values, *the International Labor Organization Indigenous and Tribal Peoples Convention No. 169/1989*, at Article 15, provides expressly that:

> *the rights of the peoples concerned to the natural resources pertaining to their lands shall be specifically safeguarded. These rights include the right of these peoples to participate in the use, management and conservation of these resources…in case in which the state retains the ownership of minerals or sub-surface resources or rights to other resources pertaining to land, governments shall establish or maintain procedures through which they shall consult these peoples, with a view to ascertaining whether and to what degree their would be prejudiced, before undertaking or permitting any programs for the exploration or exploitation of such resources pertaining to their lands. The peoples concerned shall wherever possible participate in the benefits of such activities and shall receive fair compensation for any damages which they may sustain as a result of such activities.*

Individual and Indigenous Rights to Property

As stated, while there may be no standalone provisions that justify humans' right to land, international and local treaties enshrine the alternative right of people(s) to acquire and hold properties. The definition of property rights and how land may be legitimately acquired, protected and revoked has been a source of controversies in law. Very importantly the aftermath of the world/civil wars and episodes of slavery instigates the intention of regimes that subtly prohibit acquisition of land by invasion, wars or fraud. Illegitimate acquisitions at all instances should subject the invader or illegal owner to humanitarian and international queries and condemnation. It is hence doubtful that a title acquired through invasion in contemporary times would survive international scrutiny. Governments may therefore retrieve illegitimate titles without paying compensation to the offenders.

Property ownership revolves around other tenets that ensure the realization of the right to adequate standard of living and other economic, socio-cultural, civil and political rights, especially those that promote inclusive development. However, existing laws not only protect property rights; they often have implications that suggest that land rights are limited and subject to justifiable revocations. For example, Articles 13 and 14 of the African Charter on Human and Peoples' Rights (ACHPR) 1981 state:

> *(13) the right to property shall be guaranteed. It may only be encroached upon in the interest of public need or in the general interest of the community and in accordance with the provisions of* ***appropriate*** *laws.*
>
> *(14)* ***every citizen*** *has the right to participate freely in the government of his country, the right to equal access to public services and "the right of access to public property and services in strict* ***equality*** *of all persons before the law".*

Invariably, individual or indigenous assertions on land ownership flow from claims that present the mode(s) of acquisition. In recent times, such acquisitions may be through statutory or traditional access. When claims are traditional, the government must seek ways to review affirmations based on superior claims on initial *occupation/first settlement, undisputed retention of land* or circumstances of possession through invasion (largely prohibited). On the other hand such claims are assertions based on the *historical evidence of labor* (where persons own lands because they have productive labor attached to it), that is, by making something out of the materials of nature.

The occupation theorists assert that, given that all material resources are given to mankind in common, such material resources may become the private property of individuals through the consent of the rest of mankind. This kind of title to private property is the most traditional, which laws including common law and international law would protect from trespassers and invasion. On the other hand "undisputed retention of land" gives right to ownership claims by some persons when they have lived and survived for a long period of time on property, such that it is reasonable that their title or possession would have been contradicted, if there was another person(s) with superior title.

Undisputed retention of land underlies the principles of *Laches* and Acquiesces in law. Laches and Acquiesces are principles with similar implications. Hence both often appear together or are used interchangeably. When asserted during litigation, Laches is an equitable defense, asserting that the party claiming superior title "slept on their rights," and that, as a result of this delay, circumstances have changed, witnesses or evidence may have been lost or no longer available, or at most the respondent has added his own "labor" to the property. It would hence be unconscionable and unjust to grant the plaintiff's claim. The essential element of *laches* is the unreasonable delay by the plaintiff in bringing their claim.

On the other part, Acquiesces occur when a person knowingly stands by without raising any objection to the infringement of his or her rights, while someone else unknowingly and without malice does an act that is inconsistent with this rights. The person whose rights are infringed may lose the ability to make a legal claim against the infringer. The doctrine infers a form of permission from the passiveness over an extended period of time. In the Nigerian *Kayode v. Odutola (2001)11 NWLR (Pt.725) 659 at 679*, the courts held as follows:

> *There is a duty on a person having estate or interest in land or other property for that matter to raise protest against a trespass or encroachment on the property or invasion of his right on same if he has reason to believe that such a trespasser or encroacher or invader mistakenly conceives himself to be acting lawfully, because in such a situation there cannot be said to be any misrepresentation, delusion or inaction from the owner's part, encouraging or fostering the trespasser in expending money by developing the property.*

The logic behind the thesis is that while a person who illegally interferes in another property remains a trespasser under law and would be evicted, the court of equity would not allow a situation where a stranger builds on another's land, supposing it as his own acquisition, while the legal owner, seeing this error, refuses to correct him. The court of equity will not allow such legal owner to assert his title to the land, after the stranger has expended money on supposition that the land was his own. The conscience behind the principle is that, it will be dishonest on the part of the owner to remain willfully passive, in order afterwards to reap from the labor of a mistaken owner.

On the labor theory of land ownership, the possibility of claiming a land against an owner who has abandoned it and has slept over his rights was enunciated by John Locke (1690) who posits that man owns himself and, by extension, everything that he produces. By mixing work with nature, the resulting goods should necessarily belong to the worker. This theory suggests that a person is entitled to the full produce of their labor. The concept flows from the common perspective that land is owned in common but private ownership may occur when a person commingles their labor with it and in extreme cases where original owners of land intentionally sit back, in order to fraudulently convert another's efforts simply because they claim an original title to the land in question. The labor theory therefore fits the rationale behind the Earl of Oxford's case.

The Earl of Oxford's case was about a parcel of land in England. Earlier the King's Bench (Common Law Court) had held that the respondent's (Earl of Oxford's) title was void and caught by a statute from which no one may be exempted. The consequent implication of eviction on the mistaken owner evolved from the principle *Quic quid plantatur solo, solo cedit* ("whatever is affixed to the soil belongs to the soil"). Therefore, whoever owned the piece of land owns everything affixed to it. Meaning that, the plaintiff, who had the formal title simply by the fact of law, automatically becomes the owner of every fixture that is placed on the land by the mistaken owner.

It is the implication of this decision that aroused the conscience of the Lord Chancellor at the Court of Chancery. Lord Ellesmere issued a common injunction out of the Court of Chancery prohibiting the enforcement of the common law order and granting the equitable owner (Earl of Oxford) and his tenants quiet enjoyment of the land. It stayed all common law suits against the Earl. Referencing the Bible, book of Deuteronomy, Verse 28:30, the Lord Chancellor, an ecclesiastic, rendered his intervention:

> *He that builds a House ought to dwell in it; and he that plants a Vineyard ought to gather the Grapes thereof.*

The Lord Chancellor through the Court of Chancery then issued a common injunction on the basis of an unconscionable advantage which had developed in favor of the Magdalene College. The Lord Chancellor would not allow the enforcement of the common law order against the Earl of Oxford (mistaken owner) for breaching the statute. In this instance the Earl became the equitable owner of the land in question.

Government's Economic Interest and Land Management

According to John Stuart Mill (1848), among others, private property creates the environment where maximum productivity is created based upon profit motives. He therefore regarded economic development as a function of the factors of production including land. To John Locke, private property is the center of free economy based on natural law. However, unlike other properties of value, land has special characteristics, in the sense that it is fixed and limited, and each is unique in value. Another distinctive characteristic is that, the value of land highly influences its environment and adjacent parcels. For a commodity that is fixed, unequal access would be as a result of inequality in human talents, labor or financial standing. Economic theory therefore emphasizes the profit and financial motive behind all actions on land matters. Since economic rights over private properties (including land) are not created by government but they exist before government, the role of government is to protect value and assign these rights.

The implication of this arrangement is that, since governments also retain economic rights over lands within its territory, including private properties; land reformation activities are often influenced by land use, land price and land value (Mohamed et al. 2014). To J.S. Mill, economic democracy exists where government enables equality measures that lessen impending unhealthy competition for wealth. Over the years the term globalization has achieved the tempo of international force that influences governments toward worldwide financial and trade integrations. States therefore open local contingencies up to satisfy the outlook of the interconnected and interdependent world. Globalization suggests the inability of nations to depend on their own resource in isolation. Development may, therefore, only be achieved through the extraction of domestic resources to satisfy global connections and trade. It is for these purposes that international and universal mandates have emerged to provide common and protective standards in respect of government exploitations on land. Other concerns have also arisen on the sustainable use of land to satisfy capitalists and neocolonial demands, even where governments are in denial of the impact on the environment, citizens and ecosystems.

Indigenous African System

Land management and issues arising from it may be adequately inserted within the African indigenous theories on general governance. Under almost all African customary systems, it is well understood that occupancy is generally the key to "ownership" and land is allocated by those claiming prior occupancy through lineages and clans. These systems have traditionally included indigenous communities through various context-specific social mechanisms. Muo et al. (2012) argues that indigenous people in Nigeria and Africa had their own management philosophies and strategies by which they were able to manage themselves and survive, in pre-colonial times. Such peculiar strategies are those that encompass other aspects of life in manners that suggest alternative methods of political, economic and social governance, albeit, in ways that may be more beneficial to the region and the whole world. That is, only when all stakeholders participate as a part of the universe. To R.O. Badru (2010), the concept of *Ajobi* connotes that all persons live as descendants of a source by which everyone looks out for the welfare of others within a cosmopolitan entity as distinct from a compatriotic perspective. To him then, those who have should be ready to part with little on behalf of states that lack.

The African indigenous community is rooted in the will of leaders to rule and lead in good conscience. Such ideas rely on the need for all stakeholders to in a common purpose associate with one another and combined efforts in hunting for developmental purposes. Generally, settlement of civil conflicts and disputes are made through negotiations and arbitration. More importantly, individuals are to make compromises due to the wishes and interests of the community. Such interests of the community were usually toward sustaining peace without upsetting the standards as set by the divinity. For example, the idea of *ubuntu* suggests that the human moral obligation is to enter more deeply into community with others. African governance ideas are therefore more conceiving of communal relationships as an objectively desirable form of interactions, which should determine what majorities want and which norms become dominant.

To achieve peace, each person must see himself as an indispensable part of the group that conceives of themselves as a "we," and is willing to take pride or feel shame in the group's activities. In this instance engagements and projects are coordinated and regulated to achieve shared ends. The alternative to such unity is alienation, division and opposition. Such group solidarity ensures that people engage in mutual aid and act in ways that are reasonably expected to benefit each other. It entails the positive attitudes, motives and emotions toward others. That is, the ability to sympathize and assist one another. Among the Esan, the relationship between community of people and its persons is referred to as "*Oria no riwiusuagbon*" (one in the midst of many people); that is, a communal being with others. Oghojafor, B. et al. (2015). Among Yoruba Akiwowo (1983), the concept of *Ajobi*, *Ajogbe* and *Asuwada* all represent the moral theories of brotherhood, unity, communitarianism and harmonious living. The African inherent familial approach to land and resource management underscores Locke's permissive account:

> *A small elite may appropriate all of the huge cooperative surplus produced by modern social organization. But this elite must not enlarge its share even further by reducing the poor below the state-of-nature baseline to capture more than the entire cooperative surplus.*

Conclusion

The chapter from inception argues that the state remains the most appropriate figure to regulate land issues through provisions of laws and respect for international human rights and standards. The study describes the essence of state powers and the major objectives for land managements and interventions. The internationally agreed standards are however: the need to sufficiently consult and seek the free, prior and informed consent of affected persons; the willingness of states to provide undertakings and compensations in good faith; and the endurance of reformatory actions that are legal and sustainable. In achieving these three objectives, it is important that institutions do not adopt a general approach to dispute resolution, but that they understand all stakeholders' positions before taking impacting roles.

Land regulations that disregard traditional setup, citizens' bias and historical tendencies usually cause conflicts and inequality. States are unlikely to succeed with socio-economic development plans until they harmonize or isolate diverse interests within procedures that promote equality. Extreme statutory provisions should be amended to cushion equitable regimes of land use. The role of courts is not just to administer laws, but to favor judgments of equitable precedents that reflect the willingness to correct old anomalies. Government may not therefore be sensitive to the incidental impacts of nationally valued resources that are situated within traditional homelands of indigenous communities. Within the confines of law and common sense, due respect must be attributed to peoples culture and heritage.

Meanwhile, this does not suggest that lands may only be distributed based on unwritten and historical evidence or antecedents. Rather the role of law is to ensure that land is redistributed in manners that is inclusive of all persons whether indigenes, settlers or foreigners. Stakeholders should have guiding regimes which put the reversionary interest in government. This includes the primary consideration of persons, genders and communities that have been left out. The position does not also preclude the state power to expropriate illegitimately acquired parcels or to prohibit illegal land acquisitions.

Cited theories on land ownership and dispute resolution put governments in the position to ensure that all stakeholders understand their role within the commonwealth and the sacrifices and benefits incidental to such positions. If the aim of the government is to reduce inequality and poverty, it may borrow a leaf from indigenous ideologies that do not discriminate between persons on the entitlement to use land as a means of survival. For the purpose of land redistribution, the issue of compensation cannot be nationally determined. Rather, the essence of compensation is determined by the facts of each case. By international law, compensation is an inherent part of land management schemes, and this may not be waived away by other rules unless there are genuine reasons for that. For all purposes the main ideal should be to diffuse probable tension among stakeholders. At all times the government should also ensure that its land principles are not heavily influenced by neocolonial tendencies toward usury or economic exploitation of land in unsustainable manners.

Land rules would be efficient if hinged on the equitable fluidity of decision makers with good conscience and good faith. The first concern of laws through good faith is that at all instances public institutional structures do not overtly or subtly encourage the accumulation of valuable land by a few, while the majority become disposed to unsustainable use of other resources to meet immediate survival needs.

References

Abolition of Racially Based Land Measures Act, 1991 (Act No. 108 of 1991).
Akiwowo, A. 1983. *Ajobi and Ajogbe Variations on the Theme of Socialization*. Inaugural Lecture Series 16. University of Ife Press, p. 15.
Article 6 of The ILO Indigenous and Tribal Peoples Convention (169), 1989.
Article 10 of the United Nations Declaration of the Rights of Indigenous Peoples 69/215, 2007.
Article 17 of the 1948 Universal Declaration of Human Rights 1948.
Article 17 of the Universal Declaration of Human Rights (UDHR) 1948.
Badru, R.O. 2010. Compatriotism vs Cosmopolitanism: Exploring a New Cosmo-Morality of Human Relations from the Yoruba in the Age of Globalization. In *Globalization and Identity in Contemporary Africa*, ed. A.G. Adebayo et al., 43–57. Lanham, MD: Lexington Books.
Bentham, Jeremy. 1789. An Introduction to the Principals of Morals and Legislation, ("printed" in 1780, "first published" in 1789, "corrected by the Author" in 1823.) Chapter I: Of the Principle of Utility. For Bentham on Animals, see Ch. XVII Note 122.
Boundless Biology. 2019. The Soil. *Boundless-Biology*. Accessed October 12, 2019. www.lumenlearning.com

Brunt v Carew; *Larson, Aaron (21 December 2016)*. "Acquiescence To A Boundary Line". *Expert Law*. Accessed September 28, 2017.

Campbell, A. 1811. *Journey from Edinburgh through Parts of North Britain*. Vol. 2. London, p. 197.

Central Pacific R. Co. v. Alameda County, 284 US 463, 52 S. Ct. 225, 76 L. Ed. 402 (1932).

Costello v. United States 365 US 265, 282 (1961).

Darwin, Charles Robert. 1809–1882. *Origin of Species*. The Harvard Classics, pp. 1909–1914.

Diaw, M.C. 1997. Shifting Cultivation, Land Use and Property Rights in Southern Cameroon. *Rural Development Forestry Network Paper 21e*, Summer.

Dodgshon, R.A. 1998. *From Chiefs to Landlords: Social and Economic Change in the Western Highlands and Islands, c. 1493–1820*. Edinburgh University Press; 1st Edition (June 1, 1998) Edinburgh, p. 45.

Elias, T.O. 1972. *Nature of African Customary Law*. London: Manchester University Press, pp. 162–164.

Encyclopædia Britannica. Accessed 5 August 2019.

Herbert Spencer,1916, The Man versus the State: a Collection of Essays, edited by Truxton Beale 1916

Hobbs v Norton (1682), 22 ER.

Hofstadter, R. 1955. *The Age of Reform*. New York: Random House, pp. 46–47.

Hundsen v Cheyney (1690), 23 E.R 370.

Hunter, J. 1976. *The Making of the Crofting Community*. Edited by John Donald. Edinburgh, pp. 156–160.

Immanuel Kant's; *Economic and Philosophical Manuscripts of 1844*.

Legal-lingo. 2020. *What is the Legal Definition of Land*, retrieved from www.legal-lingo.net on 5 August 2019.

Locke, John. 1690. Second Treatise of Government. Sect 27.

Mill, J.S. 1848. *Principles of Political Economy* [*PPE*] [*CW* II–III].

Mohamed, M., et al. 2014. Economic Land Use Theory and Land Value in Value Model. *International Journal of Economics and Statistic* 2: 91–98.

Muo, I., et al. 2012. The Philosophy and Practice of Decision making and Consensus Building among the Ndigbo of Nigeria. *American Journal of Business and Management* 1 (3): 154–161.

Oghojafor, B., et al. 2015. Traditional Management Philosophies and Practices: The Case of the Esans of Edo State of Nigeria. *Journal of Management Policies and Practices* 3 (1, June): 50–58.

Oxford Advanced Learners Dictionary. 2001. 6th ed. Oxford University Press.

Preamble to the Constitution of the 1999 Constitution of the Federal Republic of Nigeria.
Savage v Foster (1722), 88 E.R. 703.
Section 217 of the 1999 Constitutions of the Federal Republic of Nigeria.
The Land Use Act and Land Ownership Debate in Nigeria Resolving the Impasse at www.researchgate.net [accessed August 16, 2018].
Thomas Hobbes (Leviathan II: 17, Leviathan I: 13, Leviathan I: 14).
Verdier, R. 1964. Evolution et reformes foncieres de l'Afrique noire francophone. *Journal of African Law* 15 (1): 85–101.
Withers, C.W.J. 1990. "Give Us Land and Plenty of It": The Ideological Basis to Land and Landscape in the Scottish Highlands. *Landscape History* 12: 45–54.

3

Political Economy and the Socio-cultural History of Land Dispossession, Proselytization, and Proletarianization of African People in South Africa: 1488–1770 (Part 1)

Mbhekeni Sabelo Nkosi

Introduction

There were massive proliferation of European pre-settlement and consequent permanent settlement in the southern tip of the African continent, where Europeans of Dutch, German, French, and British extraction violently dispossessed Africans of large tracts of land and then forcefully became private owners of African land and African natural resources through land seizures. The landlessness of African people resulted in trans-generational poverty and systemic deprivation amongst the African majority and trans-generational wealth and privilege amongst the descendants of European settlers in South Africa. The descendants of European settlers still live in South Africa today. In 1994, the African National Congress (ANC) opted not to eject them out of South Africa. To date,

M. S. Nkosi (✉)
Department of Philosophy, University of the Western Cape,
Bellville, South Africa

E. Masitera (ed.), *Philosophical Perspectives on Land Reform in Southern Africa*,
https://doi.org/10.1007/978-3-030-49705-7_3

therefore, they remain private owners of large tracts of land such as agricultural land, commercial farms, buildings, residential property, commercial property, including private ownership of the mines, which they have trans-generationally owned unjustly to the impoverishment of the African majority in South African society.

This chapter (part 1) locates European settlement within the narrative of land dispossessions that included a violent expropriation of African labour that occurred through European settler encroachment. It accords importance to understanding the certainty of colonialism and apartheid in South Africa and the essence of Afrikaner ethnic construction and European missionary involvement in land and cultural dispossessions and social inculturation as elements of European settler colonialism and imperialism. It offers a reconstruction of an ecclesial thrust in the South African historical narrative of land dispossession in the colonial, apartheid, and post-apartheid period. The study notes that contemporary South Africa has not undergone a political process of decolonization. Such a process is necessary for the African majority in South Africa to experience freedom as total liberation from a colonization of a special type in its contemporary, social, political, economic, cultural, and ecclesial expression.

The Emergence of European Settlers (1488–1591)

On the 3rd of February 1488 African herdsman on the sea shores of Mossel Bay [previously named *Bahia dos Vaqueros* (Portuguese) by the Europeans because of the herds of cattle], underwent an extraordinary and unprecedented experience—European strangers from the sea emerged (Welsh 2000, 1). However, the African herdsman drove their cattle away from the shore, whereupon one of the European strangers (Antonio de Saldanha) advanced towards a fresh water source intending to fill up their containers with fresh water (Welsh 2000, 1). Hence, the African herdsman advanced towards the fresh water source and resisted, waging a fight against the European strangers. This was the first encounter between the Europeans and the Africans on the seashores on the tip of the African continent. Welsh maintains that, Antonio de Saldanha, having landed in the bay (for many years after known as Saldanha Bay), found a good supply of fresh water, only to be ambushed by some two hundred African men. His party escaped with only minor injuries, but d'Almeida was less fortunate, encountering fierce resistance from Africans in an unexpected form of warfare; describing their reception he said that:

> [Having] called their cattle, which are accustomed to this form of warfare, [they] began to whistle to them and to make signs by which to guide them, so that forming into a squadron, and sheltered by the cattle, they attacked our men with [spears] hardened by fire. Some [of our men] fell wounded and were trodden down by the cattle, and as most were without shields, their only weapons being lances and swords, in this kind of warfare they could not do much damage to the [Africans], who from among their cattle hurled their weapons against our men, which had immediate effect (Welsh 2000, 9).

The African people's resistance against European encroachment occurs immediately after the (Europeans) first appearance. The Europeans were searching for African people to capture (chain, steal) and sell in the European slave trade. But Viceroy d'Almeida and no fewer than fifty of his men were killed in this battle, which was enough to discourage others from exploiting the African inhabitants of the Cape. This was before the Cape was a colony. Welsh (2000, 9) further maintains that the English initially abstained from exploiting African inhabitants when they received first-hand accounts of d'Almeida's fate and asserts that:

> The southern coast of Africa proved both a disappointing source of slaves and a highly dangerous region, a fact emphasized when, in 1510, a strong raiding party under the leadership of Bernado d'Almeida, on his way to assume the Viceroy-ship of the Indies at Goa, landed at the Cape.

Moreover, Welsh (2000, 10) further suggests that,

> Francis Drake passed the Cape in 1580, during his circumnavigation, describing it as 'a most stately thing, and the fairest Cape [that he has ever seen] in the whole circumference of the earth.' But it was not until 1591,

> nearly a century after the first Portuguese landing, that the British arrived at Table Bay. They were more successful, and perhaps more diplomatic, than their Portuguese predecessors. Under the command of George Raymond and James Lancaster, [three ships] *Penelope*, *Merchant Royal* and *Edward Bonaventure* first [docked at] Saldanha, where they found [Africans]. They managed to [negotiate with an African person to march into the country with them; they were] in search of cattle. Finding none, the [European] sailors let the [African person] go with some trifles. Within eight days [*sic*] after, he, with some thirty or forty [Africans] brought [them] down [*sic*] some forty bullocks and oxen…very large and well fleshed.

The European sailors mentioned in the above quotation were the crews of Bartolomeu Dias (Welsh 2000, 10).[1] Dias' ships made their way up to Algoa Bay, where they landed and erected a stone pillar satisfied that their way to the Indies was open. Welsh maintains that, "on the return passage Dias did at least sight the Cape of Good Hope, to which he gave the name *Cabo de Todos los Tormentos* (Cape of all Storms) (Welsh 2000, 2).

European Pre-settlement, Settlement, and the Colonial System

In the early 1700s the British East India Company (BEIC, 1600) and the *Vereenigde Oost-Indische Compagnie* (VOC, 1602), according to Terreblanche, "moved in to contest the Portuguese monopoly, but the latter managed to retain a significant portion of it during the 17th century" (Terreblanche 2012, 153).[2] Terreblanche suggests that, "[At] least 1000 Portuguese, 600 Dutch, and 400 English and French ships landed

[1] The various designations to refer to African people such as the racial categorizations and terms: *Hottentot* or *Khoikhoi* and the classifications *Khoisan* or *Bantu* including the appellatives *Native* or *Kaffir* are deliberately not used in this chapter as they are considered to be derogatory. The word "African" is used because at this stage the term remains an acceptable designation.

[2] Maloka (2014, 9) points out that, liberalism developed as an ideology and political project in Western Europe in the seventeenth century, and over the years spread to other parts of the world. Its fundamental assumptions counter-pose the individual to the state and society. To liberalism, the individual is endowed by nature with certain rights which must be enjoyed and protected. Notwithstanding its different intellectual and political shades, the core elements of liberalism are

on the [southern] coast between 1500 and 1650. One consequence of these pre-settlement contacts by Europeans was the large-scale plundering of [natural] resources and [African] people" (Terreblanche 2012, 153).[3] However, it was Holland that first developed the colonial system. Marx (2015a, 535) asserts that,

> Holland, which first fully developed the colonial system, in 1648 stood already in the acme of its commercial greatness. It was "in almost exclusive possession of the East Indian trade and the commerce between the south-east and north-west of Europe. Its fisheries, marine, manufactures, surpassed those of any other country. The total capital of the Republic was probably more important than that of all the rest of Europe put together" [by 1648] the people of Holland were more over-worked, poorer and more brutally oppressed than those of all the rest of Europe put together.

In view of the fact that it was Holland that developed the colonial system as shown in the above quotation, the process of spontaneous, unregulated colonization in the southern tip of the African continent began when in 6 April 1652, three ships, the *Dromedaris*, the *Reyger*, and the *De Goede Hoop*, docked at the Cape, Africa's southern tip (Farisani 1990, 3). This process began the systematic social, political, cultural, and economic construction of racialized poverty and racialized inequality amongst the African people by a European and Christian colonial system. Marx (2015a, 534) maintains that,

> Of the Christian colonial system, W. Howitt, a man who makes a specialty [*sic*] of Christianity, says: "The barbarities and desperate outrages of the so-called Christian race, throughout every region of the world, and upon every people they have been able to subdue, are not to be paralleled by those of any other race, however fierce, however untaught, and however

---

arguably individualism, a state with a limited role in society, the reification of private property, and the promotion of the rule of law to protect individual freedom.

[3] It is important to note that the understanding of healing, treatment techniques, the philosophy of medicine (and medical knowledge *per se*) was not brought to African people by Europeans when they docked with ships in the Cape (named by the Portuguese to be: *Cabo de Todos los Tormentos*, and tactfully renamed *Cabo de Bõa Esperanza*—the Cape of Good Hope—by King João II; and later renamed Cape Town by the colonists).

> reckless of mercy and of shame, in any age of the earth." The history of the colonial administration of Holland—and Holland was the head capitalistic nation of the 17th century—"is one of the most extraordinary relations of treachery, bribery, massacre, and meanness." Nothing is more characteristic than their system of stealing men, to get slaves.[4]

There was a relationship between Christianity, colonialism, and slavery. The European settlers and their company had no moral, political, or legal claim to the land in the Cape. They invaded the land. The European sailors that docked at the Cape, aware of the European system of stealing men to get slaves, formed a settlement—a European settlement. Terreblanche (2012, 153) says that,

> In 1652 the VOC [which had been formed in 1602 by uniting a number of Dutch commercial undertakings] established a fortified provision station at Table Bay in order to regulate the benefits that [European] sailors had long derived from Cape stopovers. The voyage to the East took six to eight months, and was fraught with numerous dangers, including scurvy.

The emergence and development of private European capital and European commercial activity in South Africa can be traced back to this period. The VOC (formed in 1602) established a fortified station at Table Bay in 1652. As a result of their settlement, the European settlers formed a European settler colony in the Cape and began seeking for artificial means to ensure a systematic construction of poverty amongst the African people, and racialized inequality between themselves and the Africans. This period began a historical process wherein the social, political, cultural, and economic foundations of South Africa were laid. In this historical process emerged the degradation and dispossessions of African people. A mass of African people were expropriated from their land, and they were to be used as slave labour. Marx (2015a, 542) asserts that, "the

[4] Marx quotes William Howitt: "Colonisation and Christianity: A Popular History of the Treatment of the Natives by the Europeans in all their Colonies." London, 1838, p. 9. On the treatment of the slaves there is a good compilation in Charles Comte, "Traité de la Législation." 3me éd. Bruxelles, 1837. This subject one must study in detail, to see what the bourgeoisie makes of itself and of the labourer, wherever it can, without restraint, model the world after its own image. Marx also quotes from Thomas Stamford Raffles, late Lieut-Gov. of that island: "The History of Java," London, 1817.

expropriation of the great mass of the people from the [land], from the means of subsistence, and from the means of labour, this fearful and painful expropriation of the mass of the people forms the prelude to the history of capital."

The Cape Colony was to serve as a half way station and post between Europe and Asia, for the VOC—a chartered trading corporation (Welsh 2000, 12).[5] Land was consequently forcefully and violently expropriated and usurped by European settlers in order for small gardens, orchards, and farms to be cultivated so as to provide fresh vegetables, fruits, grains, meat, and water for European ships in transit (Farisani 1990, 3). In this process of invasion, land dispossession, and the expropriation of African people's land and labour was a forcible robbery of African means of subsistence. However, in the colony, "property in money, means of subsistence, machines, and other means of production, [did] not as yet stamp [European settlers] as a capitalist [class] if there be wanting the correlative—the wage-worker, the other man who is compelled to sell himself of his own free will" (Marx 2015a, 533). At this stage Africans had not yet been converted into wage-labourers. European settlers had property in money. Machines and other means of production had not yet been introduced into the economic system for the purposes of building an industry, or beginning the process of industrialization, or the exploitative system of African wage-labour, at this early stage.

Capitalism, Capital Accumulation Process and Exploitation

According to Welsh, "Europeans could not be persuaded to produce the Company [VOC]'s food; slave labour had seemed to serve the Company well in the East, where its brutal suppression of resistance had produced an ample supply of captives; [and that] slavery encouraged colonists to be idle and unwilling to labour for themselves" (Welsh 2000, 35). Slavery

[5] Welsh further maintains that, "When the VOC was formed in 1601 the lion's share naturally fell to Amsterdam—367,500 guilders of the starting capital of 6,440,200 guilders; Zeeland, always the second most important province, subscribed just under half as much."

was seen by the Europeans as a basis for colonial wealth. Therefore, the racist exploitation of African people by European settlers influenced the development of capitalism in the Cape. But Marx (2015a, 544) asserts that, "capital is not a thing, but a social relation between persons, established by the instrumentality of things;" and that, "the means of production and subsistence, while they remain the property of the immediate producer, are not capital. They become capital only under circumstances in which they serve at the same time as means of exploitation and subjection of the labourer." Unfortunately for the Europeans, when they arrived in the Cape, African men, women, and children were free, being the owners of their own means of production and subsistence. Neither were they slaves nor exploited as labourers. The European settlers forcefully and brutally occupied African land and, to reach their capitalist objectives, identified the African population as both labourers and potential labourers. Marx (2015a, 534) holds that, "Force is the midwife of every old society pregnant with a new one. It is itself an economic power." The means of force and violence were used to subjugate and enslave Africans. The expropriation of the African people and their land, formed the basis of a racialized capitalist mode of production (Marx 2015a, 544). However, there were early signs of resistance amongst the African people. They refused to work for the European settlers and to produce food for them. It is this aspect of non-compliance with European settler demands that serves as a pretext for the African resistance struggle that led to the killing of many African people. African people were converted into the private property of the European settlers through the violent use of force. African labour, fused together with the conditions of labour, were supplanted by European capitalistic private property interests which rested on exploitation of the free labour of African people and their land—this culminated into an African resistance struggle (Marx 2015a, 542). Welsh (2000, 37) maintains that,

> The first serious manifestation of the [African] resistance to the intruding Europeans took place in a skirmish [where] they saw that the Europeans were breaking up the best land and grass, were their cattle were accustomed to graze, trying to establish themselves everywhere, with houses and farms, as if they were never to move anymore.

European colonists settled and built buildings and they established themselves never to move anymore. In view of the above quotation, there were land seizures, conquests, displacements, and forced land occupation to build a European settlement. Therefore, so long as the Africans could fend for themselves—and this they could do as they remained possessors of their means of production—capitalist accumulation and the capitalistic mode of production became impossible. The racialized class of African wage-labourers, essential to these, was wanting Marx (2015a, 544). As African people were dispossessed of their land, they were consequently converted into a servant race and class during the formation of a European settlement as a capitalist society and as a colony. In this context, the racialized class formation contextualized African people and Europeans under a relationship of European masters and African servants. Africans were compelled to become suppliers of forced labour power. The descendants of the European settler and capitalist class integrated with Africans within a racialized capitalistic society and the existence and movement of African people began to depend upon these racialized, unequal, and exploitative relations. The materialist dialectic accords primacy to *content* (reality of land dispossessions) and *being* (essence of land dispossessions) over *form* (appearance of the dispossessed) and *thought* (expropriation of land—without compensation). It is important to provide a method of reconstruction and analysis for the total movement of this *content* and *being*, identifying laws of development within which to place the South African historical, political, and economic situation (Lefebvre 2001, xx). Lefebvre suggests that,

> We must start from the *content*. The *content* comes first, it is the real [being] which determines dialectical thought. The object of our method of inquiry is to take possession of matter in its detail, to analyze its various forms of development and to discover its inner laws (Lefebvre 2001, 74).

The arrival of European colonists and their forced occupation of land to form a European settlement, and the subsequent colonial conquest, formed a permanent European settler community that posed an immediate threat to the life and existence of African people.[6] There was also an ecclesial impetus in the continual land seizures that occurred in the early colonial settlement.

An Ecclesial Impetus for Racial Domination and Land Seizure

In the Cape Colony's beginnings as a garrison, according to Gerstner, "the VOC provided for Dutch Reformed services, led by officially recognized religious workers. The first permanent minister arrived in 1665" (Gerstner 1997, 16). Gerstner (1997, 16) adds that, "the VOC, in collaboration with the Amsterdam Classis (regional assembly) of the Reformed Church in the Netherlands, maintained an almost continuous string of resident ministers from that time. As the established church, the Dutch Reformed Church [DRC] exercised a virtual monopoly of Christian expression in the new colony." Serfontein reveals that the first resident minister's name was Johan van Arkel, who, as Gerstner mentioned, arrived at the Cape in 1665, "which is regarded as the founding date of the first DRC congregation in South Africa" (Serfontein 1982, 59). Between 1652 and 1665, some thirty (30) ministers passed through the post *en route* between the East and the Netherlands, and ministered to the Christian (European) "flock" settled there (Serfontein 1982, 59). The first European settlement in the Cape was intended, at first, simply to provide a port of call for Dutch ships to pick up fresh supplies, but as early as 1657, the VOC allowed some of its former employees to settle and farm (Gerstner 1997, 16). The DRC was the first denomination to occupy land in the Cape colonial period. According to Elphick, "during the first phase of this early period, from 1652 to 1795, the public expression of Christianity was, with minor exceptions, monopolized by the Dutch Reformed Church, closely overseen by the ruling Dutch East

[6] The arrival of European colonists through the occupation of land to form a settlement, and the subsequent colonial conquest, brought with it the concept of western medicine and colonial diseases. However, this arrival, occupation and consequent settlement of European settlers formed a European community that exposed an immediate threat to the life and existence of the African people and African medical knowledge systems.

India Company (VOC)" (Elphick 1997, 2).[7] There is a relationship between private company ownership of land and the ownership of land by churches in South Africa. In any discussion of expropriation of land without compensation, the DRC (or NG Kerk) and its land occupations are implicated and form part of the historical and contemporary national question. Their occupation of land came through a displacement of African people. Therefore, such land as they occupy as a church in South Africa needs to be expropriated without any form of compensation to the DRC. Also, land that is owned by private companies needs to be expropriated without any compensation to the companies that own the land.

Christian Theology and the Development of Cape Colonial Culture

The southern tip of the African continent had been used as a refreshment stop and trading post by European seafarers to nourish European mariners that were *en route* to the Eastern spice-producing countries mainly India and Sri Lanka (Ceylon) and to trade with the local land and livestock owning African population. The expropriation of the African labourer from his conditions of labour was brought about in the Cape by the co-existence of European capital and the system of African wage-labour. As a result of European settlement, there came into existence a social contract of quite an original kind—the European settlers divided themselves into owners of capital and owners of African labour. The racialized class divisions were the result of conquests and violent dispossessions and the consequent subjugation and enslavement of African people as oppressed (un-free) labourers (Marx 2015a, 544). Most slaves,

[7] It is this monopoly of the public expression of Christianity during this important period that explains my focus on the Dutch Reformed Church (DRC/NGK) as a denomination. The VOC officials then erected a makeshift hospital for the European settlement only. Russel Viljoen maintains that, ideas of western medicine, however, were not immediately imposed on the local indigenous people, even though the VOC authorities had erected one poorly equipped and [poorly] staffed hospital to provide medical care to Company employees and to sick sailors (Viljoen 2014, 1); Viljoen provides evidence for the introduction of a doctor-centric, hospi-centric approach to patient care. Viljoen points to the first hospital that was set up for the medical treatment of those that were sick amongst the European settlers.

except those who belonged to the VOC, according to Elbourne and Ross (1997), were not baptized as Christians unless they were manumitted. The Christian religion was used to pacify the dispossessed. The proselytization of African people by European settlers can be traced back to this period. Elbourne and Ross (1997) further maintain that the other main groups of the dispossessed were the slaves brought to the Cape from all shores of the Indian Ocean—from Mozambique through Madagascar, Sri Lanka, South India, Bengal, to Indonesia (Elbourne and Ross 1997, 34). The bringing of slaves from Asia into the economic system forms the structural and systematic origins of racial pluralism in South Africa. The Asian slaves came with a wide range of religious convictions. However, many Cape slaves were neither Muslim nor Hindu when they disembarked in Cape Town (Elbourne and Ross 1997, 34). Dutch Reformed church life, Gerstner adds, and Christian theology played a formative role in the development of Cape colonial culture and society. In particular, it contributed greatly to the formation of a distinct identity among the European settlers and their conviction of racial superiority to African people and slaves (Gerstner 1997, 16). Elbourne and Ross (1997) disclose that the first work by European missionary societies in the Cape Colony was among African stock herding people who inhabited most of the region and who were not as poor as they are now.[8] The poverty of African people was created, socially constructed, and ensured through artificial means through the economic ideology of racism. The significance of this problem should be understood against the background of European settlers turning the land that they had violently dispossessed into their private property. Therefore, private property law regarding private land ownership [and the private property clause in the South African constitution] needs to be evaluated from this perspective. Marx (2015a, 544) asserts that,

[8] These are African people who were discriminated against and labelled by Europeans as "Khoikhoi;" and who were subjugated and classified as "Hottentots;" and who were dispossessed and categorized as "San;" and mass murdered and referred to as "Bushmen." Mqhayi (2001, 87), depicting this tribalism and principle of "divide and rule," uses this derogatory and divisive language and maintains that, the "Hottentots" lived content with the "Ndlambe" because when the "Bushmen" met a "Xhosa" they would ask who he belonged to, "Ndlambe" or "Hahabe" (Rharhabe); yet all were African.

> The essence of a ["free"] colony, on the contrary, consists in this—that the bulk of the soil [was] still public property, and every [European] settler on it therefore [turned] part of it into his private property and individual means of production, without hindering the later [European] settlers in the same operation. This is the secret both of the prosperity of the colonies and of their inveterate vice—opposition to the establishment of [European] capital.

Land was turned into a privately owned means of production. No European settler in the colony was hindered from this operation. The secret to the prosperity of European settlers and their descendants in South Africa can be traced to the ownership of land as private property and the exploitation of African people as landless wage-labourers. The African population had been numerous and it communally or collectively owned land, and had plenty of cattle and more than enough meat and milk, as compared to the European settlers (Elbourne and Ross 1997, 37). Upon the construction of the European colony, the land that belonged to the African population was turned by the Europeans into public property, liable to be converted into private property—an antithesis to collective property. Marx (2015b, 125) affirms that, "Land, to be an element of colonization, must not only be waste, but it must be public property, liable to be converted into private property."

Re-conceptualizing Private Property and Public Ownership of Land

According to Elbourne and Ross (1997, 27), European labour-hungry local farmers and VOC officials sought to convert Africans into landless farm labourers, who were to live permanently on farms that were owned by European settlers. These farms became private property that was individually owned by European settlers. Gerstner (1997, 27) adds that, Africans knew the European settlers by their name of group identity, "Christian." Marx (2015a, 541) suggests that, "Private property, as the antithesis to social, collective property, exists only where the means of labour and the external conditions of labour belong to private individuals."[9] By the time Jan van Riebeeck arrived in the Cape, he landed with approximately 200 people at the foot of Table Mountain to establish a provision station for the ships of the Dutch East India Company on their voyages to the East Indies (Serfontein 1982, 59). Gerstner (1997, 27) points out that,

> In April 1657, there [were] 144 people on the station: a hundred company employees, ten free burghers, six married women, twelve children, ten slaves and six convicts. The number of slaves increased sharply in March the next year, when a Portuguese slaver was captured and 250 head of the cargo taken to the Cape. Many of these were too young for work and were sent to school under the chaplain, under the eye of the Commandant himself for the first few days; they were stimulated to industry by the promise of a tot of brandy and tobacco when their lessons were satisfactorily learnt. Some of the others who were fit for employment—relatively few—were transferred, on credit to the free burghers to help on the farms. A further consignment came two months later, when 228 Guinea slaves...were landed. Those who survived looked more promising than their predecessors and were sold for one hundred guilders a head to the free burghers on 9 May [1657].

The slave trade was endemic in the European settler colony. The VOC originally depended on "trading" with Africans for cattle and the company was anxious to "avoid" wars at the Cape. But the VOC and its employees plundered during this period. Race-based conflict would break out and battles would ensue between the Europeans and the Africans. African leaders who would lead the resistance against European plunder would be captured and banished to Robben Island. Terreblanche (2012, 154) further suggests that,

[9] This situation further created the necessity for healthcare facilities. According to Viljoen, the VOC was the first company to own a hospital in the Cape Colony. He further points out that, "For the most part of the late seventeenth and eighteenth centuries, colonial medical facilities, the quantity and quality of medicine remained poor. Medical supplies were not only expensive, but also scarce. Soon after taking up his post as Commander of the Cape Colony, Jan van Riebeeck, who was also a [mate to a] surgeon, was the first one to complain about insufficient medical supplies" Viljoen (2014, 1).

> Consequently, [the VOC] ordered its first commander, Jan van Riebeeck (1652–62), to treat the [Africans] with respect and to do nothing to disturb their cultural integrity and socio-economic stability. He originally applied this policy very strictly, but after the company had released some of its employees from their contracts and set them up as freeburgers (or independent farmers) in 1657, [a] war of plunder broke out between the VOC and the [Africans] in 1659. After the war, the [African] leader [who led the war] was banned to Robben Island.

The cultural identity and economic stability of African people were undermined by European settlers. The development of the European settler colony simultaneously led to the development of an import-export economy. Therefore, the dependence of the South African economy on imported products can be traced back to this period. This process would later lead to the dominance of the European settlers in the retail and commercial sector. To think of Africans as a market was a later thought that was introduced when Africans were allowed to work for an income and to earn money. In 1659, according to Viljoen (2014, 1), Van Riebeeck wrote to Amsterdam complaining and said that,

> They received 'no medicines for two years.' A year later, he again informed his superiors in Holland how sparse the medical supplies had become compared to the previous shipment. The only time medicines and medical supplies were imported were when ships docked. Even then there was no guarantee that it would be brought ashore or destined for the [Cape Colony].

In April 1660, the African leader who had led the war against the settlers (in 1659) was brought back from Robben Island for "peace negotiations." Even in later years in South African political history, African political leaders were to be banished to Robben Island and would later be brought back for "peace negotiations" with descendants of European settlers. According to Terreblanche (2012, 154), Van Riebeeck told the African leader that, "not enough grazing land was available for the cattle of both the [European settlers] and the [Africans]. [The African then asked]: 'If the country is too small, who has the greater right: the true owner, or the foreign intruder?'" European settlers, as foreign intruders, began to privately own land, livestock, and labour in the farms as independent farmers. Terreblanche (2012, 154) maintains that Van Riebeeck recorded an answer on his diary: "We have won this country in a just manner through a defensive war, and it is our intention to keep it." The private property of the labourer, according to Marx (2015a, 542), is his means of production, "[It] is the foundation of petty industry, whether agricultural, manufacturing, or both; petty industry, again, is an essential condition for the development of social production and of the free individuality of the labourer himself. Of course, this petty mode of production exists also under slavery." Petty industry was later to be developed in the European colony. The Edict of Nantes was revoked in 1685. Davenport and Saunders (2000, 22–23) adds that,

> In 1689, 180 French Huguenots who had fled France for the Netherlands after the revocation of the Edict of Nantes in 1685, settled at the Cape, German settlers were added to the mix in the eighteenth century. The dominant culture, however, remained Dutch. As the historian, Davenport, has noted that, 'An originally diverse European settler population was…coaxed into cultural uniformity, with the language of the Netherlands and the religion of the [Dutch] Reformed Church for cement.

The French and the German settlers migrated from Europe to South Africa. This process created a diverse European settler population in the colony. In the main, these European settlers came as wage workers. There was a relative surplus of European wage workers at the time. However, upon their arrival in the Cape Colony they soon ceased to be wage workers for hire; they became independent land owners and competitors with the Dutch settlers (Marx 2015a, 545). It is here that the thesis of South Africa being a colony of a special type incipiently emerges. South Africa became a colony of a special type (CST) in a sense that the European colony that evolved in South Africa after the Europeans arrived, was not a colony of Portugal, Britain, Holland, France, or Germany, thus it became a colony of a special type. British annexation of the colony occurs later which disrupts the CST thesis. The process of land dispossession, racialized capitalist exploitation, and European settler monopolistic capitalist production continued. Henceforth, was to come the internal market for capital. Money is a form in which capital appeared. Marx (2015b) points out that, "[capital] is the economic power which dominates everything." Furthermore, according to Marx (1988, 449), "The circulation of money as capital is, on the contrary, an end in itself, for the expansion of value takes place only within this constantly renewed movement. The circulation of capital has therefore no limits." Money in the colony became a product of exchange. According to Lenin (1982, 20), "Being the highest product of the development of exchange and of commodity production, money masks the social character of individual labour, and hides the social tie between the various producers who come together in the market." Marx (1988, 445) maintains that, "The circulation of commodities is the starting-point of capital." The starting point of racialized free-market fundamentalism in South Africa can be traced back to this period. The beneficiaries of the free-market system as it evolved were European settlers. Lefebvre (2001, 75) maintains that,

> [Analysis of the starting-point] determines the relations and moments of the complex content. Only then can the movement of the whole [economic system] be reconstituted and 'exposed'... In thought it appears as a process of synthesis, as a result and not as a starting-point, although it is the true starting-point.

It is in understanding this complex historical and economic process that the movement of the whole economic system in South Africa can be exposed. The South African racialized capitalist economic system, if it is to be transformed, needs to be understood according to its historical framework that underpins its racist economic foundations. The European settler population was not exclusively agricultural, excepting slaves and their employers who fused European capital and African labour. African labourers cultivated the soil and followed many other forced occupations. Within a racial-ideology-based economic system, some portion of the furniture and tools which the European settlers used was commonly and forcefully made by African people. Europeans frequently used African forced labour to build their own houses, and to carry to the market, at whatever distance, the produce of their own industry. There were spinners and weavers in the colony; soap-makers and candle-makers, as well as, in many cases, shoe-makers and producers of clothes for their own use, and to sell to the African market. There came blacksmiths, millers, and shopkeepers. Marx (2015a, 545) asks: "With such queer people as these, where is the 'field of abstinence' for the capitalists?" Capital formation became the starting-point for capitalist production in the development of commodity production. It formed the point of departure and the conclusion. Hence, South Africa is a capitalist and racially exploitative society. The economy and its concepts brought about the interconnection of various conceptual and economic categories. Race and class as conceptual categories became the ruling material force of society. The race and class which owned the means of production had ownership and control of the political economy. The economic system underwent a series of controversial changes. Commodities were traded (exchanged) in the market system. Lefebvre (2001, 77) points out that,

> The exchange of commodities tends to put an end to a natural, patriarchal economy. In relation to individuals this new social whole, functions as a superior organism. In particular, it imposes on them a division and distribution of labour in conformity with the sum of the forces of production and the requirements of society.

Commodity exchange functioned as a superior organism. It imposed a racialized division and distribution of labour. The African wage worker was produced, and the slave worker reproduced in an intercultural and interracial multiclass society. There was private capital accumulation in the colony. As the European settler population grew in the colony, the appetite for more land grew, there was also an increased demand for labour. Africans in the country were identified as a population of potential wage workers. African labour was commodified. Marx (2015a, 545) further maintains that,

> [Capitalist] production consists in this—that it not only constantly reproduces the wage-worker as wage worker, but produces always, in proportion to the accumulation of capital, a relative surplus-population of wage-workers. Thus the law of supply and demand of labour is kept in the right rut, the oscillation of wages is penned within limits satisfactory to capitalist

> exploitation, and lastly, the social dependence of the labourer on the capitalist, that indispensable requisite, is secured; an unmistakable relation of dependence, which the smug political economist, at home, in the mother-country, can transmogrify into one of free contract between buyer and seller, between equally independent owners of commodities, the owner of the commodity capital and the owner of the commodity labour.

The coming into existence and the consequent development of the European settler colony created a social and economic relation of dependence for the African labourers on the European settler capitalists—transmogrified into one of contract between "buyer" and "seller," between owners of commodities, the "owners of the commodity capital" and the "owners of the commodity labour." Yet the European settler colony became a complex system of slavery, segregation, racial discrimination, and racial domination. Most European slave-owners resisted instructing their African slaves in religion, because, at least after 1770, a converted African slave could not be sold (Elbourne and Ross 1997, 34). However, African communities were found to be deserted by the 1770s due to European settlement that caused a high African mortality rate which was a result of violence and European introduced diseases. There was in the Cape Colony the urgent desire for cheaper and more subservient labourers—for a class to whom the European capitalists might dictate terms. Converted slaves remained oppressed (un-free and forced) labourers. By Dutch law they were dependent on capitalist European settlers. In the Cape Colony, this dependence was created by artificial means.

Conclusion

This chapter (part 1) starts in 1488 with pre-settlement contacts between Africans and Europeans in South Africa and ends in 1770 where African communities were found to be deserted as a result of European settlement and territorial expansion. The chapter contests the view that European contact with African people on the southern tip of the African continent occurred starting from 1652 when Jan van Riebeek landed at the Cape. The chapter laments the fact that when such a history is told it becomes a history of Europeans as the objects of their own history and Africans become their subjects. Nevertheless, though this chapter narrates such a history starting from 1488 it alludes to the fact that by about 1350 African people managed centres of trade and commerce with connections to Arabia, India, and China. The chapter shows that Africans resisted European settlement from the very onset. The interaction in 1591 of European strangers from the sea shore with Africans forms the prelude to the history of capital in South Africa. By 1650 Africans had underwent pre-settlement contact with European settlers as foreigners. Such contact led to the plundering of natural resources and people. Europeans developed the colonial system. Before 1652, the colonial system had been fully developed in Europe. During the seventeenth century Holland was a capitalist nation. The European settlers that settled in the Cape had no moral, political, or legal right to claim the country as their own. They formed a colony that began a historical process of enslaving, degrading, dehumanizing, and impoverishing African people; forcefully expropriating their land and violently expropriating their labour—expropriating African people from their land. Slavery formed the basis of colonial wealth. African people were exploited and subjected to forced labour by Europeans. Force was used as a means of coercion. African people and African land were forcefully converted into the private property of European settlers. Europeans forcefully established themselves in the country never to move anymore.

References

Davenport, T.R.H., and C. Saunders. 2000. *South Africa: A Modern History*. Palgrave Macmillan.

Elbourne, E., and R. Ross. 1997. Combating Spiritual and Social Bondage: Early Missions in the Cape Colony. In *Christianity in South Africa: A Political, Social and Cultural History*, ed. R. Elphick and R. Davenport. Cape Town: David Philip.

Elphick, R., and R. Davenport. 1997. *Christianity in South Africa: A Political, Social and Cultural History*. Cape Town: David Philip.

Farisani, T.S. 1990. *In Transit: Between the Image of God and the Image of Man*. New Jersey: Africa World Press.

Gerstner, J.N. 1997. A Christian Monopoly: The Reformed Church and Colonial Society under Dutch Rule. In *Christianity in South Africa: A Political, Social and Cultural History*, ed. R. Elphick and R. Davenport. Cape Town: David Philip.

Lefebvre, H. 2001. *Dialectical Materialism*. London: University of Minnesota Press.

Lenin, V.I. 1982. *The Teachings of Karl Marx*. Moscow: International Publishers.

Maloka, E. 2014. *Friends of the Natives: An Inconvenient History of Liberalism in South Africa*. Durban: 3rd Millennium.

Marx, K. 1988. *Selected Writings*. Edited by D. McLellan. Oxford: Oxford University Press.

———. 2015a. *Capital: A Critique of Political Economy*. Vol. 1, Book 1: The Process of Production of Capital. Moscow: Progress Publishers.

———. 2015b. *Capital: A Critique of Political Economy*. Vol. 2. Moscow: Progress Publishers.

Mqhayi, S.E.K. 2001. *Abantu Besizwe: Historical and Biographical Writings, 1902–1944*. Edited by J. Opland. Johannesburg: Wits University Press.

Serfontein, J.H.P. 1982. *Apartheid Change and the NG Kerk*. Emmarentia: Taurus.

Terreblanche, S. 2012. *A History of Inequality in South Africa 1652–2002*. Scottsville: University of KwaZulu Natal Press.

Viljoen, R. 2014. Medicine, Medical Knowledge and Healing at the Cape of Good Hope: Khoikhoi Slaves and Colonists. In *Medicine and Colonialism: Historical Perspectives in India and South Africa*, ed. P. Bala. London: Routledge.

Welsh, F. 2000. *A History of South Africa*. London: Harper Collins.

4

Political Economy and the Socio-cultural History of Land Dispossession, Proselytization, and Proletarianization of African People in South Africa: 1795–1854 (Part 2)

Mbhekeni Sabelo Nkosi

Introduction

European settlers invaded South Africa and continued a process of systematic colonization in the historical period between 1795 and 1854. With the colonization process they brought with them the ideology of racism, liberalism, and the economic system of capitalism which resulted in the exploitation of African people as labour. Colonial encroachment brought with it a proliferation of European mainstream churches and the religion of Christianity which resulted in the proselytization, and social and cultural domination of African people. This chapter discusses colonialism and land dispossession. It shows how African people's land was

M. S. Nkosi (✉)
Department of Philosophy, University of the Western Cape,
Bellville, South Africa

E. Masitera (ed.), *Philosophical Perspectives on Land Reform in Southern Africa*,
https://doi.org/10.1007/978-3-030-49705-7_4

violently dispossessed and African labour was expropriated. Africans were subjugated and enslaved and suffered large-scale loss of land. The argument in this chapter is that the colonization, proletarianization, and proselytization of African people in South Africa led to their political, socio-cultural, and economic domination. The position that is taken in this chapter is that a racialized capitalist production process was set up in the colony amidst a feudal patriarchal master-servant property relation and system of slave ownership. The chapter also reflects on the Afrikaner ethnic and political formation that defends its own racist and separatist interests of the remaining descendants of European settlers who unjustly own vast amounts of land in the interior of South Africa. The chapter concludes that the land that is privately owned by descendants of European settler society in general in South Africa, and the Afrikaner settler community in particular, remains in their private ownership unjustly as a result of the historical process of land dispossession.

Arrival of European Imperialist Forces

The British initially arrived in the southern part of the African continent in 1795. Davenport (1997: 52) suggests that, "when the British arrived in 1795, they recognized the Reformed church (NGK) as in the de facto possession of the field and paid stipends to the NGK clergy." In the Cape Colony the European settler population increased much more quickly because many European "labourers" entered this country as adults, and yet the labour-market was always understocked. The law of supply and demand of labour fell to pieces. On the one hand, England constantly threw in capital, thirsting after exploitation of labour. When European wage workers arrived they became independent peasants and artisans, working for themselves. Thereafter, when European wage workers were transformed into independent producers, they enriched themselves. The degree of exploitation amongst European wage workers remained indecently low. Also, in retrospect, "it seems that it was inevitable that, since no church had a clear majority among the [European] settlers, the Cape would reject an established church and adopt instead a pluralist form of church organisation" (Elphick and Davenport 1997: 3). Thus, with the arrival of the British settlers was imported into the Cape Colony the ideology of liberalism. Racism had already been developed and was entrenched in the European colony in South Africa. Maloka (2014: 9) asserts that,

> [Liberalism] reached [Africa's shores] through European influence. Communism is another political movement that came [into Africa's shores] through [European] émigré during the colonial period... The same applies for Christianity. Like communism, it arrived in [Africa] through colonial contact with Europeans but in no time it was appropriated by Africans and indigenized. This appropriation took the form not only of the emergence of the home-grown hymns and the re-interpretation of the gospel, but Africans themselves within the church structures started making demands on the [European settlers] for a voice in decision making and representation in the leadership hierarchy. This was not to be so for liberalism.[1]

If capitalism was the European settler colonial cell, liberalism was the nucleus. At this stage in the historical process of the economic development of South Africa, communism had not yet been introduced. However, in the 1790s there was another attempt at revolting against the European settlers beginning in 1799. Elbourne and Ross concur that, "[the] last attempt at revolt occurred in the 1790s. In the Eastern Cape the [Africans] tried in vain to resist land dispossession, subjugation, and enslavement. In a three-year rebellion from 1799 to 1802, they suffered large-scale loss of stock, land, and access to water, and were increasingly reduced to servitude [by] local [European] farmers" (Elbourne and Ross 1997: 37). This revolt was not inspired by communism or Marxism. However, Elbourne and Ross (1997: 37) conclude by stating that,

> On mission stations, such [Africans] could regain a measure of authority over their lives. The appeal of Christianity was doubtless bolstered by the strong opposition to [European] settlers—who benefited from the equation between Christianity, a [pale skin], and economic and political dominance—to the Christianization of their [African] dependents. [Africans], particularly those born of sexually exploitive mixed-race unions, knew the

[1] Maloka further notes that, "within [a] few years of its landing [communism] indigenized and became fully Africanized."

> settlers' views and for many of them an alliance with Christian missions was a defiant move, rather than a simple acceptance of the religion of their masters.

There was a strong African opposition to European settlers even though they were politically dominant. Many children who were born of sexually exploitive and violent mixed-race sexual activities began to emerge in colonial society as a result of the enslavement and sexual trafficking of African and Asian slave women by European settlers. This emergence further consolidated the pluralist nature of European settler society. Such children would in the future be referred to as being of mixed race or coloured. However, there were those children who were not of European descent; neither were they a product of mixed-race sexual interactions. Gerstner (1997: 27) supports Elbourne and Ross' view and adds that, "when successful Dutch Reformed missions at the turn of the nineteenth century baptized [African] converts, the consequence was a virtual revolt by some [European] settlers who refused to partake at the same table with those not of European descent, or to use their term, not 'born Christian.' This led to the beginning of racialized formal church [separatism]." Herein lies the seed of apartheid. Furthermore, the ideology of separatism, liberalism and capitalism was compatible with colonialism, imperialism, and racism. Maloka (2014: 11) points out that,

> To be sure, a sizeable period of British rule in South Africa was presided over in London by the Liberal Party which was a political force in British politics in the 19th century into the early 20th century when it began to decline, giving way to the Labour Party. Not only was the Liberal Party equally committed to British imperial expansion as their Conservative Party opponents; a tendency also developed within the party, known as "liberal imperialists", which saw no contradiction between espousing liberalism and enthusiastically promoting colonial conquest overseas.

Colonial conquest in South Africa was promoted to the benefit of European imperialism. Higgs (1997: 33), in her notes, cites Thompson and records that: "The colony was originally established in 1652 by the Dutch East India Company as a station to reprovision its ships *en route* to Asia. The [Cape] colony was seized by the British in 1795, during the

French Revolutionary Wars (to prevent it falling to the French), returned to the Dutch in 1803 by the treaty of Amiens, and claimed by the British again in 1806." South Africa became the battleground for colonial and imperial forces battling for territory. In the seizure of the Cape Colony in 1795 and in 1806 by British imperial forces, South Africa became a British colony. Missionaries in the 1800s were consolidating European settler privileges, and they were attached to the land which they had colonized. Therefore, there is a period in South African history where South Africa becomes a colony of the British Empire, but not France, thus temporarily ceasing to become a Colony of a Special Type (CST). These shifts render the CST thesis weak in its analysis of the South African question. I will explain this further in the study. Maloka (2014: 5) states that,

> [In the colony, liberalism] is an offspring of the British Empire. The two are tightly linked. This connection is due to [a] few basic ingredients that are essential to the *raison d'etre* of liberalism [in the Cape Colony and the rest of the country] namely: Empire, settlers, and the "natives" [(referring to) the African people in a derogatory manner]. Liberalism [in the colony] emerged in this context with a strong British colonial connection and linkage to the system of capitalism.

South Africa develops as a racist capitalist and exploitative political economic system. The seizure of the Cape Colony by the British settlers intensified the process of systematic colonization and land dispossession. The British colonial government put upon the land an artificial price, independent of the law of supply and demand, a price that compelled European immigrants to settle and work for wages before they could purchase land and turn themselves into independent (private) landowners. Marx (2015: 546) states that,

> [This] "sufficient price for the land" is nothing but a euphemistic circumlocution for the ransom which the labourer pays to the capitalist for leave to retire from the wage labour market to the land. First, he must create for the capitalist "capital," with which the latter may be able to exploit more labourers; then he must place, at his own expense, a *locum tenens* [placeholder] on the labour market, whom the Government forwards across the sea for the benefit of his old master, the capitalist.

With the funds that resulted from the sale of African land at a price relatively prohibitory for the European wage-workers, the British colonial government was to employ European immigrant workers, on the other hand, in proportion as it grew; it was to import European have-nothings from Europe into the colony, and thus kept the wage-labour market full for the colonial capitalists. This was the great secret of systematic colonization (Marx 2015: 546). Commodification and commercialization of land and labour became the simplest element in the capitalist production process. Marx (2015: 546) (citing Wakefield) points out that,

> Wakefield cries in triumph, "the supply of labour must be constant and regular, because, first, as no labourer would be able to procure land until he had worked for money, all immigrant labourers, working for a time for wages and in combination, would produce capital for the employment of more labourers; secondly, because every labourer who left off working for wages and became a landowner would, by purchasing land, provide a fund for bringing fresh labour to the colony." The price of the soil imposed by the State must, of course, be a "sufficient price"—i.e., so high "as to prevent the labourers from becoming independent landowners until others had followed to take their place."

In the colony, there emerged dialectical interconnections and asymmetrical interrelationships in the political economic system in the context of a European colonial settlement and a mixture of private European settler interests coaxed into a colonial system wherein commodities, including commodified land and labour, were presented as both a use-value and an exchange-value (Marx 2015: 425). Hence, financing private European interests became a continuous challenge. Private European interests became socially determined interests. Therefore, competition in colonial society became indicative of liberal pluralism and individualism. In such a colonial society, differentiations, alignments, and antagonisms insofar as they influence race and class formation cannot be fully grasped unless they are situated within the process of race and class conflicts (and concrete contradictions) operating on complex levels in an evolving capitalist system (Juan 2003: 2). Land, labour, and natural resources were commodified and commercialized in an evolving colonial free-market system. African people refused to work for European settlers, opting to trade with them instead, thereby causing frustration amongst the Europeans that were desperate for cheap African unskilled labour. Hewson (2015: 25) points out that,

> [European settlers, the Dutch and the British settlers,] traded with the [African] population ... [The Africans] were mainly hunters, fishermen, and gatherers ... [they were also] herders of sheep and cattle. Despite often cruel attempts by the settlers to persuade [them] to work for [the European settler community] in providing produce for the ships, they refused to do so ... The settlers were desperate for labour.

During this time, African people were aware of the expanding European settler colony and they chose to trade with the European strangers. Africans owned their livestock and their labour power. European settlers constantly attempted to persuade African people to work for them in food production, in various industries, and domestic work for a wage. African people had refused and resisted proletarianization, instead opted to trade with the Europeans that had settled in the colony, thereby preferring to develop trade relations and enterprise. There was no project of decolonization at this stage.

European Settlement and British Imperial Integration

Welsh (2000: xxii) asserts that, "the Dutch settlement that had begun in 1652 was supplanted by the integration of the Cape into the expanding British Empire, which brought its own language and culture, including many concepts of freedom and equality, to threaten the existing order." According to Pakenham (2009: 45), "at Simonstown, a few miles south of Cape Town behind the fluffy white 'Table Cloth' was Britain's 'most important naval base and coaling station in the whole world ... to establish this base, Britain had grabbed the Cape temporarily from the Dutch East India Company during the French Revolutionary War, and made the occupation permanent after 1806." Davenport (1997: 52) then says that,

> When the British retook the Cape in 1806, the Church of England acquired semi-official status there, with the Governor authorized by the Bishop of London to exercise general control and to legalize marriages and baptisms for all denominations. The Test and Corporations Acts, which denied public office and the franchise to non-Anglican believers in Britain, were inconsistently enforced at the Cape.

There is a historical connection between the Christian religion, Christian theology, capitalism, race politics, and government which was to influence the philosophical foundations of the African National Congress (ANC) many years later when the ANC is formed and enters albeit late in the political economic context of South Africa. Despite the British takeover, many of the Dutch farmers (European settlers that became known as Boers, from the Dutch word for farmer) remained poor and unassimilated. Higgs (1997), in her notes cites Thompson (1990: 56), that British settlers clashed with the earlier European settlers (Boers who were later called: Afrikaners).[2] There was to be animosity between the two European settler colonial groups. The Boers developed a Dutch patois which was later referred to as Afrikaans. They were to prove formidable enemies to European settlers of British origin and Africans alike (Pakenham 2009: 45). Collectively, the European settlers strengthened their position against the Africans (especially amongst *Abathwa* and *AmaXhosa*) (Feinstein 2009: 28).

[2] Furthermore, a civilian hospital was founded in 1818 by Dr Samuel Bailey. In the same year a leper asylum was established by the Cape government at Hemel-en-Aarde in the Caledon District. In 1820 the British government assisted 5000 settlers to emigrate to the eastern frontier of the colony. As a result of this emigration, there was a substantial English-speaking element in the colony.

Liberalism and the Free-Market Economy in the Cape Colony

Liberalism and the market economy in the Cape Colony emerged as a branch of British imperial expansion and European settler colonialism in the country (Maloka 2014: 5). It produced political parties, think-tanks, and various pressure groups. Maloka (2014: 5) suggests that liberalism evolved as an ideology of colonial conquest and control and not as a product of the anti-colonial struggle. Maloka (2014: 13) maintains that,

> Liberal imperialism has a new meaning which is not totally unrelated to the historical evolution of the concept. It is a foreign policy intervention doctrine that justifies interference or the invasion of sovereign states for the purpose of exporting or, perhaps, imposing liberal democracy and the "market economy."

Since in the early colonial times, according to Vorster (2006: 686), "[European settlers] perceived the land as basically unoccupied. They also held the view that the land was under-utilized and could therefore be occupied and cultivated in a proper manner by the settlers." Higgs (1997: 52) further cites that, consequently an approximately 5000 British settlers arrived in 1820:

> British colonists had first arrived in the Cape Colony in substantial numbers in 1820. The British government's intent was to settle them as farmers in the eastern part of the colony, south of lands historically claimed by [Africans]. Most 1820 [European settlers], however lacked the skills and experience to farm the arid land of the eastern Cape effectively; instead they settled in the town that grew up around the British fort at Grahamstown, or in Port Elizabeth. Those who remained on the land eventually achieved a degree of prosperity by turning to sheep ranching. Thus [European] settlers remained a presence in the Eastern Cape, periodically clashing with [Africans] and encroaching further into their territory.

European churches that had their origins in Britain arrived after the Dutch settlement. Elbourne and Ross (1997: 32) maintain that,

> The first British missionaries were most often members of the upper working classes, especially in newly industrializing areas where the power of the Anglican Church was weak; but since [English] missionaries needed a measure of literacy, they were never drawn from the ranks of the completely destitute. They tended to believe in aggressive self-improvement and the need to subjugate nature to [the] human will.

Davenport (1997: 52) asserts that, "two Anglican priests accompanying the 1820 settlers to the Eastern Cape were subsequently appointed as clergymen, but Anglicans were still unable to sustain a parochial system, despite a semblance of parish life in Grahamstown and Port Elizabeth." Hodgson (1997: 75), supporting Davenport, asserts that,

> The coming of the 1820 settlers from England caused the centre of gravity of the English colonial constituency to shift to the east. [European] appetite for land and labour grew voracious until the Cape Colony's boundary finally reached that of Natal in 1881. All Xhosa-speaking people were brought under subjugation through a three-pronged attack: military might, administrative measures, and the exploiting of indigenous rivalries. Missionary expansion kept pace with these developments. A more aggressive strategy propelled the various Protestant societies to open up new areas for the 'peaceful occupation' of the country.

In view of this, Davenport (1997: 52) further shows that the British, "also encouraged the work of the Moravian missionaries, and extended the right of public worship to Cape Muslims for the first time." Elphick (1997: 53) further suggests that,

> British conquests (in 1795, and again in 1806) exposed South Africa, not only to a dynamic global economy, but also to an explosive proliferation of Protestant movements. South Africa was soon awash [with] newly imported churches—Anglican, Congregational, Baptist, Presbyterian, Methodist—and new missions from Britain, Germany, France, Switzerland, and Scandinavia.

At this stage, the process of transformation had sufficiently decomposed the old African society from top to bottom, African labourers were turned into proletarians, and their means of labour was exploited for the benefit of European capital. Moreover, with the proliferation of European missionaries in the land, the proselytization of African people was intensified. European missionaries in the 1800s consolidated European settler privileges. The European missionaries became attached to the land which they had colonized.

Genesis of Industrial Capitalism

The arrival of the missionaries into the colonies brought with them the genesis of European industrial capitalism. Marx (2015: 533) maintains that, "The genesis of the industrial capitalist did not proceed in such a gradual way as that of the farmer. Doubtless many small guild-masters, and yet more independent small artisans, or even wage labourers, transformed themselves into small capitalists, and (by gradually extending exploitation of wage labour and corresponding accumulation) into full-blown capitalists." As soon as the capitalist mode of production stood on its own feet, European proprietors took a new form. That which was to be expropriated was no longer the African labourer working for himself, but the European capitalist exploiting many African labourers. Davenport (1997: 53) adds that,

> A handful of Presbyterians arrived with the second British occupation as members of a Scottish regiment; [and that], with the arrival of the 1820 Settlers the Presbyterians set up new churches on the Cape's eastern border. Members of the Church of Scotland and the Scottish Free Church also founded more than twenty mission stations and started Lovedale (named after a minister of the Glasgow Missionary Society), which was to play an influential part in the spread of Western education through sub-Saharan Africa.

The Methodists established themselves firmly not only as pastors for European immigrants but also European missionaries among the Africans. English Baptists arrived with the 1820 Settlers five years after the first Methodists and some fourteen years after the first members of the Church of England (Davenport 1997: 54). According to Pakenham (2009: 45), the Cape Colony "represented all that was worst about the British Empire. Take one imperial problem: feuding between [European] communities." Davenport (1997: 52) maintains that, "under the ordinance of 1829, the first Anglican churches were built by joint-stock corporations of shareholders, including St. George's [Cathedral] in Cape Town and a number of other churches in the colony." Feinstein (2009: 27) suggests that, "the first private banks started operations in the 1830's, typically small 'unit' banks without branches, owned by local [European] merchants. In general, they were well managed, but banking made only limited progress." Such interconnected operations in the colony, however small progress they made, took place before the departure of Afrikaners from the Cape and into the interior north of the Orange River in a departure known as the "Afrikaner Great Trek."

European Trek into the Interior of the Country

According to Beck (1997: 111), "Boer settlers in the 1830s began their Great Trek out of the Cape Colony, and crossed the Orange River, heading northeast toward areas of higher rainfall." Pakenham (2009: 45) maintains that in 1834, "the British Parliament decreed an end to slavery throughout the Empire. Compensation to slave-owners was slowly and clumsily paid. In 1835–1836 about 6000 Boers decided to leave [the] Cape Colony in disgust. Off they trekked, with their flocks and about 6000 African slaves and other dependents, across the Orange and Vaal rivers." Their intention was to create new states which maintained a slave system and a patriarchal feudal order. Terreblanche (2012: 219) maintains that, the Great Trek was "a deliberate attempt by the Voortrekkers to recreate in their new states the labour patterns, property relations, and patriarchal feudal order that prevailed at the Cape before the arrival of the British." It is when encroaching into the interior that the Boer trekking party came into a bloody confrontation with Africans in the kingdom of king *Mzilikazi* and the Ndebele clan; and a deadly confrontation with Africans north of the Ndebele kingdom around king *Moshoeshoe*'s kingdom amongst the Sotho clan also took place. There is evidence that small-scale gold mining had been taking place in the country's greenstone belt areas some time before the arrival of the European settlers and the emergence of the modern gold mining industry. There is little recorded history about the mining of mineral resources that existed for the period prior to the 1830s (Short and Radebe 2008: 26).

European Settler Encroachment into the Interior

When the Europeans appeared to make inroads into the interior of the country during this period, Sisulu (2010: 28) asserts that, "the [Africans] fought the European invaders in nine wars of dispossession,... They scored some spectacular successes, but they could not hold back the inexorable advance of [European] colonising forces." For example, regarding the Sixth Frontier War, dubbed the War of *Hintsa* (1834–1835) Hodgson (1997: 78) adds that, "[It] was crucial in the closing of the frontier. After the war, intensified colonial penetration into [African] territory had profound economic implications." Hodgson (1997: 79), exposing the theological paradigm that shaped the trek, reveals that,

> With each successive frontier war, the animosity of Boers and British settlers towards [African] people gathered momentum that drew the [European] missionaries into dispute. In 1837–38 a large group of Boers left the Cape Colony in part out of hostility to missionary influence on British Colonial policy, but also in part to maintain "proper relations between master and servant" in accordance with their identification with the chosen people of the Old Testament. These emigrants, the Voortrekkers, viewed [African] people as "children of Ham and Canaanites," and the British as the oppressive Pharaoh. The God of the Boers, they believed, would lead them safely through the wilderness, beset by the heathen, into the Promised Land.[3]

[3] Hodgson adds that, "the War of the Axe (1847), or the Seventh Frontier War, saw a drastic erosion of Xhosa land and independence, with the area between the Keiskamma and the Kei Rivers being proclaimed the crown colony of British Kaffraria."

During this period, the Afrikaners had rebelled against encroachments of British imperialism, they found English ideas abhorrent, trekking off into the interior to establish "*Voortrekker*" communities of their own (Welsh 2000: xxii). It is in these communities that an "Afrikaner" identity emerged, with its own language, religious fervour and republican idealism, having to fight for survival through military defeat and perceived humiliation (Welsh 2000: xxii). Pakenham (2009: 45), in line with Vorster's view maintains that, here the Europeans came into conflict with Africans (from the Zulu kingdom); "some of the Voortrekkers were killed by the Zulus led by *Dingane* the successor of King *Shaka*; others were killed by the Ndebele led by *Mzilikazi*." Dubow (2013: 17) correctly asserts that, "Questions about the process of national imagining have [distorted] our understanding of nationalism and ethnic identity, especially in relation to Africans and Afrikaners." The Afrikaners remain historic enemies of African people in South Africa.

Afrikaner Ethnic Construction and Political Formation

Afrikaner families, according to (Dommisse and Esterhyse 2009: 19), "were founded by German and Dutch descendants, 33, 7% of Afrikaners of the period from 1657 to 1867 were of German descent, the second-largest group after those of Dutch descent (34, 8%). The history of the Afrikaners, as Terreblanche (2012) shows, predates gold mining but it is a history that is interwoven with the political, economic, and ecclesial history of South Africa. Short and Radebe (2008: 26) assert that, "the more recent history of gold mining in South Africa started with the mining in the greenstone belts in Northern KwaZulu-Natal in 1836 and the development of mines in the Murchison, Giyani and Pietersburg greenstone belts." Giliomee (2003: 204) records that, among the Dutch Reformed clergy, "there was an almost instinctive tendency to remain loyal to the government of the day as part of a God-willed social order. A majority of ministers at a synod of 1837 had expressed disapproval of the Great Trek as an insurrection against a God-given dispensation."

According to Feinstein (2009: 27), "further assisted immigration followed after 1837, when some 5000 artisans and labourers came from the United Kingdom to help rebuild the population of the Cape following the departure of thousands of [Afrikaner] trekkers." It is three years after 1837 that a *Volksraad* amongst the Afrikaner trekkers was held to discuss the necessity for cheap African labour. Terreblanche (2012: 219) states that,

> Between 1834 and 1840 about 15000 Afrikaner frontier farmers left the Eastern Cape in a series of Trek parties and established their own states north of the Orange River. This emigration of a large part of the Afrikaner population of the Cape [which] became known as the Great Trek ... was an act of resistance ... against British definitions of the way in which land and labour were to be 'owned' and used.

Terreblanche (2012: 225) confirms that, "in 1840 the Natal *Volksraad* provided for 'native apprenticeship'"[4] In the same period, European settlers of British extraction annexed Natal. The Natal colony was proclaimed to be a British colony on the 4th May 1843, after the annexation of the Republic of Natalia which was governed by Europeans of Dutch extraction. Giliomee states that, Abraham Faure proposed a toast to Queen Victoria as the rightful sovereign of the region when he visited the Voortrekkers in Natal, but as a result, the Voortrekkers in other parts of Natal shunned him (Giliomee 2003: 204). In 1845 the leper asylum that was established by the Cape government at Hemel-en-Aarde in the Caledon District was closed down and the patients were transferred to Robben Island—a new asylum had been built there. Robben Island in the future was to serve as a jail for leading members of the ANC and the Pan African Congress (PAC) of Azania.

[4] This was a simply a perpetuation of the 'apprenticeship' system created by Cradock in 1812 and by the Cape government when slavery was abolished in 1834.

African Resistance Against Subjugation and the Struggle Against Hut Tax

Public African reactions against Christianity began late in 1848. King *Moshoeshoe*'s second son, *Molapo*, who had become a prominent Christian convert, renounced Christianity. However, because of the demand for cheap African labour it was almost a decade later after the setting up of the *Volksraad* in Natal that the African population was faced with the implementation of the hut tax laws. Concerning this experience Feinstein (2009: 55) maintains that, "[t]he first hut tax was levied in Natal in 1849 at a rate of 7 shillings per hut." This hut tax law was designed to legally coerce African people to become a labour force in order to comply with the law; but a year later after its introduction in certain sections hut tax was met by Africans with resistance and struggle. Concerning this struggle Terreblanche (2012: 219) asserts that,

> A protracted struggle—extending from 1850 to well into the 20th century—took place in the Transorangia during which Afrikaner farmers tried by various means to mould Africans into a useful and manageable labour force. Africans vehemently resisted these attempts... Afrikaners found it so difficult to subjugate Africans in the Transorangia.

The aim of the Europeans was to force the African population into becoming a cheap African labour force. The African resistance and struggle against this aim continued throughout the 1850s well after the political construction of the two states that became known as the Transvaal and the Orange Free State (OFS). African children were hunted, captured, and enslaved as forced labour. Transvaal, such as Natal, had its own *Volksraad* which acted as a means to pass laws that protected Afrikaner interests in African labour.

European Invasion, Enslavement of African Children, and Apprenticeship Law

African chiefs were imprisoned in Robben Island in the late 1850s and 1860s. Captured African children were to be forcefully employed as slaves for the Afrikaner farmers. Some of the sons of African chiefs were sent to study at Zonnebloem College in Cape Town where Africans were being assimilated into a colonial system. African people waged a resistance struggle against the enslavement of captured African children in the 1850s. The enslavement of captured African children was later to be legalized as "apprenticeship." Terreblanche (2012: 225) maintains that,

> In 1851 the Transvaal *Volksraad* passed the apprenticeship Law. These laws also applied in the OFS. The employment of captured [African] children was not legal unless the apprentices had been registered by a *veldcornet* or *landdrost*. The children were compelled to remain in the service of their masters until the age of 25, and the latter had to provide them with food, shelter and clothing.

During 1851 as the number of Christian believers amongst Africans declined the prestige of African traditional diviners and African prophets rose, including the Xhosa prophet *Mlanjeni* whose millenarian message against all whites, including Christians, found a sympathetic ear among the Sotho (Beck 1997: 113). By this time the Voortrekkers were not considered to be independent of Britain, they were British subjects. However, this position changed a year later in 1852. The British invaded King *Moshoeshoe*'s territory in 1852 (Beck 1997: 113).

This invasion took place in the bicentenary of European settlement in South Africa. Afrikaners called for the date of the bicentenary to be recognized as a holiday. Terreblanche (2012: 222) notes that, "Britain recognised the independence of a Voortrekker republic north of the Vaal River." Giliomee (2003: 204) asserts that,

> The bicentenary of the [European] settlement in 1852 was a moment of truth for the [Christian] church and the Afrikaner colonists' attempt to claim a special place. The [Dutch Reformed Church (DRC)] clergy asked

> the government to proclaim 6 April, the day Jan van Riebeeck and his party arrived, as a religious holiday to stress the connection between the European settlement and Dutch Reformed Christianity, thus projecting the church onto centre stage of the colony's history but the government refused the request.

In view of the above, Beck (1997: 113) states that by 1852 all five of Moshoeshoe's Cape Town-educated Christian kinsmen had abandoned their acquired Christian faith (Beck 1997: 113). Welsh maintains that, in 1852 one could speak of Afrikaners of Dutch, French, German, English, Danish, Portuguese, Malay and African extractions (Welsh 2000: xxi). In due course they were joined by a further 2700 German civilian settlers, friends, and relatives of the military settlers (Dommisse and Esterhyse 2009: 20). In their conflicts with African people, Pakenham (2009: 45) reveals that,

> They were uniquely uncompromising. On the frontier, they ruled by the whip and the gun. No matter that, in Cape Town free-born Africans were equal before the law—on paper. The Boers on the frontier conceded no equality to Africans in Church or State. And the land seemed to be theirs for the taking, the land belonging to Africans who were still poorer, weaker and less united than the Boers. To work this land, like the settlers of the American South and the Caribbean, the Boers took Africans as slaves.

Higgs supports Vorster's and Pakenham's position by asserting that "the Afrikaners, however, continued to battle the African people whose lands they occupied, and the British government remained concerned about this continued unrest on the borders of its colonies; in 1853 the British granted representative government to the Cape colony; three years later the colony of Natal was granted the same privilege" (Higgs 1997: 52). Most Afrikaners that survived went on to found miniature Boer republics in what became the Orange Free State, Natal, and the Transvaal (Pakenham 2009: 45). Dommisse (Dommisse and Esterhyse 2009: 45) adds that, "the independence of the impoverished republics of the Transvaal and the Free State was guaranteed by the British in 1854."[5]

Conclusion

European settlers of British origin (English-speaking) arrive in South Africa in 1795, to seize the Dutch colony (and prevent the colony from being seized by French-speaking Europeans) thereby beginning a process of systematic colonization. Through the seizure of the Dutch colony by the British, the colony was integrated into British imperial expansion. Upon the British colonial government seizing control of the colony in South Africa, land was set up to be for sale to European settlers who were immigrating from Europe to work in the colony. British take-over of the colony marginalized the Dutch settlers (who were farmers that became known as Boers and later referred to themselves as Afrikaners). With British invasion and occupation there was missionary expansion and a proliferation of churches (Anglican, Congregational, Baptist, Presbyterian, Methodist, etc.) and the British colonial government extended rights for Muslims to hold public worship. During this time, it was not only land that was expropriated but labour as well. As much as the European settlers imported the religion of Christianity into South Africa, through colonialism and imperialism they equally imported the ideologies of capitalism and liberalism. Notably, in 1799 European colonial encroachment intensified in the Eastern Cape and Africans resisted land dispossession, subjugation, and enslavement.

By 1802 African people had suffered large-scale loss of land and access to water sources. European settlers set up Christian mission stations. The Christianization of African people led to their social, cultural, political, and economic domination. Racial separatism was practised in the colonial church. This became an element of the capitalist production process in the colony. The British colonial government put an artificial price upon the land, a price that compelled the European immigrants to work

[5] The independence of these two republics was guaranteed by the British in 1852 and 1854 respectively.

in the colony, earn wages, and purchase land, thereby converting European settlers into private land owners. African land was hereby commodified. Through the British colonial government, European have-nothings immigrated to the colony where soon after their arrival they became land and private property owners. The racialized capitalist production process was set up to employ more European settlers so that they could purchase land and become land owners. The price of the land was imposed by the British colonial government to extend the timeframe for European wage workers to work to purchase the land. The European settlers encroached into the interior of the country to recreate patriarchal feudal property and production relations and slave labour patterns.

References

Beck, R.B. 1997. Monarchs and Missionaries among the Tswana and Sotho. In *Christianity in South Africa: A Political, Social and Cultural History*, ed. Richard Elphick and Rodney Davenport. Cape Town: David Philip.

Davenport, R. 1997. Settlement, Conquest and Theological Controversy: The Churches of Nineteenth-Century European Immigrants. In *Christianity in South Africa: A Political, Social and Cultural History*, ed. Richard Elphick and Rodney Davenport. Cape Town: David Philip.

Dommisse, E., and W. Esterhyse. 2009. *Anton Rupert*, 2009. Cape Town: Tafelberg.

Dubow, S. 2013. South Africa and South Africans: Nationality, Belonging, Citizenship. In *The Cambridge History of South Africa Vol. 2: 1885–1994*. New York: Cambridge University Press.

Elbourne, E., and R. Ross. 1997. Combating Spiritual and Social Bondage: Early Missions in the Cape Colony. In *Christianity in South Africa: A Political, Social and Cultural History*, ed. R. Elphick and R. Davenport. Cape Town: David Philip.

Elphick, R., and R. Davenport. 1997. *Christianity in South Africa: A Political, Social and Cultural History*. Cape Town: David Philip.

Feinstein, C.H. 2009. *An Economic History of South Africa: Conquest, Discrimination and Development*. Cambridge: University Press.

Gerstner, J.N. 1997. A Christian Monopoly: The Reformed Church and Colonial Society under Dutch Rule. In *Christianity in South Africa: A*

Political, Social and Cultural History, ed. R. Elphick and R. Davenport. Cape Town: David Philip.

Giliomee, H. 2003. *The Afrikaners: Biography of a People*. Cape Town: Tafelberg.

Hewson, M.G. 2015. *Embracing Indigenous Knowledge in Science and Medical Teaching*. London: Springer.

Higgs, C. 1997. *The Ghost of Equality: The Public Lives of D.D.T. Jabavu of South Africa, 1885–1959*. Cape Town: David Philip.

Hodgson, J. 1997. A Battle for Sacred Power: Christian Beginnings among the Xhosa. In *Christianity in South Africa: A Political, Social and Cultural History*, ed. R. Elphick and R. Davenport. California: University of California Press.

Juan, E.S. 2003. Marxism and the Race/Class Problematic: A Re-articulation. http://clogic.eserver.org/2003/saniuan.html.

Maloka, E. 2014. *Friends of the Natives: The Inconvenient Past of South African Liberalism*, 2014. Durban: 3MS Publishing.

Marx, K. 1988. *Selected Writings*. Ed. D. McLellan. Oxford: Oxford University press.

———. 2015. *Capital: A Critique of Political Economy*, Vol. 1, Book 1: The Process of Production of Capital. Moscow: Progress Publishers.

Pakenham, T. 2009. *The Scramble for Africa: 1876–1912*. London: Abacus.

Short, R., and B. Radebe. 2008. *Gold in South Africa 2007*, in Chapter 2 - Entitled 'Reserves to doré: the Gold Mining Industry'.

Sisulu, E. 2010. *Walter and Albertina Sisulu: In Our Life Time*. Cape Town: David Philip.

Terreblanche, S. 2012. *A History of Inequality in South Africa 1652–2002*. Scottsville: University of KwaZulu Natal Press.

Thompson, L. 1990. *A History of South Africa*. Johannesburg; New Haven: Yale University Press.

Vorster, J.M. 2006. The Ethics of Land Restitution. *Journal of Religious Ethics* 34 (4): 685–707.

Welsh, F. 2000. *A History of South Africa*. London: Harper Collins.

5

Ivhu Kuvanhu/Umhlabathi Ebantwini: The 'Violent' Ubuntu in the Fast Track Land Reform Programme in Zimbabwe

Joseph Pardon Hungwe

Introduction

The objective of the chapter is two-fold. Firstly, the chapter analyses the land reform programme in Zimbabwe in relation to the ideal of common humanity as espoused in the culturally compelling notion of Ubuntu. It would be argued that a closer scrutiny on the galvanizing neologisms that underpins violence within Fast Track Land Reform Programme (FLRP) ultimately contradicts the Ubuntu imperative of common humanity. In this regard, the exclusive neologism of *ivhu kuvanhu/umhlabathi ebantwini* suggests that FLRP pitted the 'entitled' black indigenous African as human beings (*vanhu/abantu*) against the 'usurpers' white commercial farmers (*varungu/abelungu*) with their 'foreign' farmworkers. In Zimbabwe, *ivhu kuvanhu* (Shona) or *umhlabathi ebantwini* (isiNdebele) are land distribution mantras that inadvertently depict the necessity for conceptual interrogation and reconfiguration of racial and xenophobic undertones that undergird Ubuntu. Put in simple terms, the mantras of

J. P. Hungwe (✉)
College of Education, University of South Africa, Pretoria, South Africa

E. Masitera (ed.), *Philosophical Perspectives on Land Reform in Southern Africa*,
https://doi.org/10.1007/978-3-030-49705-7_5

ivhu kuvanhu and *umhlabathi ebantwini* are suggestive of appropriating land to those who qualify to be regarded as the 'people'. At the climax point of land redistribution, a process that is sometimes referred to as land invasion, land eviction or land grab because of its chaotic and disorderly nature, there was a clarion call to return land to the 'rightful owners'. As 'rightful owners' the black indigenous people had the inherent and seemingly indisputable right to confiscate land from the white commercial farmers who represented colonial left-overs. Subsequently, it would be argued in this chapter that in view of FLRP, the current conception of Ubuntu 'permits' a leeway for latent racial discrimination.

Secondly, within the discourse of FTLRP, the chapter debunks the assumption that Ubuntu is static, conservative and culturally impermeable (Murove 2014; Matolino and Kwindingwi 2013). A perception that Ubuntu is conceptually static is actually anachronistic and can perpetuate the racial and nationalities exclusive categorization of humanity. In other words, the notion of common humanity is ultimately terminated by the dichotomization of black and white race as well as foreign and local (Sadomba and Helloker 2010). In the context of Zimbabwe, the systematized violent practices and neologisms of racial discrimination that characterize land reform programme, therefore, provide an opportune academic moment to eliminate the racial and nationalities exclusivity embedded in the interrogated conception of Ubuntu. In outlining FLRP, this chapter seeks to establish a reconfigured conceptualization of Ubuntu that takes into account the racial diversification that characterize modern society.

Subsequently, the two-pronged objectives of this chapter challenge the notion of the perceived continuities of black African victimhood within the broad scope of land reform contestations in Zimbabwe. The notion of black African victimhood is here conceptualized as the perpetual claim by black Africans that they are ever under threat of land dispossession. While this chapter does not seek to dispute the historical fact of the often violent black African land dispossessions and forced relocations during the colonial era, it is essential that instances where violence is appropriated by black Africans within the discourse of land reclamations should be interrogated within the conceptual scope of Ubuntu. In juxtaposing the racially and xenophobic violent practices and Ubuntu, the theoretical framework of critical race theory is employed in the chapter.

Critical Race Theory

Critical race theory is a derivative theoretical framework from the generic critical theory. In accordance to critical theory, critical race theory asserts that in any society there are power relations that ultimately structure the society along dominance and marginalized trajectories. For instance, the politically powerful people may marginalize other people through ideologies, limited access to economic and social resources. Beyond social description and analysis, critical theories, in their multifaceted approaches, advocates that the status quo should be challenged, dismantled, rearranged and transformed so that social equality is established. To this end, Leonardo (2013) states that critical race theory is tended towards emancipating people from the unexamined assumption that certain races are superior to the other. In the FTLRP, it could be argued that black African Zimbabweans considered themselves to be a superior race in comparison to white farmers and 'foreign' farm workers.

However, the distinguishing feature of critical race theory is that it highlights the fact that the perception of phonotypical race superiority over and above race inferiority tend to determine the society. As a theory that arose in the social context of United States of America, critical race theory challenges the practices that entrench perceptions of white people as a supreme race over and above other racial categories such as black people.

For Leonardo (2004), racial privilege is the notion that white subjects accrue by virtue of being constructed as white. Primarily, race is a concept that cannot be confined to physiological appearances such as skin colour, hair texture, nose shapes and language. On the contrary, race is a social construct that is expressed through beliefs, privileges, prejudices and stereotypes (Wilson and Davis 2011). In the context of the FTLRP, *vanhu/abantu* is a racial construct that exercised social dominance and entitlement over the white farmers and the 'foreign' farm workers. Leonardo (2011) observes that superiority is recreated and reenacted through generalized negative stereotypes accorded to certain sections of the society. It is significant to state that race can be a broad categorization of social diversities beyond the binaries of white and black. In this respect, forms of social diversifications such as nationalities, sex, religious and political affiliations, ethnicity and gender can all be regarded as racial classifications. It is for this reason that the concept of race has proved rather ambivalent and difficult to define (Leonardo 2013). In the discourse of FTLRP, the categorization of *vanhu/abantu*, white farmers and farm workers are considered as racial categories. The *vanhu/abantu* claimed superiority and dominance that was/is derived from the conceptualization of indigeneity. In order to appropriately locate the land contestation between vanhu/abantu and the white farmers as well as the cohort of 'foreign' farm workers, the following subsection outlines the historiography of land in Zimbabwe.

Historiography of Land Contestations in Zimbabwe

When the Pioneer column of the British South African Company failed to locate minerals like gold and diamond, they quickly reverted to agriculture. In the execution of colonialism, the colonial administration grabbed large hectares of fertile and arable land in areas that had high annual rainfall (Fisher 2010). As a consequent of the land grabs, the black indigenous Africans were forcibly removed and constricted to drought prone areas with poor soil for agricultural purposes. The agriculturally poor land that was allocated to black indigenous Africans were known as reserved. In semantics terms, areas that were allocated to both black Africans and wild animals were known as native reserves and national park reserves respectively (Murove 2014).

The process of 'acquiring' land from the black indigenous Africans was 'legitimatized' through laws such as the Native Reserves Act, Land Apportionment act of 1930 and the 1969 Rhodesia Constitution (Shumba 2018; Mlambo 2010). The cumulative consequence of land grab is that an imbalance of land ownership between black indigenous

Africans and white farmers began to emerge. White farmers owned almost half the arable land, while black Africans were congested within agriculturally unproductive areas. As a consequence of the skewed land redistribution, black Africans who had economically relied on land for subsistence farming became impoverished while white settler farmers accumulated wealth.

In addition, to meet the required labour demands on the acquired farms, the colonial authority put in place punitive measures that literally destroyed black indigenous farming. Accordingly, monthly and annually hut, cattle and dog taxes were imposed on the black populace. The Native Affairs department, whose primary remit was to 'oversee' the welfare of Africans, ensured that there was economic under-development in the native reserves (Shumba 2018). For instance, the absence of good roads in the reserve areas meant that Africans could not easily facilitate the marketing of their agricultural products. In addition, while white commercial farming enjoyed government subsidies, African farming were denied access to both bank loans and government financial grants (Tom 2015). As tactics for suffocating and disrupting the black African indigenous farming activities, white farmers could raid the cattle and burn down crops on the African farms. The introduction of preposterous taxes such as cattle and hut taxes consequently forced Africans to offer their services as cheap labour to pay the prescribed taxes.

The dispossession of land and the consequent economic poverty among black Africans precipitated the first and second war of liberations (*Chimurenga/umvukela*). The 1896 and 1897 Ndebele and Shona uprising against colonialism chiefly centred on the contestations of land. For Moyo, the three phases of land reform were tended towards establishing land equilibrium among the Zimbabwean populace. Owing to the military superiority of colonial authority, Africans were suppressed and massacred in the battles against colonial authority.

However, the protracted second *Chimurenga/umvukela* culminated in the political negotiations that involved Zimbabwe African national Union Patriotic Front, Zimbabwe African People's Union (ZAPU), the British government and the colonial government of Ian Smith. This political negotiation settlement was held at the Lancaster House in London. As one of the prerequisite for political independence in 1980, it was negotiated that white farmers would gradually and voluntarily give their land to the government on a willing buyer and willing seller arrangement (Gwekwerere et al. 2018). The willing buyer-willing seller that was negotiated at the Lancaster house was inserted into the constitution to remain legally binding for a period of ten years. Regrettably, the legal arrangement proved restrictive and not much land was transferred from the white farmers to the 'needy' ordinary black Africans. It is often argued that the slow pace of land transfer from white to black people triggered the 'fast track' and often violent method that the programme later on took. Though the political negotiations in London culminated in the transfer of political independence from minority white to the black majority government, it is critical to note that the tendency to resort to political violence to achieve political and economic goals had been nurtured during the liberation war (Nyarota 2006). During the colonial period, the land-centred violence drew its 'validation' from the rationale of rectifying the economic imbalance which entailed the subjugation of the black masses. After attaining political independence, it could be argued that the dehumanizing tendencies that were to be evident in the fast track land reform drew justification from exclusive misconceptions on Ubuntu as common humanity. As discussed in the following subsection, the practices of violence to access land in the post-independence Zimbabwe are couched in the distinction between the 'people' (*Vanhu/abantu*) and the white commercial farmers.

Outlining the *vanhu/abantu* of Ubuntu in FTLRP Discourse

In its simplistic, naïve and romantic conceptualization, Ubuntu is touted as pacification, non-violent, 'giving the other cheek' and an ever-seeking reconciliation communitarian value system. Ubuntu is a multifaceted, multilayered and variegated concept that has become so elusive to define. Muller and Traher (2016) succinctly observe that Ubuntu is "fluid, evading and difficult to control." As a concept, it indexes hospitality, courteous, empathy and care for others. Owing to the geographical specifications that the Bantu people find themselves in, the cultural expressions of Ubuntu tend to vary. However, Ubuntu find constancy in its high regard for its emphasis on communal solidarity. Its overarching principle that *umuntu ngumuntu ngabantu* (a person is a person because of others) crystallizes the supremacy of community. The point of departure for Ubuntu is that an individual draws his or her sense of humanness from the community. By abiding to communally prescribed values and norms, an individual is considered human. By the same token, an individual whose conduct is judged not to be in tangent with the moral prescriptions of the community, then consequently such a person can 'lose' their humanity. In Shona a person whose conduct is not pliant to the community is said to be *haana hunhu* (he does not have humanness).

The discourse on the post-2000 FTLRP in Zimbabwe has generated two polarized scholarly literature 'camps'. On one hand, there are proponents of the programme who generally argue that such an undertaking was long overdue as a corrective measure to the colonial legacy of land imbalance (Moyo 2005). Critics on the other hand, however, advance the position that land distribution was and has remained a gimmick for the political survival of Zimbabwe African National Union Patriotic Front (ZANU PF) (Shumba 2018). However, the two contesting scholarly 'camps' apparently converge on some semblance of agreement in condemning the violence that accompanied the land reform programme. Nevertheless, in analysing the violence, there is not much attention given to the interface of land reform programme and the concept of Ubuntu as common humanity. In delineating the interplay between fast track land reform and Ubuntu as common humanity, this subsection outlines the emergence of violence on those perceived as not possessing 'appropriate' common humanity within the trajectory of fast track land reform.

A referendum on the proposed government constitution was held on the 12–13th of February 2000. During the campaign period, the government through both state and private media campaigned vigorously for the acceptance of the constitution (Manzungu 2004). The government campaign's coercive narrative was that a rejection of the proposed new constitution was tantamount to reversing the country to colonialism. The acceptance and consequent adoption of the new constitution would have empowered the government to confiscate white-owned farms without paying them compensation except for development on the land (Shumba 2018). In this regard, a caption of white 'farmers' signing some fund donations to the Movement for Democratic Change was broadcast in television advertisement by the government to 'remind' the people that the opposition was working in cahoots with the white people to return the country to colonialism. The advert was inscribed "don't follow them back to the dark days of the past when they were kings and queens". Right from the beginning of the land reform, the government gave the impression that black people had to challenge the white farmers. The struggle of land was about the 'children of the soil' demanding and reclaiming their 'stolen' land from the white farmers (Willems 2004). Mugabe further argues that "we say no to whites owning our land and they should go" (ibid.). As a non-people category, it is noted that white farmers were colloquially referred to with the Afrikaans label of *amabhunu* (Boer/farmer).

Though the then president had admitted to referendum defeat in March 20 as processes of democracy, the government endorsed the wanton invasion of white commercial farms. The president publicly pronounced that "let us bring it home to the commercial farmers of the Commercial Farmers Union that they have declared war on the people of Zimbabwe who have every determination to win it" (Shumba 2018). In commenting on the consequent bloodshed that occurred on some farms, the president pointed out "the people are at war with white landowners". The framing of the public pronouncements on land invasion in which there is dichotomization of 'the people' against white farmers is central in juxtaposing fast track land reform and Ubuntu in this paper. Tom (2015) opines that land reform in Zimbabwe was done to 'correct' the legacy of colonialism in which land was disproportionately distributed.

The insinuation is that land reform of characterized by the banality between 'people' on one hand, and on another, there are white commercial farmers. Consequently, from an Ubuntu perspective, people (*vanhu/abantu*) are the deserving owners of the land, while white farmers and farm workers are racially and 'xenophobically' excluded from the category of people. Land is an entitlement of black indigenous Africans. To that end, Ubuntu entrenches the monolithic conceptualization of people only as black indigenous Africans.

In July 2000, the government of Zimbabwe launched the Fast Track land reform ostensibly to give land to the landless black majority. While there are numerous instances of land invasions in the pre-2000 era, July 2000 witnessed a government orchestrated operation that specifically targeted white commercial farmers (Muzondidya 2009). Without dismissing the fact that minority white commercial farmers comparatively owned more land than the black majority, it is essential to state that there had been a growing population of black political elite and military who equally were multi-farm owners (Shumba 2018). Such black African political elite and some senior military officials who had amassed land since independence were 'exempted' from the 'corrective' intentions of the FTLRP. Murove (2014) points out that Ubuntu became more explicitly pronounced as a cultural way of countering the practices of dehumanizing that occurred during the colonial period. In this regard, colonial tendencies of forcibly displacing black African people and relocating them to arid and drought-prone areas had been chiefly undertaken on the assumption that black Africans were 'lesser' human beings.

With specific reference to land, Ubuntu connotes that land is incontestably owned by the community in its collectiveness. *Ivhu ravanhu/umhlaba wabantu* connotes the indispensability of the community ownership of land. Consequently, it could be argued that the notion of *ivhu kuvanhu/umhlabathi ebantwini* is always given in plurality. Hansungule (2000) states that in Africa the fact that land is communally owned, entails that no individual member of the community can at any point be excluded from access and use to land. While land is used for economic activities such as crop plantation and cattle rearing, the benefits are in some ways supposed to cascade to the rest of the community members. It is for that reason that the model of *dura raIshe/isiphala senkosi* in which each community member offers some of their agricultural produce to the chief. Such produce which are usually in the form of grain are supposedly distributed to less-privileged, the disabled, and the sick and widowed members of the community. Ideally, what the individual harvests from his or her agricultural field is supposed to benefit other members of the society. It is important to state that while some of these points on communal ownership of the land can be dismissed as rather archaic, communality has remained deeply entrenched in the conceptions of land.

Socially, land is conceived as belonging to the dead, living and the unborn members of the community. Land is highly important in the performance of social functions such as weddings and funerals. Before the post-2000 economic morass in Zimbabwe, it was the norm that if a person dies in the urban areas, the corpse would be transported to the rural land for burial purposes. The land where relatives are buried therefore becomes a treasure not only for economic agricultural purposes but for socially burying the dead. Ultimately, the often violent removal of black Africans from the land was patently an anti-thesis to humanness as encapsulated in Ubuntu.

Jambanja in FTLRP: An Antithesis to Ubuntu

Jambanja is a Shona street lingo for chaotic, violent, disruptive, offensive and combative social activities. Precisely, the term connotes a disorderly conduct that is associated with protests and public demonstrations. Essentially, it is noteworthy to highlight the point that *jambanja* is not just violence for the sake of violence. Rather, *jambanja* is tended towards the accomplishment of a specific goal. In relation to the land reform programme, *jambanja* was tailored towards the reclamation or repossession of land. *Jambanja* is couched in the imperative of correcting the anomalous land pattern in which white farmers owned much land while black majority remained confined and congested in poor arable soil with less rain. The argument for the violent 'fast' track land reform is drawn from an observation that equitable land redistribution had proved difficult since the dawn of political independence in 1980.

It is highly important to state that appropriation of humanity as encapsulated in Ubuntu entails that a person who is referred to as human is accorded respect, hospitality, right to life, tolerance and courtesy. On the other hand, a person who is, because of racial or nationality differences, not regarded as human may be exposed to violent inhumane treatment. Specifically, in the context of Zimbabwe, the narrative in the land reform of *ivhu kuvanhu*/*umhlaba ebantwini* delineated who is and who is not human being. To that end, white farmers and farm workers who mostly originated from foreign countries such as Malawi, Mozambique and Zambia were excluded from the ambit of human beings (Sadomba and Helloker 2010). To that end, land reform was conceptualized as binary between the natives Shona and Ndebele or *vana vevhu/abantwan bomhlabathi* versus white farmers (*varungu*) and farm workers who were given dehumanizing and derogatory collective names such as *mabwidi/MaNyasarand/mabvakure/amadingindawo* (Muzondidya 2007). In that regard, violence on both white farmers and workers that was theorized as *jambanja/hondo yeminda/third chimurenga/dubula ibhunu* in Zimbabwe drew its 'rational justification' from exclusion of whiteness in the concept of Ubuntu. Using the racial pattern of land reform in Zimbabwe, the primary objective of this chapter is to reconfigure the notion of Ubuntu so that conceptualization of common humanity is not restricted to racial and tribal confines. In Zimbabwe, a non-black person is often categorised as being outside the auspices of *umuntu/munhu*. Accordingly, Murove (2014) notes that, *munhu ari kufamba nemurungu* which translates to the idea that if a white man is walking with a black person, people will not recognize the common humanity. It is imperative to state that such human distinctions have had social ramifications on the fast track land reform programme in Zimbabwe.

Jambanja occurred in two forms; verbal and explicit physical confrontation. Verbally, white farmers were constantly denigrated and portrayed as economic looters who perpetuated black indigenous African subjugation. The then president of the country, Mr Robert Mugabe publicly declared that "we must strike fear in the heart of the white man and the white man must tremble" (Newsday, 17th March 2000). Additionally, the then president further reiterated that white farmers are the enemies of the people's revolutionary objectives. Consequently, the anti-white diatribe permeated the generality of black indigenous African Zimbabweans.

On the physical level, white farmers were maimed, kidnapped and some were brutally murdered. Of the 4500 white farmers who had occupied 80% of arable fertile land, only 400 have been made to remain farming (Mararike 2018). By the end of June 2000, about five white farmers had been brutally murdered as *vanhu/abantu* (people) demanded their land back. The government sanitized the land grab by providing the invaders with logistics such as food, transport, guns and intelligent services. In nearly all the cases, the police were not allowed to arrest the invaders even after the high court declared the land invasions as illegal. The police would stand by and watch as farm properties were vandalized and white farmers were beaten. Under national and international pressure to remove the invaders and restore peace, the government adamantly responded that they will not evict their people. The government and its supporters coined the Zimbabwe for Zimbabweans mantra for the farm invasion. The president alluded to the fact that as a government there were contend that the people have taken up the struggle to self-emancipation and self-determination. Mlambo (2013) aptly observes that the farm invaders sang liberation war rendition as they 'reawaken' the revolution.

The FTLRP Neologisms that Contradict Ideal Ubuntu

Shedding Blood as the Symbol of Sacrifice (*Zimbabwe ndeye ropa ramadzibaba*)

The glorification of shedding of blood in the song *Zimbabwe ndeye ropa ramadzibaba* (Zimbabwe is born from blood-shed) that was replayed in the FTLRP succinctly captures the violent Ubuntu perpetrators. In the FTLRP, the symbiotic sacrifice of shedding of blood was ubiquitous and was equally celebrated as a historic reminder of the war of liberation fought between *vanhu/abantu* and the colonizers. Tracing from the historical setting of the liberation struggle, Chitando and Tarusarira (2017) note that the song *Zimbabwe ndeye ropa ramadzibaba* (Zimbabwe was/is realized through the blood of the forefathers). In this respect, Ndlovu-Gatsheni (2009) states that for Africans, land is not so much of a commercial commodity but rather a cultural marker of African identity.

The song *Zimbabwe ndeye ropa* was appropriated within the FTLRP not as a historical recall of the liberation struggle but rather to contextualize the imperative for sacrifice in the reclamation of land. In this regard, there was often a reminder that liberation was hard won and therefore land as one of the gains of independence will not be returned cheaply (Chitando and Tarusarira 2017). Of importance to note is the fact that it is precisely the blood of the enemy that must be shed to attain the set objectives. In the context of FTLRP, the white farmers and farm workers were constantly referred to as the enemies of the people. As noted in this chapter, the FTLRP was projected as a struggle between the sons and daughter of the soil (black Africans) against the white farmers and 'foreign' farm workers.

In resonance with the shedding of blood as encapsulated in the *Zimbabwe ndeye ropa* mantra, a number of white farmers and farm workers were killed during the FTLRP. The killing of the first white farmer in the southern part of the country was actually celebrated and endorsed as 'necessary evil' by both the ZANU PF and war veterans (Ndlovu-Gatsheni 2009).

Rambai makashinga: A Call for Perseverance in FTLRP

As a direct address to the *vanhu/abantu,* a rendition titled *rambai makashinga* which means people must remain resilient was a direct exhortation to the Zimbabweans (Shonas) to preserve during the tumultuous period of land reform. Despite the racial and ethnic diversity in Zimbabwe, it is informative to note that this rendition was exclusively sung in Shona to indicate its direct intended target population group. As *vanhu*, the rendition encourages people to endure the collateral privations that are consequential to the land reform programme. From a statistical point of view, it is noted that the rendition was played 288 times per day on the radio and 70 times per day on the state television (Muzondidya 2010). Furthermore, *siyalima* (we farm) and *huya uone kutapira kokurima* (experience the rewards of farming) were the Ndebele and Shona neologisms that endeavoured to draw *abantu/vanhu*'s attention to the possible benefits of farming. In so doing, a misconception was always created that since political independence, the white farmers had constantly 'enjoyed' the benefits of farming to the exclusion of black people. It is explained that "we fight to get back our land which was stolen from us by the pink-nosed imperialists" the land is ours. The term 'our' has consistently been used to refer to the black masses. To that end, there was never an understanding of Zimbabweans in their social diversity of race and ethnicity.

'Our Land Is Our Prosperity'

Land reform process was regarded as "a declaration of total independence and an empowerment of Africans in consolidating their self-determination" (Hughes 2010: 35). Equally so, the programme was referred to as the 'unfinished business', defeating imperialism or 'resolving the land question' to depict the resurgence of offensive struggle against 'white settlers' (Ncube 2016). To all intents and purposes, embarking on land reform programme was considered as the culmination and completion the independence revolutionary trajectory. Land reform was referred to as Third *Chimurenga* or *hondo yeminda* (war for land) (Maposa et al. 2010). Like in any other militarily contested situation, a war involves two antagonistic parties in which offensive and combative activities are systematically conducted. In most cases, the two conflicting parties carry out operations with the sole purpose of eliminating each other. In the historical context of Zimbabwe, the first and second *chimurenga* uprisings pitted the black indigenous Africans against white settlers. Subsequently, the use of third *chimurenga* as a coinage for land reform depicts the perpetuation of black indigenous Africans' struggle against white people as symbols of colonialism. In Zimbabwe, the land distribution is couched in euphemism of equitable land distribution. The process was equally touted as "a declaration of total independence and empowerment of Africans on consolidation their self-determination" (Mararike 2018).

Towards the supposed end of the land distribution in Zimbabwe, it was constantly pronounced by the political authority that Zimbabwean land beneficiaries must not return the land to the white people (The Herald 24th February 2004). It is pointed out that "the people have taken their land and must not return it back to the white people" (Sadomba and Helliker 2010). The logical consequent that can be drawn from such political utterances is that there is a clearly marked distinction between

Zimbabweans as the people (black indigenous Africans) and the white people. In so many ways, land reform programme entrenched the conceptions that only black indigenous Africans can be rightfully accorded the humanness that is derived in Ubuntu.

In summation of the violent neologisms that characterizes FTLRP in Zimbabwe, it is evident that the mantras of *ivhu kuvanhu/umhlabathi ebantwini* dichotomized the Zimbabwean citizenry along race and nationalities. The racial and xenophobic dichotomization is ultimately an affront to the claimed assertion that Africans are the custodians of the communally binding imperatives of Ubuntu. Perhaps the pertinent question to inquire is: Where was Ubuntu during FTLRP? It is in the endeavour to provide some response to that question that the following subsection deals with an inclusive version of Ubuntu. The objective of such an endeavour is undergirded by the imperative to combat recurrences of racial and xenophobic competition to natural resources in Zimbabwe.

Towards a Racial and Foreign Inclusive Version of Ubuntu in Land Reform Issues

In conceptually interrogating the current concept of Ubuntu, justification is drawn from the fact that identity Ubuntu as an African perspective on humanity is historically located to pre-colonial era (Murove 2014). Before the advent of colonialism, black Africans used to live within minuscule, closely knitted and related communities. In other words, everyone knew each other, spoke the same language and generally practised similar cultural norms. The 'unavailability' of transport means that to cover long distance essentially entailed that community members could only interact within those who were in their precincts. There was simply limited contact with 'strangers' as people lived in exclusive community (Matolino and Kwindingwi 2013). Even though most traditional African communities used to be nomadic for the purposes of agricultural needs, a community would always avoid settling with strangers in occupied areas. Depending on its military strength, the mobile community would either drive off the residential community or settle in an 'unoccupied' territory. The avoidance of living with strangers ultimately meant that the appropriation of humanness was an exclusive term for affiliated members of the community. In cases where 'strangers' were kidnapped, the incorporation meant that they had to be proselytized and 'baptized' into the humanity of the capturers. A case in point is the minority ethnic groups such as the Basotho, Batswana and Kalanga that were 'incorporated' into the Ndebele nation. In most African societies, it is still a challenge to tolerate and interact with culturally non-members of one's group. It is often 'puzzling' for average African person to conceive that there are some black Africans who cannot speak or understand their language.

It is precisely for that reason on initial contact with white Europeans, the black African Shona group of Zimbabwe referred to them as *vanhu vasina mabvi* (people without knees). Since wearing a trouser covers one's knees, the Shona people could not see the knees of the white Europeans. Owing to their 'otherness', black Africans described white Europeans as *varungu/abelungu/amakiwa* and as those white people who took up farming were known as *mabhunu*. Essentially, the standard definition of humanness during the pre-colonial era was strictly arrogated to 'familiar members of one's community. In the absence of 'strangers', human beings are only those who you interact with and possibly share the same worldview. *Munhu/umuntu* was therefore, constructed, developed and entrenched out of culturally fortified communities.

In the post-colonial Africa, the ideals of Ubuntu are reinvigorated as counter-factor to the dehumanizing systems of colonialism (Murove 2014). Moreover, from a functional perspective, Ubuntu is described as an endeavour to reclaim, reassert and restore the colonially disrupted African heritage. While this researcher does not seek to dismiss such superlatives associated with Ubuntu, it is essential to note their logical implications lead to latent social exclusion. If Ubuntu is a unique perspective of cohesive human life, does this imply that there is a uniquely ideal conception of humanity? Is it conceptually feasible that white farmers and 'foreign' farm workers could have been regarded as *vanhu/abantu* in the same understanding of land claimers? The selectively violent method to land reform in Zimbabwe denied Ubuntu to white people because of their perceived historical baggage of colonialism.

Apparently, the 'I am because we are' underlying principle of Ubuntu is exclusive of the perceived strangeness that is encapsulated by the white farmers and foreign farm workers.

The dichotomization between *vanhu/abantu* and the white farmers gave 'legitimacy' to the acts of vandalism and murder that occurred during land reform in Zimbabwe. The supposedly unifying concept of common humanity was compartmentalized between *vanhu/abantu* and the white farmers. In fact there are no instances during the land reform in which white people were referred to as fellow Zimbabweans as was the case in the 1980 president's speech.

Shayanana and Waghid (2016) state that the underlying assumption in the existing conception of Ubuntu as a communal practice is seeing humanity in others. Put in other words, the sense of humanity should provide the common basis upon which respect, care, compassion and other socially harmonious characteristics should be shared. In the same regard, Chitumba (2013) observes that Ubuntu is essentially an affirmation of humanity that ultimately leads to social bonding. It is imperative to state here that in all the conceptual description of Ubuntu, there is no allowance for 'othering' social categories of human beings through discrimination.

To that end, practices such as racism, tribalism, xenophobia, religious intolerance and many other forms of social discrimination subvert the very basis of Ubuntu. In Ubuntu, the assumption is that humanity transcends all forms of social categorization. The racial and xenophobic undertones that defy Ubuntu are explicit in the discharge of land reform programme in Zimbabwe. Mlambo (2013) rightly points out that it is incorrect to assume that all white farmers in Zimbabwe were of British origin with historical links to colonialist. Besides the white farmers with British heritage, there were Italians, Greeks, Germans, Afrikaans, Poles and European Jews. However, the popularized narrative in land reform programme was that white farmers are all direct descendants of British colonialists. Therefore as direct descendants, they amassed land through black subjugation and mass extermination. All white farmers were depicted as either owning multiple farms or owned exceedingly vast tracts of land. It is ironic that in all this rhetoric, there is researched evidence that points that many elite black African indigenous people had acquired numerous farms since 1980. Such black indigenous' farmers were not targeted for acquisition and redistribution.

'Zimbabwe for Zimbabweans' is one mantra that was used ZANU PF as the ruling party to galvanize its supporters and possibly the rest of Zimbabweans towards land reform (Ndlovu-Gatsheni 2015). For Maposa et al. (2010), every black person in Zimbabwe is *mwana wevhu/umntwana womhlabathi* (son/daughter of the soil). In this regard, it is preposterous in the mind of an average black person as a subscriber to Ubuntu to consider a white farmer as munhu. Pointedly, the exclusion of white farmers from Ubuntu's humanness is primarily based on their race as white people. It is always surprising for black people to come across a white person who is fluent in indigenous language such as Shona and Ndebele. In those rare cases when a white person speaks local language, eat local staple food such as *sadza/isitshwala* then black people would say *haasiri murungu ave munh*u (no longer a white but now a person). The insinuation is that non-black person can assume some semblance of humanness (Ubuntu) if he or she lives out some values associated with Ubuntu.

Conclusion

This chapter has exposed the interface between land distribution and the conception of Ubuntu in the context of Zimbabwe. Accordingly, the violence that played out during the FTLRP can only be adequately understood in consideration of conceptions of humanness in Ubuntu. It is advanced that in its current conception, Ubuntu paradoxically includes and excludes other human beings. It is precisely in the Ubuntu paradox of human inclusion and exclusion that violent conduct during LRP drew justification. Through the LRP, this chapter exposes the conceptual internal contradiction within Ubuntu. Beyond this exposition, the chapter advances the argument that LRP occasions an imperative to reconfigure the tenet of Ubuntu so that it takes into account the ever-changing social demographics of any society. Using the LRP neologisms, this chapter outlines the conceptual exclusion embedded in Ubuntu which was and is employed to exclude white people as a racial group and foreign farm workers.

References

Chitando, E., and J. Tarusarira. 2017. The Deployment of a 'Sacred Song' in Violence in Zimbabwe: The Case of the Song 'Zimbabwe ndeye ropa ramadzibaba' (Zimbabwe Was/Is Born of the Blood of the Fathers/Ancestors) in Zimbabwe Politics. *Journal of the Study of Religion* 30 (1): 5–25.

Fisher, J, L. 2010. *Pioneers, Settlers, Aliens, Exiles.* New York: Anu Press.

Gwekwerere, T., Mutasa, D, E.& Chitofiri, K. 2018. Settlers, Rhodesians and supremacists white authors and the Fast Track Land Reform in the post-2000 Zimbabwe. *Journal of Black Studies, 49*(1), 3–28.

Hansungule, M. 2000. Who owns land in Zimbabwe? In Africa? *International Journal on Minority and Group Rights*, (7), 305–340.

Hughes, D. M. 2010. *Whiteness in Zimbabwe: Race, Landscape, and the problem of belonging.* New York: Palgrave Macmillan

Leonardo, Z. 2004. The Color of Supremacy: Beyond Discourse of 'White Privilege'. *Educational Philosophy and Theory* 36 (2): 138–155.

———. 2011. After the glow: Race ambivalence and other educational prognoses. *Educational Philosophy and Theory, 43*(6), 46–67.

———. 2013. The Story of Schooling: Critical Race Theory and the Educational Racial Contract. *Discourse: Studies in Cultural Politics of Education* 34 (4): 599–610.

Manzungu, E. 2004. Water for all: Improving water resource governance in Southern Africa. *International Institute for Environment and Development Gatekeeper* (113): 1–18.

Maposa, R, S., Gamira, D. & Hlongwane, J. 2010. 'Land as sacrificial lamb': A critical reflection on the effects of colonial and post-independent land management policies in Zimbabwe. *Journal of Sustainable Development in Africa, 12*(6), 20–41.

Mararike, M. 2018. Theoretical locations of Mugabeism, Land "Terrorism" and Third Chimurenga neo-coloniality discourse in Zimbabwe: A rejoinder of a revolutionary. *Journal of Black Studies, 49*(3), 191–211.

Matolino, B., and W. Kwindingwi. 2013. The End of Ubuntu. *South African Journal of Philosophy* 32 (2): 197–205.

Mlambo, A,S. 2010. 'This is our land': The racialization of land in the context of the current Zimbabwe crisis. *Journal of Developing Societies, 26*(1), 39–69

Moyo, S. 2005. The politics of land distribution and race relations in Southern Africa. UNRISD Programme on Identities, Conflict and Cohesion, (Paper number 10), 1–32.

Muller, J. & Trahar, S. 2016. Facing our whiteness in doing Ubuntu research: Finding spatial justice for the researcher. *HTS Teologiese Studies/ Theological Studies, 72*(1), 1–7

Murove, F.M. 2014. Ubuntu. Diogenes.

Muzondidya, J. 2007. *Jambanja* Ideological Ambiguities in the Politics of Land and Resources Ownership in Zimbabwe. *Journal of Southern African Studies* 33 (2): 325–343.

———. 2010. The Zimbabwe crisis and the unresolved conundrum of race in the post-colonial period. *Journal of Developing Societies, 26*(1), 5–38.

Ncube, L. 2016. 'Bhora mugedhi versus Bhora musango'. The Interface between Football Discourse and Zimbabwean Politics. *Sociology of Sport* 51 (2): 201–218.

Ndlovu-Gatsheni, S.J. 2009. Making Sense of Mugabeism in Local and Global Politics: 'So Blair Keep Your England and Let Me Keep My Zimbabwe'. *Third World Quarterly* 30 (6): 1139–1158.

———. 2015. Decoloniality as the future of Africa. *History Campus* 13(10): 485–496.

Nyarota, G. 2006. *Against the Grain: Memoirs of a Zimbabwean Newsman.* Cape Town: Zebra Press.

Sadomba, W., and K. Helloker. 2010. Transcending Objectifications and Dualism: Farm Workers and Civil Society in Contemporary Zimbabwe. *Journal of Asian and African Studies* 45 (2): 209–225.

Shumba, J, M.2018. Zimbabwe's predatory state: Party, military and business. Pietermaritzburg: University of KwaZulu-Natal.

Tom,T. 2015. Post Zimbabwe's Fast Track Land Reform Programme: Land conflicts at Two Farms in Goromonzi district. *Journal of Humanities and Social Science, 20*(10), 87–92.

Wilson, D.C., and D.W. Davis. 2011. Re-examining Racial Resentment: Conceptualization and Content. *ANNALS, AAPSS* 634: 117–134.

Willems, W. 2004. Peasant demonstrators, violent invaders: representations of land in the Zimbabwean press. *World Development, 32*(10), 1767–1783.

6

A Logical Evaluation of the Fast Track Land Reform Economic Argument in Zimbabwe

Ephraim Taurai Gwaravanda

Introduction

The economic argument has been repeated over the Fast Track Land Reform Programme (hereafter called FTLRP) in Zimbabwe and it has been presented by defenders of land reform as one of the strongest arguments to justify the post-2000 land reform process in Zimbabwe. Critics of the land reform argument have expressed doubts on the strength of the argument, and attempts to weaken the argument are based on isolated cases of empirical claims that tend to contradict one or two of the premises within the argument. From the point of view of logic, such isolated refutation attempts have not yielded much result because they serve to weaken without necessarily dislodging the argument. The purpose of this chapter is to offer a sustained logical evaluation of the fast track economic argument through steps that examine the assumptions, premises and the conclusion of the argument. It has to be clear from the beginning that the

E. T. Gwaravanda (✉)
Department of Philosophy and Religious Studies,
Great Zimbabwe University, Masvingo, Zimbabwe

E. Masitera (ed.), *Philosophical Perspectives on Land Reform in Southern Africa*,
https://doi.org/10.1007/978-3-030-49705-7_6

type of argument under scrutiny is an inductive one; hence, the tools of inductive evaluation shall be used. While an inductive argument may not offer a proof as in a deductive argument, the strength of the argument lies in the extent of the probability claimed by the premises and the relationship between the premises and the conclusion.

Philosophical contributions to land reform in Zimbabwe have looked at debating expropriation of white farms (Shaw 2003a); application of Nozick's principles of justice to land reform in Zimbabwe (Shaw 2003b); land justice within the context of Sen's capability approach (Daka 2006); reconciliation and the land question in Zimbabwe (Mawondo 2008); land contestations within an economic crisis (Masaka 2011); and distributive justice and capability approaches to land reform in Zimbabwe (Masitera 2017). While these scholars use logical tools to assess arguments, this is done within a broad philosophical area such as social and political philosophy or economic philosophy. The contribution of this chapter, beyond the above scholars, is to show a sustained logical examination of the fast track land reform economic argument by demonstrating how the assumptions, premises and conclusion of the argument can pass the proof reasoning test.

While the attempt in this chapter is to provide a logical evaluation of a key argument used in the land reform debates, it has to be clarified that the logical examination cannot be done in isolation from other philosophical areas that have contributed to land debates such as ethics, social and political philosophy and economic philosophy. In addition, the chapter also relies on economists, sociologists and agricultural experts to check the truth of the claims that are implied and expressed in the fast track land reform economic argument in Zimbabwe.

The chapter is divided into four sections. The first section examines the fast track land reform process in Zimbabwe in terms of history and background of the process. The second section is a logical examination of two key assumptions that have been used in the fast track land reform economic argument. The third section discusses the nature of the premises used in the argument using the criteria of strength and cogency. The last section scrutinises the relationship between the premises and the conclusion of the fast track land reform argument to determine the extent of probability to which the conclusion follows from the premises.

Brief Background of the Fast Track Land Reform in Zimbabwe

The government of Zimbabwe initiated the process of setting up a 'fast track' land reform programme (FTLRP). In June 1998, the Zimbabwe government published its policy framework on the Land Reform and Resettlement Programme Phase II (LRRP II), which envisaged the compulsory purchase over five years of 50,000 square kilometres from the 112,000 square kilometres owned by white commercial farmers, public corporations, churches, NGOs and multinational companies (Utete 2003). Broken down, the 50,000 square kilometres meant that every year between 1998 and 2003, the government intended to purchase 10,000 square kilometres for redistribution. In February 2000, the Zimbabwean government, headed by Robert Mugabe, launched a controversial plan to seize white-owned farms and redistribute the land to black peasant farmers, in order to comply with a promise made to the country's war veterans who helped liberate Zimbabwe in 1980 (Tonini 2005).

There are different interpretations of the causes, processes and outcomes of the FTLRP, also termed Jambanja or Third Chimurenga or radical land reform (Mutondi 2012). However, there is consensus that the programme cannot be divorced from the colonial processes of accumulation by dispossession and the post-colonial resistance to change in agrarian structure. Land dispossession was seen as the main cause of poverty, famine and unemployment, among other economic ills. The FTLRP is an unprecedented nationwide occupation of white-owned farms by the landless blacks due to the slow pace of land and agrarian reforms (Sadomba 2013; Tom and Mutswanga 2015). The process of fast track land occupations is mainly divided into two phases. Phase I was the 1998 to 2000 occupation of white-owned farms by war veterans. Such occupations resulted from non-realisation of their negotiations with the ZANU (PF) led government for seizure and redistribution of white commercial farms, and an additional demand that 20 per cent of the land be set for the war veterans (Sachikonye 2005a). Phase II of the fast track land reform was the formalisation of land acquisition and speedy redistribution on 15 July 2000. July 2000 to December 2001 was the planned initial life span of the FTLRP was expected to be from (Sachikonye 2005b). According to Sachikonye (2005a), the objectives of the FTLRP were: (1) the immediate identification for compulsory acquisition of not less than 5 million hectares for Phase II of the Resettlement Programme, for the benefit of the landless peasant households; (2) the planning, demarcation and settler emplacement on all acquired farms; and (3) provision of limited basic infrastructure (such as boreholes, dip tanks and schemes roads) and farmer support services (such as tillage and crop packs). According to Moyo and Chambati (2013), after its formalisation, the FTLRP was divided into two models. Model A1 is a communal organisation that is based on subsistence farming. This model was intended to decongest communal areas. Small-, medium- and large-scale black commercial farmers are served by the Model A2. The economic justification of the fast track land reform programme can be summarised in an argument form as shown in the next section.

Assumptions

1. The land is the economy and the economy is the land
2. Poverty is due to land deprivation

Fast Track Economic Argument

The fast track land reform economic argument can be summarised into five premises and a conclusion. The argument presented is a summary of views from literature that defends the economic argument in the justification of the fast track land reform in Zimbabwe. The argument presented is an inductive argument that relies on evidential support (Hawthorne 2018) to give on several premises to come up with a conclusion. The argument can be summarised as follows:

Premise 1: Land reform promotes household and national food security.
Premise 2: Land reform creates employment.
Premise 3: Land reform generates foreign currency.

Premise 4: Land reform promotes industrialisation.
Premise 5: Land reform results in economic growth.

Therefore: land reform is good for the overall economic well-being of Zimbabwe.

Evaluation

Inductive arguments can be evaluated along a continuum from weak to strong. The evaluation is based on two aspects which are (1) content strength (truth and acceptability of the premises) and (2) formal strength (relevance and sufficiency of the support provided by the premises for the conclusion (Okasha 2005). Inductive arguments can fail because of a problematic premise, that is, because of the lack of the truth or acceptability of the premise (Roush 2006). The premises of inductive arguments are more vulnerable than the premises of other arguments because these claims are often empirical claims and as such based on (1) human observation, which is often unreliable (Maher 2006; Williamson 2007); and (2) based on categorisation, which is relative (McGrew and McGrew 2008). In the context of the FTLRP economic argument, it is important to examine the assumptions underlying the argument so as to assess the logical foundations of the argument.

Rebuttal of Assumptions

The first assumption of the fast track land reform argument claims that the land is the economy and the economy is the land. The assumption is made up of two phrases that are joined by a conjunction. The assumption has been coined to appear like a conceptual truth so that the conversion of the concept of land and the economy can remain true even if the conversion is done. Before examining the assumption is detail, it is important to show that statements are divided into two main types, that is, relations of ideas and matters of fact (Hume 2000; Allison 2008; Garrett 2015; Ainslie 2015). A phrase or statement that expresses a relation of ideas can be converted without implying falsity or a contradiction. For example,

(S1) a triangle is a three-sided figure; and
(S2) a three-sided figure is a triangle.

The two statements remain true despite the interchanged subject and predicate. This means that it is conceptually true that a triangle is a three-sided figure and the other way round.

On the other hand, matters of fact admit of contradictions and the negation of a matter of fact is logically conceivable. In matters of fact, a statement and its negation are logically conceivable without implying a contradiction.

Having looked at Hume's distinction, I now turn to the application of the first assumption. Is the statement 'the land is the economy and the economy is the land' a logically necessary statement? A statement is logically necessary if its negation yields a contradiction. The land and the economy are conceptually distinct notions and there is no way one can logically derive the idea of land from the economy or vice versa. So the assumption is not a logically necessary statement.

If the assumption fails the first disjunct of Hume's fork, does it pass the second aspect? In the second aspect of Hume's fork, a statement can fit into matters of fact. In matters of fact, there is no contradiction involved when a statement is negated and it is equally conceivable to hold the opposite statement without violating any rules of logic. The statement 'the land is the economy and the economy is the land' can therefore be considered as a matter of fact and existence. However, even if the claim can in principle be considered as a matter of fact, the truth of the statement is subject to empirical verification or falsification. To claim that 'the land is the economy' is empirically controversial since it involves a reduction of parts to a whole. In addition, the other conjunct that maintains that the 'the land is the economy' raises further questions. While it may be a truism that economic production takes place on some piece of land or property, it does not necessarily follow that all land is economically productive since it is logically and empirically conceivable to have idle land or barren land. When linked to the issue at hand, it can be argued that the fast track land reform is based on a questionable and misleading assumption.

The second assumption claims that 'poverty is caused by land deprivation.' The causal link that can be drawn between poverty and land can be clearly understood if quantifiers can be used to examine the claims. Since the assumption is a general statement it may take at least one of the following forms:

C1 all poverty is caused by all land deprivation
C2 all poverty is caused by land deprivation
C3 poverty is caused by all land deprivation

While the general statement may seem to resemble C1 above, the weaker claims of C2 and C3 may be implied by the strong statement C1. Since the statements are contingent, they can be true without implying a contradiction. This means the statements can be true in one context and false in another. Within the land reform fast track context within Zimbabwe, the claims seem to follow the contingent nature and their truth varies with contexts. However, the assumption can be rebutted by scenarios where land deprivation can exist without poverty and vice versa. Still further questions arise whether land deprivation is relative to white farmers or indigenous Zimbabweans or both. The question of causality is subject to further logical scrutiny since what may be seen as causality may be a mere correlation. Having examined the assumptions of the argument, I now turn to the premises of the argument in the section that follows.

Examination of Premises

The first premise claims that 'Land reform promotes household and national food security'. It may be important to point out that the premise can be understood as an empirical claim or a prescriptive statement. However, since the statement is coming from facts of observation, it can best be seen as an empirical claim. As an empirical claim, it is subject to verification or falsification. In order to test the veracity of the claim, it is necessary to subject the claim to empirical test. Soon after the post-2000 land-grabbing programme, Zimbabwe changed from being a bread basket to a basket case (Tonini 2005). Although defenders of the land reform programme seem to bring evidence that may contradict claims of food insecurity, the principle of non-contradiction may be helpful. According to the principle, a statement cannot be true and false at the same time and under the same respect (Gwaravanda 2011). In the context of the present study, claims of food security and their contradictories cannot be simultaneously true.

Defenders of the land reform programme are often economical with truth in the context of food security. Economy with truth is 'selective withholding of information with intent to deceive' (Warburton 1996: 47). The situation in Zimbabwe has become more complex, because even those with entitlements have been failing to access food on the markets, while food production declined substantially during the FTLRP period for various reasons (Moyo 2005; Chambati 2011). These reasons include land reform as the main cause, though drought and policy inconsistencies are also contributory. Since the post-2000 land reform programme, Zimbabwe has seen main cereal (maize, wheat and sorghum) and the key nutrition giving commodities (milk, groundnuts, beef and soyabeans), as well as oil seed derivatives being in short supply (Musodza 2015). This expanded food insecurity beyond the normal effects of drought, and broadened the band of the food insecurity. The access effects were mostly in marginal and remote areas, and among the urban poor and socially vulnerable (women and children, HIV/AIDS affected, farm workers etc). Added to this is the fact that the Strategic Grain Reserve held by the Grain Marketing Board (GMB) was depleted from 2001, thereby limiting the opportunities to enhance food security and to support the poor during drought. The result has been the expensive reallocation of scarce foreign currency to food imports. Evidence therefore shows that the claim of food security is contradicted by evidence on the ground. Having established that the first premise of the argument contradicts truth, it is important to check the veracity of the second premise.

According to the second premise, land reform creates employment. In examining the second premise, it is equally important to consider the truth content of the premise. Evidence on the ground appears to point to the contrary. As a result of the fast track land reform programme, about 300,000 farm workers are estimated to have lost their jobs (Moyo 2005; Zikhali 2008). The FTLRP has had numerous effects on the residential status of former farm workers, who had resided on their employer's property for the greater part of their employment life. Some former farm workers have been forced to move off the farms to make way for new settlers, under either the A1 or A2 models, while some are still resident on farms acquired under FTLRP, either as squatters or in agreement with the new owners. Those displaced in this manner are often stranded on the outskirts of the farms or they trek to the fast-growing 'informal settlements' where social conditions are desperate, especially in areas where there were higher proportions of former farm workers perceived to be truly 'foreign' migrant workers. In addition, line industries processing agricultural products have cut down production capacity since the FTLRP, and there has been a proportional reduction in employment.

Premise 3 holds that land reform generates foreign currency out of the sale of tobacco, maize and cotton. Foreign currency earnings from agricultural production has been declining over the years since the time of the FTLRP. Major crops like tobacco and cotton have declined in production and this has led to a proportional decline in foreign currency earnings. Output of tobacco, Zimbabwe's traditional major hard currency earner (a third of total exports), fell from 173 million kg in 2002 to 103 million in 2003, the lowest level since independence in 1980 (Musodza 2015). The drop was due to the one-third reduction in crop area (from 69,000 hectares to 46,500 over the year). About 85 million kg was auctioned off at an average of US$2.26/kg during the April/October 2003 sales (compared with 165.7 million kg in 2002, itself a sharp fall from the 2000 record of 237 million kg) (Musodza 2015). The sales earned only US$183 million—compared with US$368.6 million in 2002 and way below the 1996 peak of US$593.4 million—further exacerbating the foreign currency crisis (Musodza 2015). Tourism earnings have also nose-dived—'not only because of international anxiety surrounding civil unrest but because of the widely publicised poaching of endangered wildlife in game conservation parks, where some 60% of wildlife has been lost'.

In the fourth premise, the claim goes 'land reform promotes industrialisation'. In the Zimbabwean context of land reform, manufacturing industry was supposed to grow after the fast track land reform but the opposite was obtained on the ground. The main crops such as maize, wheat and tobacco declined in production soon after the fast track land reform and thereafter, thereby causing a decline in production in the line industries that depended on those crops. Moyo (2005) identifies both quantitative and qualitative declines in the production patterns. Reasons for the decline include but are not limited to poor policies, droughts, lack of capital and failure to strategize by the new farmers (Moyo 2005). Specialised and mechanised farming that has been producing horticultural products, milk and meat was highly disturbed by the fast track land reform programme and billions of potential revenue have been lost (Sadomba 2013). The drop in agricultural production has resulted in proportional decline in food processing and related industries. This shows that premise 4 is contradicted by evidence on the ground.

Premise 5 claims that 'land reform results in economic growth'. However, the infrastructure and technologies around the agricultural industry collapsed as a result of the FTLRP (Moyo 2005). Industries that supported agriculture with machinery, equipment, infrastructure, seeds, fertilisers and chemicals declined or closed due to lack of business after the FTLRP. Service industries that promoted agriculture, such as extension, research and market information, also faced decline. Overall, the country's real Gross Domestic Product (GDP) declined for the sixth consecutive year in 2003 (Mutondi 2012). Further, GDP was expected to shrink by 18.5 per cent in 2003 (after 12 per cent in 2002) and by 14 per cent in 2004 (Musodza 2015). It can be argued that the GDP decline cannot be a result of some chance or coincidence but a direct consequence of the negative economic impact caused by the FTLRP.

The conclusion of the argument that states that 'land reform is good for the overall economic well-being of Zimbabwe' is also affected by the problems of its premises. If the claims in the premises are false, there is no way truth can be introduced in the conclusion. Well-being as a result of land reform can be measured in terms of distribution of welfare among Zimbabweans. I use the distribution of individual well-being as a measurement of the success or lack of it in the FTLRP argument because it reflects the ethical dimension of happiness rather than income. The use of income has been avoided to prevent circularity since it appears in premises 4 and 5. Health, assets and happiness can be used to assess individual well-being and the overall well-being of members (Fleurbaey 2008). For the conclusion of this argument to carry weight, considerations for well-being, as a consequence of the FTLRP, must depend on food security (premise 1), employment creation (premise 2), availability of foreign currency (premise 3), industrial growth (premise 4) and economic growth (premise 5). While each of the premises individually fails to support the conclusion, the problem persists when the premises are considered jointly. Overall, the conclusion of the FTLRP economic argument contradicts the truth on the ground. Having examined the premises of the FTLRP economic argument, I now turn to the evaluation of the logical inference that relates the premises and the conclusion.

Relationship Between the Premises and the Conclusion

The fast track land reform argument, in theory, meets the form and structure of an inductive argument in the sense that empirical evidence is used to support a conclusion. The premises in the inductive land reform argument are, in principle, relevant in supporting the conclusion to provide a probabilistic inferential claim. The inference in an argument is the relationship of support between the premises and the conclusion (Hurley 2011; Buchak 2014). Since all the premises and the conclusion are based on claims about the FTLRP, they are relevant and sufficient for the argument. The inference in an argument is the process by which one asserts a conclusion on the basis of given evidence or reasons (Gwaravanda and Masaka 2008; Gwaravanda 2012). Inductive strength admits of degrees: an argument can be moderately strong or very strong. Even the best inductive inference still leaves some room for doubt regarding the conclusion. Often, the inference in an argument can be made stronger if the conclusion is appropriately qualified to match the degree of evidence (Kelly 1996: Huber 2005). A strong inductive argument is one that establishes its conclusion with *probability* (see Carnap 1952). If the premises are taken to be true, then the conclusion is likely. The premises provide good reasons, though not logically conclusive ones, to accept the conclusion. The premises make the conclusion of the argument more likely than any other possible conclusions drawn from the same evidence (Hacking 2001; Fleurbaey 2008).

However, when tested in the actual world, the connection between the premises and the conclusion of the land reform economic argument is weighed down by problematic premises in the sense of false premises. The argument becomes more deceptive than convincing. The deception occurs in the sense that the argument is structurally correct but the truth content of the premises is lacking. This reduces the degree of probability with which the conclusion follows from the premises within the land reform economic argument. The argument is therefore a weak form of inductive argument whose premises contradict reality on the ground.

The argument fails the logical test although it has been pushed emotively in political spheres. I argue that the inductive argument fails and it is important that scholars should seek what is convincing rather than what is persuading in evaluating the FTLRP economic argument. The political push of the FTLRP economic argument is fallacious in the sense of hasty generalisation to a conclusion that cannot be supported by premises.

Conclusion

It has been shown that the basic assumptions to the FTLRP economic argument are logically questionable due to their controversial nature. The assumptions are not only unwarranted but they also lack sufficient logical justification. The five premises that form the inductive argument may provide a good structure for the argument in terms of the form. However the content of the premises is contradicted by empirical findings. The contradiction weakens the overall state of the inductive argument. The inferential pattern that relates the premises and the conclusion follows the rules of logic and it gives a satisfactory inferential claim. The conclusion follows with a weak probability due to the lack of truth in the premises. However due to a relationship between false claims and a false conclusion, the entire FTLRP economic argument lacks cogency. While the chapter has focused on the logical evaluation of the inductive FTLRP argument, room for further research on inductive logic can still be found in the areas of statistical reasoning, analogical reasoning and inductive generalisation.

References

Ainslie, D. 2015. *Hume's True Scepticism*. Oxford: Oxford University Press.

Allison, H. 2008. *Custom and Reason in Hume*. Oxford: Oxford University Press.

Buchak, L. 2014. *Risk and Rationality*. Oxford: Oxford University Press.

Carnap, R. 1952. *The Continuum of Inductive Methods*. Chicago: University of Chicago Press.

Chambati, W. 2011. Restructuring of Agrarian Labour Relations after Fast Track Land Reform in Zimbabwe. *Journal of Peasant Studies* 38 (5): 1047–1068.

Daka, L. 2006. Towards a Human Empowerment Approach to Justice: An Appropriation of Amartya Sen's Capability Approach with Particular Reference to Zimbabwe Land Reform, PhD Thesis, Boston: Boston College.

Fleurbaey, M. 2008. *Fairness, Responsibility, and Welfare*. Oxford: Oxford University Press.

Garrett, D. 2015. *Hume*. London: Routledge.

Gwaravanda, E. 2011. Philosophical Principles in the Shona Traditional Court System. *International Journal of Peace and Development Studies* 2 (5): 148–155.

———. 2012. Shona Indigenous Knowledge Systems and Critical Thinking: Lessons from Selected Shona Idioms. *Dzimbahwe: Journal of Humanities and Social Sciences* 1 (1): 78–102.

Gwaravanda, E.T., and D. Masaka. 2008. Shona Reasoning Skills in Zimbabwe: The Importance of Riddles. *The Journal of Pan African Studies* 2 (5): 193–208.

Hacking, I. 2001. *An Introduction to Probability and Inductive Logic*. Cambridge: Cambridge University Press.

Hawthorne, J. 2018. Inductive Logic. *The Stanford Encyclopedia of Philosophy*. Spring. https://plato.stanford.edu/archives/spr2018/entries/logic-inductive/.

Huber, F. 2005. Subjective Probabilities as Basis for Scientific Reasoning. *British Journal for the Philosophy of Science* 56: 101–116.

Hume, D. 2000. *A Treatise of Human Nature*. Oxford: Oxford University Press.

Hurley, J.P. 2011. *A Concise Introduction to Logic*. 7th ed. Belmont: Wadsworth.

Kelly, K. 1996. *The Logic of Reliable Inquiry*. Oxford: Oxford University Press.

Maher, P. 2006. A Conception of Inductive Logic. *Philosophy of Science* 73 (5): 513–523.
Masaka, D. 2011. Zimbabwe's Land Contestations and Her Politico-Economic Crises: A Philosophical Dialogue. *Journal of Sustainable Development in Africa* 13 (1): 331–347.
Masitera, E. 2017. *A Critical Analysis of Distributive Justice in Zimbabwean Land Redistribution: Making use of the Capability Approach and Entitlement Theory to Formulate a Land based Compromise.* PhD Thesis, University of Pretoria, Pretoria.
Mawondo, S. 2008. In Search for Social Justice: Reconciliation and the Land Question in Zimbabwe. In *Struggle after Struggle: Zimbabwean Philosophical Studies 1*, ed. D. Kaulemu. Washington, DC: The Council for Research in Values and Philosophy.
McGrew, L., and T. McGrew. 2008. Foundationalism, Probability, and Mutual Support. *Erkenntnis* 68 (1): 55–77.
Moyo, S. 2005. *A Review of the Zimbabwean Agricultural Sector Following the Implementation of the Land Reform: Overall Impacts of the Fast Track Land Reform Programme.* [Online]. http://archive.kubatana.net/docs/agric/aias_land_reform_040513.pdf. Accessed 19 July 2019.
Moyo, S., and W. Chambati. 2013. *Land and Agrarian Reform in Zimbabwe: Beyond White-Settler Capitalism.* Dakar: CODESRIA.
Musodza, C. 2015. *Zimbabwe's Fast Track Land Reform Programme and the Decline in National Food Production: Problems of Implementation, Policy and Farming Practices.* MA Thesis, Saint Mary's University, Halifax, Nova Scotia.
Mutondi, P. 2012. *Zimbabwe's Fast Track Land Reform.* London: Zed Books.
Okasha, S. 2005. Bayesianism and the Traditional Problem of Induction. *Croatian Journal of Philosophy* 5 (14): 181–194.
Roush, S. 2006. *Tracking Truth: Knowledge, Evidence, and Science.* Oxford: Oxford University Press.
Sachikonye, L.M. 2005a. *The Promised Land: From Expropriation to Reconciliation and Jambanja.* Harare: Weaver Press.
———. 2005b. The Land Is the Economy: Revisiting the Land Question. *African Security Review* 14 (3): 31–44.
Sadomba, Z.W. 2013. A Decade of Zimbabwe's Land Redistribution: The Politics of the War Veteran Vanguard. In *Land and Agrarian Reform in Zimbabwe: Beyond White-Settler Capitalism.* Dakar: CODESRIA.
Shaw, W. 2003a. They Stole Our Land: Debating the Expropriation of White Farms in Zimbabwe. *Journal of Modern African Studies* 45 (1): 75–89.

———. 2003b. Nozick in Zimbabwe. *Journal of Social Philosophy* 34 (2): 215–227.

Tom, T., and P. Mutswanga. 2015. Zimbabwe's Fast Track Land Reform Programme (FTLRP): A Transformative Social Policy Approach to Mupfurudzi Resettlement (Shamva District, Zimbabwe). *Journal of Humanities And Social Science* 20 (8): 51–61.

Tonini, D. 2005. The Bread Basket Goes Empty: Zimbabwe - A Country in Crisis. *Education in Emergencies and Post-Conflict Situations* 2 (Spring): 93–105.

Utete, C. 2003. *Report of the Presidential Land Review Committee under the Chairmanship of Dr Charles M. B. Utete*, Volume 1: Main Report to His Excellency the President of the Republic of Zimbabwe. Harare: Government Printers.

Warburton, N. 1996. *Thinking from A to Z*. London: Routledge.

Williamson, J. 2007. Inductive Influence. *British Journal for Philosophy of Science* 58 (4): 689–708.

Zikhali, P. 2008. Fast Track Land Reform and Agricultural Productivity in Zimbabwe. In *Land Reform, Trust and Natural Resources Management in Africa*, ed. P. Zikhali, 47–57. Gothenberg: University of Gothenberg Press.

Part II

Restitution, Compensation, and Development

7

We Acknowledge that We Reside On…: Canadian Land Acknowledgments and South African Land Reform

Yolandi M. Coetser

Introduction

When I attended the Environmental Philosophy Conference at the University of Guelph in Ontario, Canada, in 2018, I was struck by the opening of the conference. The organiser, as well as a number of speakers, read the following statement:

> *We acknowledge that we reside on the ancestral lands of the Attawandaron people and the treaty lands and territory of the Mississaugas of the Credit. We recognize the significance of the Dish with One Spoon Covenant to this land and offer our respect to our Anishinaabe, Haudenosaunee and Métis neighbours as we strive to strengthen our relationships with them. Today, this gathering place is home to many First Nations, Métis and Inuit peoples and acknowledging them reminds us of our important connection to this land where we learn and work.*

Y. M. Coetser (✉)
Department of Philosophy, Practical and Systematic Theology, University of South Africa, Tshwane, Gauteng, South Africa

E. Masitera (ed.), *Philosophical Perspectives on Land Reform in Southern Africa*,
https://doi.org/10.1007/978-3-030-49705-7_7

The above is a 'land acknowledgment' (University of Guelph n.d.). Winona LaDuke (1999, p. 5) eloquently says "[t]he question of who gets to determine the destiny of the land, and of the people who live on it—those with the money or those who pray on the land—is a question that is alive throughout society." Similarly, Stephen Marche (2017) says, "acknowledgment forces individuals and institutions to ask a basic, nightmarish question: Whose land are we on?" Indeed the same questions can be asked of South African land, and of the land of any other country that has been colonised. Land is a focal point since "only by land ownership and possession can people have a stake, or a sense of stake, in a community" (Tatz 1972, p. 15).

In this chapter, I ask whether Canadian land acknowledgements' underlying philosophical tenets could be applied equally, or similarly, to the South African land context. I argue that employing a similar practice in South Africa would aid in bringing awareness of land injustices to the wider community, and would serve as a small step toward equitable land distribution. Even though land acknowledgements may seem trivial—it is, after all, a few lines of spoken or written word—I argue that it can hold immense value, if done right. Since Africa has also been extensively colonised, like North America, it follows that land acknowledgements could similarly form a part of decolonisation and land reform on the African continent.

In North America[1] and Australia,[2] there has been significant literature, both academic and otherwise, on land acknowledgements. The concept is, however, largely unknown and therefore unexplored from within the African, and specifically South African, context. As such, this chapter adds to the literature in two important ways. First, it adds to the ongoing debate on land reform in South Africa. Second, it contributes to the discussion on land acknowledgements that are already taking place in Canada, North America, and Australia.

The purpose of this chapter is not to propose a particular practicality of land reform, but rather to emphasise the importance of the work to be done in terms of land awareness. If we do not know whose land we are

[1] Robinson et al. (2019), Wikes et al. (2017), Asher et al. (2018).

[2] McDonnell (n.d.), Kowal (2015).

on, and how we came to be on it, then how can the land be distributed equitably? I also centre the South African context, although the argument likely extends to other African countries where settler colonists still have significant influence.

In what follows, I first discuss Canadian land acknowledgements, and the philosophical tenets that underlie their usage in Canada. Thereafter, I look at the current situation of land in South Africa, and argue for a similar practice to be employed here.

A Brief History

For the First Nation People of North America, land is of inestimable value. Their lives are built on a special relationship with 'Mother Earth', who guides them to practice "reverence, humility and reciprocity" (Assembly of First Nations 2019). Their connection with land is evident as "Native American teaching describe the relations all around—animals, fish, trees, and rocks—as our brothers, sisters, uncles and grandpas" (LaDuke 1999, p. 2). LaDuke elaborates,

> *We are nations of people with distinct land areas, and our leadership and direction emerge from the land up. Our commitment and tenacity spring from our deep connection to the land. The relationship to land and water is continuously reaffirmed through prayer, deed, and our way of being*—minobimaatisiiwin, *the 'good life'.* (LaDuke 1999, p. 4)

Before the arrival of European colonisers in the 1400s in North America, there was a low ratio of people to land, allowing freedom of movement over large areas (Bailyn 2012, p. 12). This nomadic lifestyle was imperative to the survival of many people—a yearly agricultural cycle dominated much of their lives.[3] Like historian Bernard Bailyn says, "[n]o

[3] This does not entail that all Native Americans were nomadic, as there were also "sedentary Natives" who practiced agriculture before the arrival of the European settlers (Wolfe 2006, p. 396). This means that the accusation of 'savagery' often levelled against the Native Americans was unfounded, and their "unmistakeable aptitude for civilization", as demonstrated by their ability to cultivate agriculture, scared the settler colonist (Wolfe 2006, p. 396).

one possessed—'owned'—land. 'Ownership'—exclusive possession, with the publicly approved right to sell as a commodity or otherwise alienate and use as one saw fit—was unknown" (Bailyn 2012, p. 14). Their understanding of 'ownership' was a communal one, where "communities were collectively entitled to control and use", and "rights of use derived from membership in the group—rights that were never exclusive, were commonly shared with others and were impermanent" (Bailyn 2012, p. 14). Pre-Columbian America was "a diverse world—polylingual, polyethnic, regionally disparate in political and social structure, and economically multiform" (Bailyn 2012, p. 22).

However, with the arrival of European settlers in the fifteenth century a period of colonisation, genocide and dispossession began, the repercussions of which are felt until today. Within a few generations of European colonisation of the Americas, 95% of Native Americans were wiped out (Stannard 1992, p. x). Even though many were killed by physical violence, more were killed by the 'invisible killer'—"the barrage of disease unleashed by the Europeans among the so-called 'virgin soil' populations of the Americas" (Stannard 1992, p. xii). Native Americans were enslaved, in "practices of captivity [that] came to resemble the kinds of human trafficking that are recognizable to us today" (Reséndez 2016, p. 3).[4]

This period of colonisation lasted a couple of hundred years, and, some may argue, continue until today. Needless to say, the five hundred or so years that followed the arrival of colonisers harmed First Nations people in immeasurable ways, and had dire effects on their relationship to the land they occupied.

The Current Situation

In 2008, Canada established a Truth and Reconciliation Commission, named, in part, after the South African Truth and Reconciliation Commission. This commission was established to deal with the cultural

[4] See Guasco (2007). By some accounts, slavery started as early as Columbus' arrival in 1492, who sent "four caravels loaded to capacity with 550 Natives back to Europe, to be auctioned off" (Reséndez 2016, p. 4).

genocide brought about by the Indian Residential Schools Settlement Agreement. This agreement saw tens of thousands of children being taken away from their parents to 'Residential Schools' in the Nineteenth Century. The children were taken away in order to reduce the influence of their 'savage' parents and break their "Indian habits, training, and mode of thought" (Truth and Reconciliation Commission of Canada 2015, p. 4.). Aboriginal culture was seen as inferior to European/Christian culture, with the former being seen as savage and brutal, and so they needed to "acquire the habits and thoughts of white men" (Truth and Reconciliation Commission of Canada 2015, pp. 2–4). The Truth and Reconciliation Commission of Canada released a summary report of their findings in 2015, and emphasised the importance of acknowledging the harms that were done to the indigenous people by the settlers. From there, the use of land acknowledgements has become commonplace across Canada.

Currently, under differing legislation in the United States and Canada, portions of land has been designated as 'Indian Reservations' or 'Indian Reserves'. An Indian Reserve is defined as "a tract of land set aside under the Indian Act and treaty agreements for the exclusive use of an Indian band"[5] (First Nations Studies Program 2009b).[6] These reserves are often rural pieces of land, with little or no access to basic amenities. Eve Tuck and K. Wayne Yang remind us that "in the United States, many Indigenous peoples have been forcibly removed from their homelands onto reservations, indentured, and abducted into state custody" (Tuck and Yang 2012, p. 5). Most of the reserves are owned by the state, but are in possession of the Native Americans—and this distinction between ownership and possession remains a point of bitter contention (Tatz 1972, p. 15).

Since the land is now legally held privately, and prosperity in Northern America is built on property rights, which in turn gives one access to credit from financial institutions, the people inhabiting reserves are often very poor (Koppisch 2011). A former Chief in British Columbia laments,

[5] "A "Band", or "Indian Band," is a governing unit of Indians in Canada instituted by the *Indian Act,* 1876. The Indian Act defines a "band" as a "body of Indians (First Nations Studies Program 2009a).

[6] See Bartlett (1990), and Harris (2002).

> *We've been legislated out of the economy. When you don't have individual property rights, you can't build, you can't be bonded, you can't pass on wealth. A lot of small businesses never get started because people can't leverage property.* (Koppisch 2011)

That is just one of the problems. A further problem is that the reservations "are subject to some of the most invasive industrial interventions imaginable", like toxic waste, nuclear waste dumps, resource extraction and development activities (LaDuke 1999, pp. 2–3). These industrial invasions impact the health of the communities on the reserves. For instance, in Native American populations there "are a high incidence of cancer and lack of access to cancer treatment, screening" (Lynch and Stretesky 2012, p. 107). In one case, there are worrisome links between elevated rates of cancers in members of the Native population exposed to Uranium in Colorado (Lynch and Stretesky 2012, p. 107). Research indicates that there is a "connection between environmental toxins and disease and other negative outcomes in Native communities" (Lynch and Stretesky 2012, p. 108).

The land issue in North America is therefore a tricky one, with many intersecting problems, ranging from environmental injustice, to land reform, to legal ambiguities, to medical questions. The question can now be raised about what role land acknowledgements play in this complex situation.

Land Acknowledgements

Acknowledging the land is a tradition that dates back centuries for indigenous people (Shahzad 2017), and has been part of the start of gatherings, ceremonies, and events for as long as can be remembered (City of Toronto 2019). However, it was with the release of the Canadian TRC report that land acknowledgements were taken up by the wider population. Acknowledging territory

> *shows recognition of and respect for Aboriginal Peoples. It is recognition of their presence both in the past and the present. Recognition and respect are essential*

elements of establishing healthy, reciprocal relations. These relationships are key to reconciliation.... (Canadian Association of University Teachers 2019)

As this quote shows, acknowledgement leads to recognition, recognition to respect, which in turn, hopefully, leads to reconciliation. More practically, "[a]n Indigenous Land or Territorial Acknowledgement is a statement that recognises the Indigenous peoples who have been dispossessed from the homelands and territories upon which an institution was built and currently occupies and operates in" (Garcia 2018). Land acknowledgements are either verbal or visual. Verbal land acknowledgements take the form of spoken word acknowledgements at the opening of sports events, academic conferences, art exhibitions, corporate meetings, or any other type of event. Visually, land acknowledgements take the form of plaques, signs, or web pages.

Territorial acknowledgements should not be viewed as the beginning and end of land reform, but rather serve as "a necessary first step toward honouring the original occupants of a place" (Mills 2019). Acknowledgments do not aim to place blame, but rather serve to show "how systemic and institutional systems of power have oppressed Indigenous peoples, and how that oppression has historically influenced the way non-Indigenous people perceive and interact with Indigenous peoples" (Mills 2019). In what follows, I have identified some possible underlying philosophical tenets of land acknowledgements, and unpack them in some depth. Thereafter, I move on to arguing that this is a practice that could be usefully applied in South Africa.

Underlying Philosophical Tenets of Canadian Land Acknowledgments

This list of underlying philosophical tenets is not an exhaustive one, and may very likely be a flawed list—it is a South African's interpretation of a practice happening thousands of kilometres away in Canada. I look at three specific ideas that underlie Canadian land acknowledgments—these are (1) undoing indigenous erasure, alienation, and invisibilisation; (2) decolonisation; and (3) reconciliation.

Undoing Indigenous Erasure, Alienation and Invisibilisation

One of the first underlying tenets of territorial acknowledgements is that "they can be transformative acts that to some extent undo Indigenous erasure" (âpihtawikosisân 2016). Colonisation is an attempt to erase indigenous people from the place that the settlers want to make their own (Tuck and Yang 2012, p. 6). This erasure of indigenous communities was done, in part, by recasting land as property and as a resource (Tuck and Yang 2012, p. 6). Like Patrick Wolfe argues, "[w]hatever settlers may say … the primary motive for elimination… is access to territory" (2006, p. 388).

For the settler, his anthropocentric view of land, influenced by his Christianity, awards him dominion over the land, and so, in making a new home, he views 'wild land' and 'wild people' as made for his benefit (Tuck and Yang 2012, p. 6). To survive, he needs to produce, and to produce, he needs labour, which he finds in making the indigenous people chattel slaves (Tuck and Yang 2012, p. 6). Once the elders die out, the settler's desire to erase is sped along, since the death of the elders hasten the death of their way of life. To colonise means to either absolutely destroy the original inhabitants, or to assimilate them into the settler's way of life (Tuck and Yang 2012, p. 9). Like Andrea Smith holds "'America' itself can exist only through the disappearance of indigenous people" (2010, p. 5). This is not only true of America, but also of most colonised lands where the indigenous people were largely annihilated, including Canada.

Part of working towards undoing erasure is centring indigenous interests. For settlers in settler spaces, being uncentred may be shocking, uncomfortable, and even unwelcome (âpihtawikosisân 2016), since for so long their own interests have been privileged. As such "territorial acknowledgments continue to have the power to disrupt and discomfit settler colonialism" (âpihtawikosisân 2016). If one thinks of Land

Acknowledgements as sites of disruption, then they need to unnerve and unsettle both those speaking and those hearing the words (âpihtawikosisân 2016). It forces non-indigenous peoples to "confront their own place on these lands" (âpihtawikosisân 2016). By unnerving the settler, the land acknowledgement forces her to reflect on how she came to be on the land. It forces the settler to critically reflect on history, and engage with what the role of her forefathers were in the erasure of indigenous people and their culture, and how she is perpetuating their actions. With acknowledgement comes reflection—and this uncomfortable reflection is one of the purposes of land acknowledgements.

Of course, the critical question is whether erasure can ever truly be undone? One can never restore what was before—that which was erased cannot be unerased. The focus then should be on centring the interests of the indigenous people who remain today, since for too long the interests of the settler were centred. Like Selena Mills says

> *It's not so much about focusing on the omission of belonging, and all of us having a right to a home, but rather about introducing non-Indigenous people to this land's accurate confederate history and the importance of relationship to land despite the dominant worldview of owning the land. All we're asking you to do is to remember, and remember with us.* (Mills 2019)

Steps Towards Reconciliation

Another underlying tenet of land acknowledgements is that they form part of a process of reconciliation. A defining characteristic of settler colonial systems is "ill-gotten control over land and resources" (Finegan 2018, p. 2). The Canadian TRC sought to neither shame, nor point out wrongdoing, but rather to determine the truth in order to lay the foundation for reconciliation (Truth and Reconciliation Commission of Canada 2015, p. vi). It is important not to think of reconciliation as the "re-establishment of a conciliatory state" since conciliation has never "existed between Aboriginal and non-Aboriginal people" (Truth and Reconciliation Commission of Canada 2015, p. 6). Rather, for the Canadian Truth and Reconciliation Commission, "reconciliation is about establishing and maintaining a mutually respectful relationship between Aboriginal and non-Aboriginal peoples" (Truth and Reconciliation Commission of Canada 2015, p. 6) and this means there has to be "awareness of the past, acknowledgement of the harm that has been inflicted, atonement for the causes, and action to change behaviour" (Truth and Reconciliation Commission of Canada 2015, pp. 6–7).

A paramount aspect of reconciliation is acknowledging and rejecting paternalism and racism, and thereafter developing a relationship based on mutual respect (Truth and Reconciliation Commission of Canada 2015, p. vi). In its report, the Canadian TRC acknowledges the physical, biological, and cultural genocide that was perpetrated against Aboriginal people (Truth and Reconciliation Commission of Canada 2015, p. 1). Importantly, reconciliation, as understood in the Canadian context, is not viewed as "an exercise in warmth, coziness or security" for the settlers who are "facing up to" past (Finegan 2018, p. 4). Rather, it is about centring indigenous interests, which means that a "process of dismantling of oppressive structures and coming-to-terms with how settlers continue to benefit from, enable, and perpetuate settler colonialism is a fundamental part thereof" (Finegan 2018, p. 4). The reality is that settlers, even generations after first arriving, remain privileged "because of their ongoing complicity in settler colonialism" (Finegan 2018, p. 4). A process of reconciliation thus implores settler colonists to attempt to "understand how indigenous peoples have been, and continue to be, systematically oppressed by settler colonialism" (Finegan 2018, p. 4). The Canadian interpretation of reconciliation is therefore forward looking in as much as "[r]econciliation must inspire Aboriginal and non-Aboriginal peoples to transform Canadian society so that our children and grandchildren can live together in dignity, peace, and prosperity on these lands we now share" (Truth and Reconciliation Commission of Canada 2015, p. 8).

Decolonisation

A third underlying philosophical tenet of land acknowledgement is decolonisation. Franz Fanon, in *Wretched of the Earth,* holds that "[d]ecolonization, which sets out to change the order of the world, is, obviously, a program of complete disorder" (Fanon 1963, p. 2). Worldwide, however, decolonisation has been a slow and unsure process. One of the pertinent issues of decolonisation across all countries with a colonial past is land—land ownership and land entitlement (Korteweg and Russell 2012, p. 7). This is because colonisation relied on the physical occupation of spaces, and the simultaneous violent removal and/or extermination of those already occupying the land. Like Tuck and Yung say "[w]ithin settler colonialism, the most important concern is land/water/air/subterranean earth ... [it] is what is most valuable, contested, required" (Tuck and Yang 2012, p. 5).

Centuries later, these colonised spaces are now office blocks, highways, suburbs, shopping malls, homes, and airports, which means that, legally at least, others (and usually settler-colonists) now 'own' the land. The implementation and subsequent transference of ownership occurred "because the settlers make Indigenous land their new home and source of capital, and also because the disruption of Indigenous relationships to land represents a profound epistemic, ontological, cosmological violence" (Tuck and Yang 2012, p. 5). In addition, the original inhabitants of the land who survived the concomitant genocide are often no longer around, having been displaced and their offspring living in other spaces, either by choice or by force. The offspring of the original inhabitants who want to lay claim to their forbearers' land, face difficult legal and political battles, since the new structures were designed to favour the coloniser. As such, it is important to understand colonisation not as an event, but as a structure. This structure is a violent one, and the violence of the arrival of the settler is "reasserted each day of occupation" (Tuck and Yang 2012, p. 5). Within the violent structure of colonisation, "land is remade into property and human relationships to land are restricted to the relationship of the owner to his property" (Tuck and Yang 2012, p. 5). This means that "[e]pistemological, ontological, and cosmological relationships to land are interred" (Tuck and Yang 2012, p. 5).

In Canada "decolonization is directly connected to treaty and traditional rights to Land, or Land entitlement and determination" (Korteweg and Russell 2012, p. 7). This is because "one of the legacies and continuing practices of colonialism in Canada is the continuing perception that the land is separate from people" (Scully 2012, p. 152). What decolonisation then does, is eliminate "settler property rights and settler sovereignty", which means it "requires the abolition of land as property and upholds the sovereignty of Native land and people" (Tuck and Yang 2012, p. 26). As Rebecca Shrubb holds,

> *The sheer fact that Indigenous Nations' cultures, knowledges, traditions, symbols, and languages continue to flourish despite every attempt at erasure, illustrates the initial and ongoing existence of the resistance rooted within decolonial thought.* (Shrubb 2014, p. 31)

South African Land Acknowledgements

Against this background, how can we start to think about South African land, and possibly the implementation of South African land acknowledgements? If undoing indigenous alienation, decolonisation, and reconciliation underpins Canadian land acknowledgements, then do these three concepts apply similarly to South Africa? In this section, I briefly explore some of the similarities and differences between South Africa and Canada. Then, I move on to discussing the South African case, and argue that land acknowledgements may be a useful practice to employ in South Africa too.

Similarities and Differences Between SA and Canada

There are substantial similarities, but also key differences between South Africa and Canada that may impact how we approach land acknowledgements from within South Africa. Both South Africa and Canada were colonised by European settlers. In both cases, these were violent colonisations, which led to a lot of bloodshed. In both cases, the remaining settlers still have a strong influence on the land and the way of life. This means that in neither situation did the settler adapt to the local way of life, but rather, imposed his own ways on the indigenous people.

An interesting similarity is that in both countries, separate areas were given to the indigenous people. In Canada it is the 'Indian Reserves' and in South Africa, it was the homelands. The homelands in South Africa were a product of the Apartheid government, under the banner of 'separate development'. The majority Black population were forcibly moved to these so called 'Bantustans', preventing them from residing in the urban, white areas of South Africa (South African History Online 2019). The guise of 'separate development' meant that Whites and Blacks were separated, and Blacks were given the opportunity to run their own independent governments, thereby stripping them of any remaining rights they may have had (South African History Online 2019). Significantly, however, the homelands were abolished in 1994, and were incorporated into South Africa proper. Contrastingly, in Canada, reserves are still in use, and do not allow for a separate government from the rest of Canada.

A further similarity is that both countries went through a truth and reconciliation process. The Truth and Reconciliation Commission of Canada started in 2008, and dealt specifically with the consequences of the Indian Residential Schools Settlement Agreement. It was concluded in 2015. The Truth and Reconciliation Commission (TRC) of South Africa was set up to deal with the atrocities of Apartheid in 1996 and concluded in 1998. The mandate of the South African TRC "was to bear witness to, record and in some cases grant amnesty to the perpetrators of crimes relating to human rights violations, reparation and rehabilitation" (South African History Online 2011). The Canadian Truth and Reconciliation Commission shared similar values[7] with the South African TRC, except for granting amnesty to offenders.

One pertinent difference in South Africa (and most of the continent) is that even though many indigenous people were killed by settlers, they were not wiped out to the extent that the First Nations were in North America. In the 2006 Canadian census, just over 1.1 million indigenous people were identified (Statistics Canada 2008), which represents less than 1% of the total population. In South Africa, by contrast, Black and Coloured Africans represent close to 90% of the current population (StatsSA 2018).

[7] For example, it aimed to acknowledge the harms arising as a consequence of the Residential Schools, it provided a safe space for families to tell their stories, promote awareness, create a historical record, and support commemoration (Truth and Reconciliation Commission of Canada n.d.).

Another difference between South Africa and Canada is described by Colin Tatz. He says that 'assimilation' was an ideal in Canada, but not in South Africa (1972, p. 5). In Canada, for the First Nations to be successful, assimilation required the abandonment of traditional behaviour, culture, manner of thinking and doing, and the adoption of 'white models' as quickly as possible. In South Africa, segregation was the dominant ideology in the 1970s and 1980s, and this had two implications. First, racial differentiation was the basis for separate laws, administrations, facilities, and services. Secondly, with the ideology of 'separate development', indigenous people were supposed to have their own land where they can "develop their own languages, customs, traditions, and social and political institutions" (Tatz 1972, p. 6). However, just like assimilation, segregation "is a process of generalization, ethnocentrically oriented, designed to make the coloured people accommodate to white-based models and white determinations" (Tatz 1972, p. 6).

Furthermore, in Canada, and the rest of North America, Whites have remained in political power (Wolfe 2006, p. 404). Contrarily, in South Africa, since 1994 the African National Congress has been the ruling party, and so there has been a predominantly black parliament since liberation. While they may not possess political power, it is nevertheless true that White South Africans still enjoy many privileges bestowed on them by the remnant structures of Apartheid, and so maintain a significant portion of the socio-economic power.

With the above differences and similarities in mind, the question of the conceptualisation of land acknowledgements within the South African context arises. I discuss this in the next section.

Constructing SA Land Acknowledgements

In this section, I argue that even though there are significant differences between South Africa and Canada, the similarities are enough to allow for the practice of land acknowledgements in South Africa.

After "centuries of colonial rule and decades of apartheid rule, democratic South Africa set out to redistribute rights in land as a way to remedy past racial injustice and lay the basis for more equitable development"

(Kepe and Hall 2016, p. 6). To obtain figures of who owns what land in South Africa is difficult. In many cases, land is owned by trusts or companies, so it is difficult to ascertain whether that land belongs to 'white' or 'black' South Africans—and attempting to establish this percentage of land ownership by race is fraught with oversimplification since "overall picture is considerably more complex" (Walker and Dubb 2013). However, a Land Audit revealed that "individuals, companies and trusts own 90% of land in South Africa", with Whites owning 72% of the total farms and agricultural holdings. Farms and agricultural holdings represents 97% of the total land (Department of Rural Development and Land Reform 2018, p. 2). Even though South Africa has gone through a series of land expropriations,[8] the colonial legacy has meant that expropriation of land continues to be fraught with difficulties. Although many of the insidious Acts[9] that dispossessed black South Africans from their land have been repealed, their legacy remains part of the South African psyche (Isaacs-Martin 2015, p. 120). In 2018, political activists pushed 'land expropriation without compensation', which saw an evolution of land expropriations, with the lack of compensation being the contentious point. Late in 2018, the Joint Constitutional Review committee resolved to amend Section 25 of South Africa's constitution[10] to allow for land expropriation without compensation (Parliament of the Republic of South Africa 2018).

The character of land reforms in South Africa, however, should be about more than just undoing racial discrimination. Rather, the character of land reform should "be pro-poor and would promote gender equality and, by changing production and investment patterns, start to transform dualism in agriculture by blurring the lines between the commercial and communal areas of the country" (Kepe and Hall 2016, p. 6). I hold that land acknowledgements would be a useful addition to land reform.

---

[8] This is detailed by Kepe and Hall (2016).

[9] These acts were the Native Land Act [Act 27 of 1913], Native Trust and Land Act [Act 18 of 1936], Groups Areas Act [Act 41 of 1950] and the Population Registration Act [Act 30 of 1950] (Isaacs-Martin 2015, p. 120).

[10] At the time of writing this chapter (mid-2019), Chapter 25 of the Constitution allows for property to be expropriated, but only when it is in the public interest, and it expropriation must be compensated (Constitutional Assembly 1996, p. 10).

When constructing a land acknowledgement, certain key questions need to be asked, such as,

- “Why is this acknowledgement happening?
- How does this acknowledgement relate to the event or work you are doing?
- What is the history of this territory? What are the impacts of colonialism here?
- What is your relationship to this territory? How did you come to be here?
- What intentions do you have to disrupt and dismantle colonialism beyond this territory acknowledgement?” (Jones 2019)

These questions, and other related ones, impel the person (or institution) doing the land acknowledgement to action. In order to do the land acknowledgement, the person should conduct research about the land that she is on, examine why and how she came to be there, and reflect deeply on her relationship to the land. The final question is also the most important one, which is how we act beyond simply acknowledging the land. This question makes explicit the fact that land acknowledgements are simply a small step towards decolonisation and reconciliation.

In Canada, because of the population demographic and the genocide of the First Nations, the overwhelming majority of people doing the acknowledgement would be settler colonists, whereas in South Africa, one may argue that it would be less so. However, it is also the case that in many contexts in South Africa, the settler colonists still hold a lot of socio-economic power. It may be especially those socio-economic spheres where land acknowledgements are needed the most. Some examples may be corporations, schools, churches, and communities. Think of the former Model C School with young students who have inherited the privilege concomitant with their colonial history, but without having corresponding awareness of how they came to be on the land. In this case, the teacher or principal may yield power to create awareness of land injustices, through reading land acknowledgements in classrooms or assemblies. Another example is the wealthy CEOs who possess privileges bestowed on them by their colonial past. By setting a precedent in their corporate sphere that meetings are opened with land acknowledgements, they indicate awareness of the colonial past, the injustices that it informed, and start a process of decolonising these spaces. We have to remember that "contests for land can be—indeed, often are—contests for life" (Wolfe 2006, p. 387), and this is true in South Africa as well.

It may be that the resistance to land reform, and especially to land expropriation without compensation, comes from the large-scale adoption of rainbow-nationism. Rainbow-nationism was the catch-phrase to describe South Africa under the new dispensation in 1994, used to describe the 'new South Africa' where non-racialism was supposed to rush in a new utopia. For the first decade post-democracy, "it became necessary to stress unity, sameness and 'rainbow nation' identity as crucial markers of being South African" (Gqola 2004, p. 6). The debate on race has evolved away from rainbowism and non-racialism, to uncovering and celebrating diversity. However, many white South Africans still find themselves caught up in rainbowism, and problematically wanting to 'move forward, and forget the past'. Since many of these white South Africans are the ones who are holding on to land, one can see that the resistance to land reform generally, and land expropriation without compensation specifically, could be an ideologically difficult pill to swallow. The resistance to land reform is possibly even more sinister, insofar as during Apartheid, "[t]he construction of a white South African identity was predicated on the control of the apparatus of state and privileged access to resources by the white minority" (Baines 1998, p. 1). Those who are still holding on to land, may very well be holding on their Apartheid identities, which sees them in control of land and resources. It is therefore especially important that people who are still in control of land be made aware of the injustices that took place on the soil they own, and land acknowledgements could be one step in this direction.

A Critique of Land Acknowledgements

Land acknowledgements are not the solution to land reform, and some have argued that it may in fact harm the process, as the following quote indicates,

> *"[Land acknowledgements] may start out as radical push-back against the denial of Indigenous priority and continued presence, may end up repurposed as "box-ticking" inclusion without commitment to any sort of real change. In fact, I believe this is the inevitable progression, a situation of familiarity breeding contempt (or at least apathy)."* (âpihtawikosisân 2016)

It is difficult not to fall into the trap that Tuck and Yang describes. They hold that "[d]ecolonization is about the repatriation of Indigenous land and life", and attempts to "improve our societies and schools" through decolonising discourse may "have objectives that may be incommensurable with decolonization" (Tuck and Yang 2012, p. 1). It may be inevitable that land acknowledgements, for those who are not serious about the restitution of land, may simply be a 'box-ticking' exercise. However, even if this is the case, it may be that a person hearing or reading the land acknowledgement could be impacted thereby, just like I was when I attended the conference in Canada. It may well be impossible to get an entire nation on the same page when it comes to something as contentious as land reform. Therefore, starting with something simple, but significant, like land acknowledgements could be the start of an awareness campaign that could eventually lead to substantial and long-lasting change.

Conclusion

I ask you to imagine a practice like land acknowledgements widely adopted in South Africa—imagine attending conferences, sports events, religious settings, school events, cultural activities, or even just going to a shopping centre, and at every turn, being made aware of history of the land. By so doing, many would be exposed to the names of the communities who called this land their own before the occupation thereof by settlers. This would, at the very least, increase awareness, and at best, inspire significant action.[11] What is most important, however, when

[11] This paragraph was inspired by a quote from the U.S. Department of Arts and Culture. The original quote reads "Imagine this practice widely adopted: imagine cultural venues, classrooms, conference settings, places of worship, sports stadiums, and town halls, acknowledging traditional lands.

implementing land acknowledgements, is the space beyond it—"stopping at territorial acknowledgments is unacceptable" (âpihtawikosisân 2016). Like Stannard holds "[w]e must do what we can to recapture and to try to understand, in human terms, what it was that was crushed, what it was that was butchered. It is not enough merely to acknowledge that much was lost" (1992, p. xi).

This chapter examined the practice of acknowledging territories in Canada, and asked how this practice can be applied to the South African context. I argued that land acknowledgements can serve at least three functions, which are undoing indigenous erasure, decolonisation, and reconciliation. I argued that even though there are some differences between the South African and Canadian context, the shared histories of colonisation, racism and continued privileging of the settler colonist means that land acknowledgements can form part of significant land reform in South Africa.

In conclusion, I would like to say that I acknowledge that this chapter was written on the ancestral land of the San people of South Africa, the Sotho-Tshwanas, notably the BaRolong, BaThlaping and BaFokeng people, and other Bantu-speaking people like the Ndebele. I recognise the significant damage that followed from the European settlers arriving on these lands, and offer my respect to the indigenous communities who were custodians of this land, as I strive to strengthen my relationship with them as a settler colonist. Today, this land is occupied by many different peoples, including many African neighbours. Acknowledging them reminds me of my connection to this land where I choose to live, learn, and work.

References

âpihtawikosisân, 2016. *Beyond Territorial Acknowledgments.* [Online]. https://apihtawikosisan.com/2016/09/beyond-territorial-acknowledgments/. Accessed 29 April 2019.

Millions would be exposed—many for the first time—to the names of the traditional Indigenous inhabitants of the lands they are on, inspiring them to ongoing awareness and action" (U.S. Department of Arts and Culture n.d.).

Asher, L., J. Curnow, and A. Davis. 2018. The Limits of Settlers' Territorial Acknowledgments. *Curriculum Inquiry* 27 (3): 316–334.

Assembly of First Nations. 2019. *Honouring Earth.* [Online]. http://www.afn.ca/honoring-earth/. Accessed 29 April 2019.

Bailyn, B. 2012. *The Barbarous Years: The Peopling of British North America: The Conflict of Civilizations, 1600-1675*. New York: Alfred A. Knopf.

Baines, G. 1998. The Rainbow Nation? Identity and Nation Building in Post-Apartheid South Africa. *Mots Pluriels* 7: 1–12.

Bartlett, R.H. 1990. *Indian Reserves and Aboriginal Lands in Canada: A Homeland*. Saskatoon: University of Saskatchewan.

Canadian Association of University Teachers. 2019. *Guide to Acknowledging First Peoples & Traditional Territory.* [Online]. https://www.caut.ca/content/guide-acknowledging-first-peoples-traditional-territory. Accessed 28 April 2019.

City of Toronto. 2019. *Land Acknowledgement.* [Online]. https://www.toronto.ca/city-government/accessibility-human-rights/indigenous-affairs-office/land-acknowledgement/. Accessed 26 April 2019.

Constitutional Assembly. 1996. *Constitution of the Republic of South Africa.* Pretoria: Department of Justice.

Department of Rural Development and Land Reform. 2018. *Land Audit Report.* Tshwane: Department of Rural Development and Land Reform.

Fanon, F. 1963. *Wretched of the Earth.* New York: Grove Press.

Finegan, C. 2018. Reflection, Acknowledgement, and Justice: A Framework for Indigenous-Protected Area Reconciliation. *International Indigenous Policy Journal* 9 (3).

First Nations Studies Program. 2009a. *Bands.* [Online]. https://indigenousfoundations.arts.ubc.ca/bands/. Accessed 5 May 2019.

———. 2009b. *Reserves.* [Online]. https://indigenousfoundations.arts.ubc.ca/reserves/. Accessed 23 May 2019.

Garcia, F. 2018. *Guide to Indigenous Land and Territorial Acknowledgments for Cultural Institutions.* [Online]. http://landacknowledgements.org/wp-content/uploads/2018/10/Acknowledgement-Guide-finalfinal.pdf. Accessed 30 April 2019.

Gqola, P. 2004. Where Have All the Rainbows Gone. *Rhodes Journalism Review* 24: 6–7.

Guasco, M. 2007. To "Doe Some Good upon Their Countryme": The Paradox of Indian Slavery in Early Anglo-America. *Journal of Social History* 41 (2): 389–411.

Harris, C. 2002. *Making Native Space: Colonialism, Resistance, and Reserves in British Columbia*. Vancouver: UBC Press.

Isaacs-Martin, W. 2015. Issues of Race, Ethnicity, Socio-economic Position and Spatial Acknowledgement in South Africa: How Spatial Access and Expression Still Perpetuate Notions of Difference, Separation, and Uncertainty Amongst the South African Coloured Populations. *International Journal of African Renaissance Studies Multi-, Inter- and Transdisciplinarity* 10 (1): 120–140.

Jones, A. 2019. *Territory Acknowledgement.* [Online]. https://native-land.ca/territory-acknowledgement/. Accessed 2 May 2019.

Kepe, T., and R. Hall. 2016. *Land Distribution in South Africa.* Tshwane: Parliament of South Africa.

Koppisch, J. 2011. *Why are Indian Reservations so Poor? A Look at the Bottom 1%.* [Online]. https://www.forbes.com/sites/johnkoppisch/2011/12/13/why-are-indian-reservations-so-poor-a-look-at-the-bottom-1/#e1438193c079. Accessed 5 May 2019.

Korteweg, L., and C. Russell. 2012. Decolonizing + Indigenizing = Moving Environmental Education Towards Reconciliation. *Canadian Journal of Environmental Education* 17: 5–14.

Kowal, E. 2015. Welcome to Country: Acknowledgement, Belonging and White Anti-Racism. *Cultural Studies* 21 (2): 179.

LaDuke, W. 1999. *All Our Relations: Native Struggles for Land and Life.* Cambridge, MA: South End Press.

Lynch, M.J., and P.B. Stretesky. 2012. Native Americans and Social and Environmental Justice: Implications for Criminology. *Social justice* 38 (3): 104–124.

Marche, S. 2017. *Canada's Impossible Acknowledgment.* [Online]. https://www.newyorker.com/culture/culture-desk/canadas-impossible-acknowledgment. Accessed 14 June 2019.

McDonnell, M. n.d.. *Acknowledgement of Land.* [Online]. https://www.michaelamcdonnell.org/acknowledgement-of-country. Accessed 14 June 2019.

Mills, S. 2019. *What Are Land Acknowledgements and WHY DO THEY MATTER?.* [Online]. https://locallove.ca/issues/what-are-land-acknowledgements-and-why-do-they-matter/#.XL6tuNhS-po. Accessed 30 April 2019.

Parliament of the Republic of South Africa. 2018. *National Assembly Approves Process to Amend Section 25 of Constitution.* [Online]. https://www.parliament.gov.za/press-releases/national-assembly-approves-process-amend-section-25-constitution. Accessed 5 May 2019.

Reséndez, A. 2016. *The Other Slavery: The Uncovered Story of Indian Enslavement in America*. New York: Houghton Mifflen Publishing Company.

Robinson, D., et al. 2019. Rethinking the Practice and Performance of Indigenous Land Acknowledgement. *Canadian Theatre Review* 177 (1): 20–30.

Scully, A. 2012. Decolonization, Reinhabitation and Reconciliation: Aboriginal and Place-based Education. *Canadian Journal of Environmental Education* 17: 148–158.

Shahzad, R. 2017. *What Is the Significance of Acknowledging the Indigenous Land We Stand on?*. [Online]. https://www.cbc.ca/news/canada/toronto/territorial-acknowledgements-indigenous-1.4175136. Accessed 30 April 2019.

Shrubb, R. 2014. *"Canada has no history of Colonialism." Historical Amnesia: The Erasure of Indigenous Peoples from Canada's History*. Victoria: University of Victoria.

Smith, A. 2010. Indigeneity, Settler Colonialism, White Supremacy. *Global Dialogue* 12 (2): 1–14.

South African History Online. 2011. *Truth and Reconciliation Commission (TRC)*. [Online]. https://www.sahistory.org.za/article/truth-and-reconciliation-commission-trc-0. Accessed 5 May 2019.

———. 2019. *The Homelands*. [Online]. https://www.sahistory.org.za/article/homelands. Accessed 5 May 2019.

Stannard, D.E. 1992. *American Holocaust: Columbus and the Conquest of the New World*. Oxford: Oxford University Press.

Statistics Canada. 2008. *2006 Census Topic-based Tabulations*. [Online]. http://www12.statcan.ca/census-recensement/2006/dp-pd/tbt/Rp-eng.cfm?LANG=E&APATH=3&DETAIL=0&DIM=0&FL=A&FREE=0&GC=0&GID=837928&GK=0&GRP=1&PID=89122&PRID=0&PTYPE=88971,97154&S=0&SHOWALL=0&SUB=0&Temporal=2006&THEME=73&VID=0&VNAMEE=&VNAMEF=. Accessed 2 May 2019.

StatsSA. 2018. *Mid-year Population Estimates 2018*. [Online]. https://www.statssa.gov.za/publications/P0302/P03022018.pdf. Accessed 2 May 2019.

Tatz, C.M. 1972. *Four Kinds of Dominion*. Armidale: The University of New England.

———. 2003. *With Intent to Destroy: Reflecting on Genocide*. London: Verso.

Truth and Reconciliation Commission of Canada. 2015. *Honouring the Truth, Reconciling for the Future: Summary of the Final Report of the Truth and Reconciliation Commission of Canada*. Toronto: Truth and Reconciliation Commission of Canada.

———. n.d. *Our Mandate.* [Online]. http://www.trc.ca/about-us/our-mandate.html. Accessed 5 May 2019.

Tuck, E., and K.W. Yang. 2012. Decolonization Is Not a Metaphor. *Decolonization: Indigeneity, Education & Society* 1 (1): 1–40.

U.S. Department of Arts and Culture. n.d. *Honor Native Land: A Guide and Call to Acknowledgement.* [Online]. https://usdac.us/nativeland. Accessed 15 May 2019.

University of Guelph. n.d. *Territorial Acknowledgement.* [Online]. https://www.uoguelph.ca/studentexperience/aboriginal/territorial-acknowledgement. Accessed 14 June 2019.

Walker, C., and A. Dubb. 2013. *The Distribution of Land in South Africa: An Overview.* [Online]. https://www.plaas.org.za/sites/default/files/publications-pdf/No1%20Fact%20check%20web.pdf. Accessed 6 May 2019.

Wikes, R., A. Duong, L. Kesler, and H. Ramos. 2017. Canadian University Acknowledgment of Indigenous Lands, Treaties, and Peoples. *Canadian Review of Sociology* 54 (1): 89–120.

Wolfe, P. 2006. Settler Colonialism and the Elimination of the Native. *Journal of Genocide Research* 8 (4): 387–409.

8

Must Land Reform Benefit the Victims of Colonialism?

Thaddeus Metz

Introducing the Question of How to Enact Land Reform

In this chapter I presume that land in South Africa was allocated by the state on an unjust basis for much of the twentieth century. Most glaringly, many white people wrongfully acquired land as a result of the Natives Land Act 27 of 1913, which denied black people the ability to hire or buy land across 93% of South Africa (later decreased by the Native Trust and Land Act 18 of 1936 to 87%). White South Africans also took over physical property unjustly in the wake of the Group Areas Act 41 of 1950 and the Natives Resettlement Act 19 of 1954, which required black people to leave urban and especially well-developed areas, deemed by the government to be properly white, and to relocate to townships. I also

T. Metz (✉)
Department of Philosophy, University of Johannesburg,
Auckland Park, South Africa
e-mail: tmetz@uj.ac.za

E. Masitera (ed.), *Philosophical Perspectives on Land Reform in Southern Africa*,
https://doi.org/10.1007/978-3-030-49705-7_8

assume for the sake of argument in this chapter that, in the light of this injustice, at least some white people (including descendants who have inherited land[1]) owe some kind of compensation to black people. The question on which I focus here is which kind of land reform would be just to advance in South Africa and in similar post-colonial contexts.

According to one answer, the right kind of compensation in respect of land is a strict function of the past, and, specifically, of what would have happened in the absence of white-controlled governments unjustly distributing land on a racial basis. By this approach, white people should give to black people precisely whichever land the latter would have possessed had the racist laws not been adopted. Although it can be hard to apply this principle, viz., difficult to tell in practice who exactly would have owned which land in the absence of white injustice, the principle itself is clear.

That, however, is not the answer I have favoured in previous work (Metz 2011: 551–554). Appealing largely to southern African values associated with *ubuntu* such as communion and reconciliation, I have argued that they require compensating in the light of certain facts about the future, and specifically doing so in ways that are likely to improve the lives of those who had been wrongfully dispossessed of land and not to impose substantial burdens on the broader society. In the context of land reform, I have further contended that this principle probably entails not transferring unjustly acquired land *en masse* and immediately to dispossessed black populations, because doing so would likely lead to capital flight, food shortages, and other weighty socio-economic disadvantages. Compensation must proceed in some other way, one more likely to help the victims of the racial injustice and less likely to harm innocent third parties.[2]

[1] For the most part I avoid discussing the complication of what is owed to the descendants of colonial and similar land distributions, and tend to focus on the simpler case of immediate victims who were unjustly dispossessed. For some discussion of whether and why compensation is owed to descendants, including those who would not have existed were it not for injustice done to their parents or older relatives, see Cohen (2009), Perez (2011), and Boxill (2014).

[2] For a recent approach that is broadly similar, see the claim that the 'unjust acquisitions and transfers must be revisited for the sake of normalising conditions for humanity to be possible for African people' (Molefe 2018: 363).

In two recent works, Oritsegbubemi Anthony Oyowe (2013, 2017) has argued against my conception of compensatory justice, and he has done so specifically in the context of land reform. Oyowe maintains that 'while a state of affairs in which compensatory justice brings about certain collective benefits is desirable, it doesn't follow that compensatory justice is contingent upon such benefits' (2013: 131). In addition, although I take myself to be arguing that offenders must compensate in a way that is likely to be good for their victims, Oyowe contends that, applied to the case of land in southern Africa, this principle when combined with some empirical claims 'inadvertently privileges the interest of the offender over that of the victim' (2013: 131) and 'seems to imply that they (white land holders—ed.) own lands justly' (2013: 131).

In this chapter, I expound Oyowe's original and powerful argumentation and respond to it in defence of my initial position. I argue that the principle that compensation should be done in a way expected to benefit victims and not to burden other innocents remains plausible, particularly—but not solely—if one is drawn to a broadly African morality (and does not subscribe to, say, a Kantian moral theory of respect for autonomy). In addition, I show that when the principle is applied to land reform in South Africa, it does not end up entailing that the interests of offenders should be favoured over those of victims.

In the following, I proceed by first sketching my initial position on compensation in response to land theft, indicating why I had found it plausible in the light of a characteristically African morality ("From *Ubuntu* to Beneficial Compensation" section). Next, I lay out Oyowe's major criticisms of the position ("Oyowe's Critique of Beneficial Compensation" section), after which I respond to them ("Responding to Oyowe's Critique" section). I conclude by noting the need for input from economists and other social scientists if my approach to land reform is justified ("Conclusion" section).

From *Ubuntu* to Beneficial Compensation

I first took up the issue of land reform in an essay indicating how an *ubuntu* ethic could plausibly ground public policy (Metz 2011). In this section, I lay out just enough of that material to facilitate debate between myself and Oyowe on the subject of how to enact land reform in South Africa and similar contexts.

By my moral-philosophical interpretation of *ubuntu*, a policy is right if and only if it treats individuals with respect in virtue of their capacity to relate communally or harmoniously. What gives people a dignity, by this account, is their ability to be party to communal relationships both as subjects, those who commune, and as objects, those with whom others commune. Communion involves two ways of interacting, namely, by identifying with others and exhibiting solidarity with them. Identifying with others means enjoying a sense of togetherness with them and engaging in cooperative projects, while exhibiting solidarity consists of helping others, particularly by meeting their needs, and doing so for their sake.

If what makes people special is their ability to commune and to be communed with, then the default position for a state (or at least officials acting on behalf of it) is for it to commune with residents in its territory and also to foster communion amongst them. However, where people have misused their capacity to commune, by for instance having initially acted discordantly against innocent parties in the form of forcibly taking their land, then respect for both them and their victims can mean that the state should also respond to the guilty with discord. Specifically, I have argued that it can be just for the state to subordinate and harm wrongdoers insofar as doing so is necessary to get them to make reparations to victims whom they had subordinated and harmed (Metz 2010, 2011). More recently I have also contended that the state may rightfully act discordantly towards the guilty as a way to disavow the mistreatment of others' capacity to relate communally, which could involve making the guilty effect restitution to their victims in ways the guilty find burdensome (Metz 2019). In a nutshell, forcing the guilty to compensate their victims is respectful of the latter's dignity and not disrespectful of the former's dignity, as least insofar as their dignity is grounded on their social nature.

Regarding the right way to make compensation, given that people's dignity is constituted by their capacity to commune and be communed with, it seems natural to conclude that the compensation should normally be communal. That is, the way for a party who has wrongfully harmed innocents to make restitution to them should take a form that is expected to help them, where help is a matter of meeting needs (as opposed to, say, satisfying variable desires, which is a more utilitarian than African view of people's good). At the very least, the form of compensation should not be expected to produce further harm, that is, to reduce victims' quality of life all the more.

Furthermore, it is not merely harm to victims that is relevant when considering how to implement land reform, but also harm to other innocent people. Compensatory justice is not the only sort of justice, and it implausibly takes lexical priority over all other kinds. In particular, there is also distributive justice owed to individuals, and compensatory justice ought to be realized in a way that does not greatly infringe on what they are owed. Although advancing certain kinds of justice can intuitively be right when *some* harm to innocent third parties is foreseen, for instance emotional suffering on the part of the relatives of a punished offender, the harm to them should be minimized where feasible.

Applying these claims to land reform, I had made the following suggestions. It is clear that those who forcibly took land (and those who have received it but have not given it back) owe something to those whose land was taken (and their descendants), but it is not as simple as merely returning what had been taken in the past, without regard for the future. Instead, land reform should be undertaken in a way that is likely to improve victims' quality of life while not greatly reducing the quality of life of those in the broader society.

So far as I can tell, Zimbabwe's Fast Track Land Reform Programme,[3] adopted in 2000, failed on both counts and did so foreseeably. The case of Zimbabwe is of course contested, and, while not essential to illustrate the moral point I want to make, it is nonetheless plausibly (even if not obviously) a useful example of it. If the reader believes I have the following empirical outcomes or causes of them wildly incorrect, she may substitute her own case.

As is well known, despite the transition to a more democratic government and to black rule in Zimbabwe in 1980, land reform had not been well effected, leaving much arable farmland in the hands of white

[3] For overviews of the policy and practice, on which I draw below, see Cliffe et al. (2011), Echanove (2017), Irigoyen (2017).

descendants of those who had acquired it illegitimately. Putting the Programme into practice in 2001, the Zimbabwean government supported guerrilla war veterans in their forcible ejection of thousands of white people from commercial farms and without compensation. Although there was reportedly cronyism, whereby farms were allocated to those with political ties, it is also the case that hundreds of thousands of black people, many of whom sought to become farmers, did receive land after the confiscations.

Setting aside the issue of corruption, confiscating white held farmland all in one go in itself was likely to cause capital flight and lead to such things as grotesque hyperinflation, reported rates of 90% unemployment, and a much greater difficulty of purchasing essential goods (Hobbes 2014). According to one estimate, about a decade after the *en masse* land appropriations in Zimbabwe, the private sector was 'operating at 10 percent of its former capacity' and about 15 years later 'Zimbabwe's per capita GDP is $600, the third lowest in the world' (Hobbes 2014).[4]

In addition, transferring the farmland immediately to those who lacked the capital, funding, and training to make it productive was likely to lead to impaired agricultural production. According to a policy analysis by CARE International that substantially draws on Zimbabwean sources,

> The subdivision of commercial farms and settling of new farmers substantially reduced agricultural output. Between 2000 and 2008 production of maize dropped 76% (Mutenyo, 2011). Agricultural exports declined by 53% during the same period (AMID, 2012). Zimbabwe, which used to be a net food exporter to neighboring countries, turned into a country with severe food shortages (Ncube, 2015), and a net importer. (Echanove 2017: 15; see also Irigoyen 2017)

There are some scholars who highlight the benefits to small-scale farmers that came in the wake of Zimbabwe's fast-track approach to land

[4] It is true that Zimbabwe was vulnerable to capital flight because of the interdependence of the world economy, which is dominated by Western and Asian forces. However, that dynamic is the reality, and needs to be considered when making political decisions that will affect the lives of millions of domestic citizens.

reform, but, even here, two of them conclude that 'a significant proportion of beneficiaries are managing only to "hang in", while others "drop out". Land and agrarian reform by itself is clearly not the sole solution to rural poverty' (Aliber and Cousins 2013: 162; for nearly identical phrasing see Scoones et al. 2011: 975).

Instead of reducing the harmful effects of colonial land dispossession, the Zimbabwean approach to land reform foreseeably caused more harm to colonialism's victims and the populace more generally. Even if things were to get better in Zimbabwe after, say, 30 years, that would mean little to those who suffered most directly from colonialism; those individuals would not have been compensated (beyond knowing their descendants might eventually come out well), instead having lived worse lives for those decades (with many soon to die, given their age).

Although I am not an economist, other approaches to land reform on the face of it would have been more likely to benefit black victims and without burdening members of the broader society. For instance, Zimbabwe could have required white farmers to transfer truly substantial portions (though not all) of the farmland in their possession to their black workers, with the expectations that the farmers would also undertake the labour of transferring skills and that the government would provide title deeds and loans to the new farmers. This approach would have been more communal, including being better for the lives of victims who had suffered from white domination.[5]

If one holds a different sort of ethic, one that is more Western, then one might be less inclined to see a problem with the Zimbabwean case. For example, if one holds a basic natural rights view, in the way that John Locke is sometimes read, then justice was obtained insofar as black people now possess the object, land, that had been stolen from them. For another example, if one's ultimate value is Kantian autonomy or utilitarian preference, then again it is more likely to appear that justice was done,

[5] Some readers will find this sort of accountability to be insufficient, with the prospect of compensation, reform, and improved relationships not being important enough to forgo a harsher penalty such as imprisonment for those in unjust possession of land. However, if *ubuntu* is our touchstone, then we have to let go of vengeful or retributive reactions, accepting that other demands for accountability remain apt. And, again, *ex hypothesi*, the alternative would be worse lives for black victims. See the land reform proposals advanced by the National African Farmers Union of South Africa, which are motivated by similarly pragmatic grounds (Dlamini 2019).

insofar as black people are now in charge and living in ways they would have chosen or preferred had there not been colonialism (cf. Goodin 1989: 67–68).

In contrast, by my understanding of *ubuntu*, since part of what gives us a dignity is our capacity to care and to be cared for, when force is justified it is so normally when necessary in order to care, that is, to improve people's quality of life. The parallel here is with *ubuntu*'s clear rejection of retribution as a primary way to respond to wrongdoers when it comes to criminal justice. Instead of calling for an eye for an eye, that is, punishing the guilty merely because they deserve it for a crime committed in the past, the dominant theme amongst southern African normative thinkers is the need for punishment to do some good in the future, ideally rehabilitating the offender and protecting the society (for just a few examples, consider Constitutional Court of the Republic of South Africa 1995: para. 129–131, 223–244; Tutu 1999; Masitera 2018). My account of civil justice runs parallel to this approach to criminal justice, such that the state should forcibly redistribute land in ways expected to improve the lives of victims of land dispossession, while taking care not to make society much worse off in the process. Compensatory justice should normally be expected to advance people's good, including their virtue and well-being, at least if we are adherents to an *ubuntu* ethic of some kind or other.

Oyowe's Critique of Beneficial Compensation

Oyowe is principally concerned to question my approach to land reform, but he also suggests an alternative approach to it, according to which just compensation is a matter of putting victims in the condition they would have been in absent the initial injustice. '(T)he restitution of land is independent of any benefits to previous victims or prospective wider social benefits of land redistribution…. (R)estitution constitutes returning victims to a condition they would have been in in the absence of the wrong'

(Oyowe 2017: 239).[6] Indeed, this account of just compensation is a common one to encounter. For example, it is central to the construal of corrective justice in the *Stanford Encyclopedia of Philosophy* (Miller 2017) and in a classic discussion by Robert Goodin (1989). In this section, I spell out Oyowe's argumentation for this position, responding to it only in the following section.

Central to Oyowe's reasoning is a purported counterexample to my principle:

> Suppose that an intruder breaks into my property, steals my Ferrari and then gets caught. Suppose further that, being a careless driver, if I were to have my Ferrari back I might pose a threat to myself and to other motorists. Now, it seems that it would be unjust to retain my Ferrari until such a time that it is established that I no longer pose any threat to others and myself. (Oyowe 2017: 239; see also Oyowe 2013: 131)

By analogy, given that land had been unjustly taken from black people in Zimbabwe and in South Africa, the land should be immediately returned to those who had rightfully owned it, regardless of whether doing so would pose a threat to them or to other innocent parties. The case is *prima facie* powerful, and deserves a reply.

Relatedly, Oyowe maintains that the logic of my approach ends up counterintuitively entailing that white beneficiaries of injustice may rightly retain the land either indefinitely or at least until such time as black victims are likely to live better lives consequent to its redistribution. Oyowe also remarks:

> For what this approach implies is that whether one justly owns land depends on whether one has the capacity to 'run farms and keep the economy stable.' And since whites possess this capacity, and are better placed to keep the economy stable, Metz's position seems to imply that they own

[6] Sometimes the word "restitution" is meant to connote not the same as compensation, but rather the act of returning an object back to its rightful owner (e.g., Goodin 1989: 59; Boxill 2013: 954–955). If one elects to use "restitution" in this narrow sense, then one way to frame the debate between me and Oyowe is whether compensation must (whenever possible) take the form of restitution. However, I instead use "restitution" and "compensation" interchangeably, as does Oyowe.

> lands justly … (which) unfairly privileges the interests of the offender vis-a-vis those to be compensated. (Oyowe 2013: 131)

So, in the light of certain empirical claims, Oyowe is contending that my approach not only cannot show that dispossessed blacks should receive land, but also ends up showing that unjust white landholders may retain it. Instead, according to him, the proper principle is that compensation ought to restore people to the state they would have been in had there not been injustice, which principle would clearly justify taking land from whites and giving it to blacks without regard to whether doing so would benefit the latter.

If my approach to compensatory justice could not justify land reform in post-colonial societies such as Zimbabwe and South Africa, I would forsake the approach. However, I believe that my approach can justify it, as I reply to Oyowe in the next section.

Responding to Oyowe's Critique

One way to reply to Oyowe would be to address our differing fundamental ethical views. Mine is a relational interpretation of *ubuntu* according to which individuals matter morally because of their capacity to be party to communal relationships. In contrast, Oyowe takes it to be an 'uncontroversial intuition that the individual has *intrinsic* value or that rights belong primarily to the individual' (2013: 129), where by 'intrinsic' I am supposing that Oyowe means not merely that the individual has a final value, but does so in virtue of her non-relational properties, perhaps her autonomy or preferences.[7] Above I suggested that different ethical foundations have different implications for how to conceive of compensatory justice, and that an *ubuntu* ethic prescribes a form of restitution that is likely to benefit victims. Hence, one strategy by which to question

[7] If Oyowe means merely that an individual and not a group is what has a dignity and is the ultimate bearer of rights, then there is no real disagreement between us. It is incorrect to describe my view as 'community-based' or appealing to a 'collective right' (Oyowe 2013: 131, 132). By my account, individual persons have a dignity, albeit because of their relational properties, specifically their inherent ability to commune with others, where what appear to be group rights are ultimately rights of individuals in virtue of their social nature (see, e.g., Metz 2014: 142–144).

Oyowe's approach to restitution would be to cast doubt on his moral foundation.

However, that would be a large project not squarely centred on issues of land reform. In addition, the force of Oyowe's criticisms of my approach is independent of his foundational ethic—after all, I did not mention his ethic when expounding his criticisms in the previous section, but I presume the reader appreciated their power nonetheless. Therefore, in the following, while I believe those drawn to an Afro-communal ethic should find my conception of restitution attractive, I instead focus on Oyowe's specific objections to this conception.

Consider, then, the Ferrari case. Oyowe's intuition is that if I have stolen it from him, I may not keep it until he no longer poses a threat to himself or other motorists. There are two distinct issues here, viz., how long I may retain the Ferrari and when he should get it back. Although neither I nor Oyowe separated those issues in our discussions, they should be distinguished. Part of the pull of his case comes from the thought that it would be wrong for me, the thief, to keep the car for any amount of time. However, the principle that compensation must benefit victims need not entail that those who unjustly took goods from others may keep them until such time as victims will benefit from them. Instead, a third party such as a court could confiscate the goods from those who wrongfully took them and then determine how to return them in a way that would improve victims' quality of life without harming innocent third-parties. I presume this point removes much of the sting from the case.

Imagine, now, a court deciding whether to return the car to Oyowe despite him being a menace on the road. Or imagine me, the thief, having had a 'come to Jesus moment' and now wanting to compensate Oyowe in the right way. It might seem that the only choices are either to give the car to Oyowe despite him posing a threat to himself and others or not giving him the car. However, there is a third alternative that I advance, which would be for the court or the thief to return the car in a way that would reduce the threat to himself and others. For example, if part of the threat were due to Oyowe's car having mechanical troubles, then it would be just for the court to order me, the thief, to go out of my way to make those repairs before giving the car back to Oyowe. For another example, if the threat were due to Oyowe being a careless driver, then the court could order that I, the thief, pay for training classes for him. Are these not intuitively desirable forms of compensation?

It is true that repairing the car or attending driver's education would take some time. At some points, Oyowe expresses concern that it 'would not be in the interest of justice to delay compensation until some subsequent benefit is realized' (Oyowe 2013: 131) and that, applied to land reform, my approach would 'slow down the process of compensating victims of unjust land dispossession' (Oyowe 2017: 239).

In a way, this phrasing begs the question, because, according to me, compensation is not merely victims getting back what was taken from them, but rather getting that or something else back in a way that is likely to make victims' lives better. It would be ideal if it did not take any time at all, and it would of course be wrongful of thieves to be obstructive when it comes to returning stolen property. However, the sort of delay involved in fixing up a Ferrari so that it is safer is intuitively justified. And while it would of course take longer than that to transfer skills and other resources so that black victims of colonialism could benefit from the land, consider the alternative: not benefiting from the land, and perhaps being even worse off as per the case of Zimbabwe.

A final poignant aspect of Oyowe's criticism of my position concerns the requirement that compensation should not cause great harm to innocent third-parties and, in the context of land reform, that it ought not be pursued in a manner that would greatly upset the economy, viz., to the point of hyperinflation, 90% unemployment, food shortages, and extreme poverty. Recall that Oyowe points out that if an appropriate form of land redistribution must avoid economic disaster, then it appears to follow that whites may keep the land if necessary to avoid that condition, thereby privileging the wrongdoer over the victim.

In reply, much depends on the empirical details. It could well be that right after independence from colonialism, white people were mainly the ones with the knowledge, training, capital, and the like needed to 'run farms and keep the economy stable', but there is of course no reason to think that must have been true for very long. With support from white farmers and the state, a transfer of land could have been made in a way that did not cause substantial capital flight, impair agricultural production, and hence bring terrible hardship to the victims of colonialism and members of the broader society.

Furthermore, those in unjust possession of the land could reasonably be expected to compensate victims not merely for the land in their possession, but also for any delays involved in returning the land in a way that would improve their quality of life. For instance, they could in the meantime help to fund housing, education, and healthcare for victims. With that additional expectation, a natural complement to my approach of beneficial compensation for wrongdoing, offender interests would not be privileged.

Before concluding, I provide some additional reason for doubting the central alternative to my principle that compensation should be likely to benefit victims while not greatly burdening other innocents. Recall that Oyowe's preferred principle is that 'restitution constitutes returning victims to a condition they would have been in in the absence of the wrong' (2017: 239).

For one thing, this principle is too narrow, for there are cases in which it would be impossible to return a stolen object and yet a kind compensatory justice could be made nonetheless (Boxill 2013: 953–955). If the Ferrari had been destroyed in a tornado at my house, I, the thief, could not give it back to Oyowe. However, I could and should make, say, financial reparations to him (at the very least if the tornado would not have destroyed his car had it been in his possession). Applied to land, the logic of the point is that there will be situations in which, say, because of mining or urbanization, land cannot be returned in its original state to the victims of colonialism. In those cases, compensatory justice is still entirely possible even though victims cannot live in the way they would have in the absence of the unjust thievery. Basically, wrongdoers and beneficiaries of wrongdoing could and intuitively should go out of their way to offer goods likely to make victims' lives better.

Furthermore, sometimes returning victims to the condition they would have been in without theft would be intuitively wrong, or at least not as just as another option. Suppose that while the Ferrari was in my unjust possession, the state adopted an extremely heavy tax specifically on Ferraris but not on Maseratis. Imagine, too, that I had a Maserati (one that was actually mine). The right form of compensation would surely be for me, someone who had stolen Oyowe's Ferrari, to offer him the option of taking my Maserati, supposing it were comparable in desirability to the Ferrari. In terms of *ubuntu*, that gesture, which is aimed at improving

Oyowe's quality of life, would be at the heart of a desirable reconciliation between us. Applying the point to land, because of the economic change in South Africa since 1913, there will likely be some victims of dispossession who reasonably judge that they would be better off if they did not receive land but instead, say, higher education or job training. Simply returning the land to them (even with additional compensation for the time it had been withheld from them) would not intuitively be as preferable as giving them what would make their lives go well.

Conclusion

As I have pointed out in this chapter, I lack economic and more generally social scientific training, and hence cannot with confidence indicate the precise contours of the land reform that would satisfy the moral principle I have advanced. By this principle, land reform should serve the function of benefiting the victims of unjust land dispossession while not placing weighty burdens on the rest of society. I suggested that the Zimbabwean fast-track programme failed to live up to this conception of compensatory justice. While I have proposed another tactic that appears more promising, whereby white farmers would make large transfers of land and skills without being forced to leave their plots entirely and the state would provide financial support to black farmers, it is ultimately up to those with empirical expertise to determine which would fit the bill.[8]

References

Aliber, Michael, and Ben Cousins. 2013. Livelihoods after Land Reform in South Africa. *Journal of Agrarian Change* 13 (1): 140–165.

Boxill, Bernard. 2013. Compensatory Justice. In *The International Encyclopedia of Ethics*, ed. Hugh LaFollette, 953–959. Malden, MA: Blackwell Publishing Ltd.

[8] For comments on a prior draft of this chapter, I thank Erasmus Masitera, Motsamai Molefe, Oritsegbubemi Oyowe, and participants in the Workshop on Philosophical Approaches to Land Reform in Africa that was held at the University of Johannesburg in 2019.

———. 2014. Compensation and Past Injustice. In *Contemporary Debates in Applied Ethics*, 2nd ed., ed. Andrew Cohen and Christopher Wellman, 191–202. Malden, MA: Wiley-Blackwell.

Cliffe, Lionel, et al. 2011. An Overview of Fast Track Land Reform in Zimbabwe. *Journal of Peasant Studies* 38 (5): 907–938.

Cohen, Andrew. 2009. Compensation for Historic Injustices: Completing the Boxill and Sher Argument. *Philosophy and Public Affairs* 37 (1): 81–102.

Constitutional Court of the Republic of South Africa. 1995. *The State versus T. Makwanyane and M. Mchunu*. Case No. CCT/3/94. http://www.saflii.org/.

Dlamini, Penwell. 2019. No Expropriation of Productive White Farms without Compensation, Says National African Farmers Union. *Sowetan Live*, 15 August. https://www.sowetanlive.co.za/news/south-africa/2019-08-15-no-expropriation-of-productive-white-farms-without-compensation-says-national-african-farmers-union/.

Echanove, Juan. 2017. *Food Security, Nutrition, Climate Change Resilience, Gender and the Small-scale Farmers: Zimbabwe*. CARE International. https://www.fanrpan.org/sites/default/files/publications/Zimbabwe%20policy%20analysis%20final.pdf.

Goodin, Robert. 1989. Theories of Compensation. *Oxford Journal of Legal Studies* 9 (1): 56–75.

Hobbes, Michael. 2014. How Did Zimbabwe Become So Poor—and yet So Expensive?. *The New Republic*, 6 January. https://newrepublic.com/article/115925/zimbabwe-prices-why-are-they-high-new-york-citys.

Irigoyen, Claudia. 2017. *Fast Track Land Reform in Zimbabwe*. Centre for Public Impact. https://www.centreforpublicimpact.org/case-study/fast-track-land-reform-zimbabwe/.

Masitera, Erasmus. 2018. Ubuntu Justice and the Power to Transform the Modern Zimbabwean Rehabilitation Justice System. In *Power in Contemporary Zimbabwe*, ed. Erasmus Masitera and Fortune Sibanda, 109–120. Abingdon: Routledge.

Metz, Thaddeus. 2010. Human Dignity, Capital Punishment, and an African Moral Theory: Toward a New Philosophy of Human Rights. *Journal of Human Rights* 9 (1): 81–99.

———. 2011. *Ubuntu* as a Moral Theory and Human Rights in South Africa. *African Human Rights Law Journal* 11 (2): 532–559.

———. 2014. African Values, Human Rights and Group Rights: A Philosophical Foundation for the Banjul Charter. In *African Legal Theory and Contemporary Problems*, ed. Oche Onazi, 131–151. Dordrecht: Springer.

———. 2019. Reconciliation as the Aim of a Criminal Trial: *Ubuntu's* Implications for Sentencing. *Constitutional Court Review* 9: 1–22. https://journals.co.za/content/journal/10520/EJC-19f0c78b6b.

Miller, David. 2017. Justice. In *In Stanford Encyclopedia of Philosophy*, ed. Edward Zalta. https://plato.stanford.edu/entries/justice/#CorrVersDistJust.

Molefe, Motsamai. 2018. Personhood and (Rectification) Justice in African Thought. *Politikon* 45 (3): 352–367.

Oyowe, Oritsegbubemi. 2013. Individual and Community in Contemporary African Moral-Political Philosophy. *Philosophia Africana* 15 (2): 117–136.

———. 2017. *Ubuntu*, Rectification and the Land Question. In *Jurisprudence in an African Context*, ed. David Bilchitz et al., 234–239. Cape Town: Oxford University Press.

Perez, Nahshon. 2011. On Compensation and Return. *Journal of Applied Philosophy* 28 (2): 151–168.

Scoones, Ian, et al. 2011. Zimbabwe's Land Reform: Challenging the Myths. *Journal of Peasant Studies* 38 (5): 967–993.

Tutu, Desmond. 1999. *No Future without Forgiveness*. New York: Random House.

9

Reconciling "Title to Land and Productivity" in Land Debates in Africa

Dennis Masaka

Introduction

The land question is one of the most controversial issues that are yet to be conclusively settled in Africa. Arguments have been proffered on the need to resolve it though the means of doing it have often differed. Some defend and prefer a more robust and radical approach where those land owners of colonial extraction are dispossessed of the land which is then set aside for redistribution to the indigenous people, while others seem to opt for a more "fairer" redistribution irrespective of whether one is indigenous or not (*see* Binswanger-Mkhize et al. 2009: 21). In some quarters, such land ownership transformations have generally been conceived as redistributive (Adams and Howell 2001, 1–6; Moyo 2011a: 257–267). However, I hasten to say that policy has not always been complemented

D. Masaka (✉)
Department of Philosophy, University of the Free State, Bloemfontein, South Africa

Department of Philosophy and Religious Studies, Great Zimbabwe University, Masvingo, Zimbabwe

E. Masitera (ed.), *Philosophical Perspectives on Land Reform in Southern Africa*, https://doi.org/10.1007/978-3-030-49705-7_9

with action especially in relation to how the repossessed land has been redistributed in some countries that have undertaken to reverse settler-colonial land dispossessions (de Villiers 2003: 1–3). The tendency has been to replace colonial-settler elite ownership with an indigenous elite ownership much to the detriment of the not-so-privileged. However, what seems common among these efforts is to correct land ownership disparities between the indigenous people and people of colonial extraction (Cotula et al. 2004: 8).

My focus in this chapter is not to necessarily labour over merits of land redistribution in Africa but to consider how title to land ought to be realistically complemented by productivity. This is necessary if countries in Africa are to attain some level of self-sufficiency that they yearn for. Though the call to use repossessed land productively is not new, it is now especially more important in present times as countries in Africa seek to assert their independence from significant dependency on others in the terrain of food production. Commitment to use repossessed land productively ought not to be mere rhetoric intended to justify repossession principally for its own sake. The clarion call to take seriously title to land and productivity as countries in Africa seek to emerge from significant dependency on other geopolitical centres is a response to some instances in Africa where land repossession has in fact increased and not lessened levels of dependency. In this light, I refer to Zimbabwe's resolution of the land question that has temporarily increased the country's level of dependency as a case in point. This is precisely why I argue that title to land ought to be complemented by productivity as countries in Africa resolve the land question.

I begin by highlighting the land question in Africa. In the second section, I show that reclamation of title to land and productivity ought to be taken as equally important if countries in Africa are to attain some level of self-sufficiency and lessen their levels of dependency on other geopolitical centres in matters of production and provision of food. This is necessary because oftentimes the urge to reclaim title to land in some countries in Africa has often been taken as primary with theoretical commitments given to its productive use. In order to show that productivity might not be given the same level of importance as accorded to the imperative to reclaim title to land, I refer to how Zimbabwe has so far resolved the land question. In the last section, I argue that when repossessed land is used productively, it is likely to reduce vulnerabilities of countries in Africa to the problem of dependency and problems associated with it. I now turn to a discussion on the problem of the land question in Africa.

Problematic Land Question in Africa

The land question is one of the most important questions that African countries that have suffered colonisation need to resolve (Moyo and Chambati 2013: 3). It is a question that touches on one of the aspects that define sovereignty (*see* Ramose 2016: 549) because without ownership of land, it is very difficult for countries in Africa to claim that they have attained independence when land is still not under their control. It might be correct to say that without the control and ownership of land by the indigenous people of Africa, these countries may not be defined as "African countries" but as "countries in Africa". In this section, I seek to present briefly the background to the land question in Africa. I then identify the land question as one of the prime reasons behind the struggles for independence across the African continent. I hasten to say that in discussing the land question in Africa, I am proceeding from the position that there are similarities between their colonial experiences revolving around conquest of both the peoples and their lands.

The incoming colonial settlers presented a very difficult scenario to the indigenous people of Africa. Generally, across the African continent, the approach was to subdue the indigenous people in preparation for the expropriation of their lands (Byamugisha 2014: 2). In such a scenario, it is reasonable to say that the indigenous people suffered a double tragedy as a result of colonial conquests. As the indigenous people battled to come to terms with their subjugation, they also found themselves excluded from the control of their own rich lands and the resources contained in them. The injustices of such actions are more telling especially when one considers the primacy of land in the lives of the indigenous people of Africa as a source of life and wealth. The extent of alienation from their rich lands through forced displacements had implications on their status as rightful owners of their lands as well as beings entitled to rights as extended to human beings elsewhere.[1] The indigenous people of Africa despised the colonisers because of the injustices that they inflicted on them.

In addition, such land dispossessions inaugurated vulnerabilities among the dispossessed. These vulnerabilities are still very alive in present times. This is despite the questionable deployment of the discourse of "industrialisation", partly through land dispossessions, as a necessary cure to the assumed "backwardness" that faced some parts of the world marked for conquest. As Sam Moyo, Praveen Jha and Paris Yeros (2013: 95) note, "this binary of backwardness/industrialization became the basis of latter-day myth-making." Following this reasoning, attempts at land ownership transformation are conceived as retrogression into "backwardness" of the past where land was underutilised. As I will show later in this chapter, this contested thinking is invoked whenever and wherever there are attempts to redistribute land. Yet, concealed in this myth of industrialisation are the injustices that inaugurate it.

The struggle for liberation across the African continent ought to be conceived as primarily a fight to overturn these injustices through restoring the dignity of the indigenous people of Africa as well as title to their land resource. This serves to show that though the imperative to reclaim expropriated land might have been a major reason behind the struggle for liberation from colonial settler rule, it was not the only one. However, for the purposes of this chapter, the focus is on land as a major driver of struggles for liberation from colonial settler rule. Because of the importance of land as a political and economic resource, it is not surprising that it has been given so much prominence in the struggles for liberation across the African continent.

The land question thus revolves around contestations concerning its assumed ambivalent ownership status inaugurated by its expropriation

[1] Though couched in non-indigenous legalistic terms that may not be applicable to their indigenous notions of ownership, the idea that "most land in sub-Saharan Africa has no registration of who owns it or has rights to use it" (Toulmin 2009: 10) might be wrongly construed to mean no one has title to land in that part of Africa unless it is "registered" in one's name. Non-indigenous people and entities could manipulate such alien interpretations of "ownership" to engage in land grabbing. Yet, it can hardly be debated that land in Africa is a birthright of its indigenous people with or without the so-called "registration".

from the indigenous people of Africa by the colonial settlers (*see* Mafeje 1997: 9). The transactional status given to it means that it could change hands on payment of agreed monetary value. This has created problems as countries in Africa move towards resolving the land question through repossessing, for purposes of redistribution, land originally expropriated from the indigenous people of Africa. However, the turning of the originally expropriated land into private property has often invoked moral questions as some governments in Africa are opting for repossession of the land without compensating its "owners" for the reason that it was originally stolen from the indigenous people of Africa whose land, by right, ought to be restored to them. As a result, the fact that some of the land exchanged hands over the years through buying and selling seems to be trashed. The reason could be that selling or buying stolen property may not absolve parties to such transactions from the "original sin".

Because of the importance and value given to land in Africa, its reclamation has often been conceived as one of the foundational problem that ought to be overcome if countries in Africa are to move towards realistic liberation from colonial subjugation. In this light, it is necessary to establish some possible reasons for the clamour for land reclamation in countries in Africa. I will consider them under the following categories: sentimental/nationalistic, ethical and economic reasons highlighting what appears to be the dominant reason(s) in some countries that have attempted land ownership transformation. The reality that land in countries in Africa is still largely possessed by non-indigenous people and entities could be an affront to those who hold nationalistic views. Such people may feel that their independence is not authentic if it does not translate to reclamation of title to their land conceived as a birthright. As a result, repossession of land marks reclamation of the humanity of the indigenous people of Africa and other peoples who have suffered unjust land dispossessions. As I argue elsewhere, "the land resource is a very vital aspect of any human race because it embodies people's sense of belonging, humanhood and livelihood" (Masaka 2011: 333–334). On this score, land assumes a nationalistic and sentimental mode. Mere repossession of land is read as an important phase in the quest for the restoration of the humanity and dignity of the indigenous people of Africa conquered in the unjust wars of colonisation (Ramose 2010: 1). It could be conceived as a necessary foundation for the restoration of other forms of rights. This will then make land repossession even more important and immediate prerequisite in the indigenous people of Africa's quest for significant liberation. In this way, repossession of land by the indigenous people of Africa could be motivated by nationalistic/sentimental reasons.

Connected to the above is the ethical imperative of land repossession in countries in Africa. The conquest of land of the indigenous people of Africa is an ethical issue that ought to be corrected by restoration of their title to it. On the bar of ethical reasoning, it is questionable to maintain asymmetries in land ownership between the indigenous people of Africa and people, and entities of colonial extraction. As such, the need to reclaim title to land by the indigenous people of Africa could be an ethically necessary step in the quest for liberation from various colonially inaugurated injustices that are still subsisting across the African continent. Such a programme is an ethical necessity if the indigenous people of Africa are to make more visible their dignity and humanity compromised by the circumstances of colonisation (Ramose 2003: 118). In this connection, it will be a misnomer epistemically and ethically for them to continue to be called "indigenous people of Africa" when mineral and agriculturally rich lands in Africa remain largely in the hands of non-indigenous people and entities. It appears fair and just for the indigenous people of Africa to be its rightful owners. Land ought to surely be reverted to the indigenous people of Africa who, at present, seem to have title to names of their respective countries yet the sum total of spaces thus named continue to be subdivided into pieces largely owned by non-indigenous peoples and entities as private property. This translates to a paradigm change from talk of "land in Africa" (Quan et al. 2004: 30) to "African land" in the sense of realistic ownership of land bounded by their respective country borders.

Land is also an important economic factor whose ownership has a strong bearing on economic power relations in any given state. Besides sentimental or nationalistic reasons for the quest to assert title to land by the indigenous people of Africa, it is also endowed with various minerals that, if reasonably exploited, could enhance the economic statuses of countries in Africa. For this reason, ownership of land and what resides in it has turned to be a contested terrain in some countries in Africa that still have to overcome the problem of land ownership structure that predominantly favours non-indigenous people and entities. The dominance of economies in countries in Africa by non-indigenous people and entities has been a source of worry since colonial times. As such, there has been a drive to increase the participation of indigenous people in economic affairs of their countries through land repossessions and commitments to use it productively (Moyo 2010: 286). This may not be construed to mean that they are averse to investment from non-indigenous sources. The call is simply to ensure title to land principally returns to the indigenous people. Having considered some reasons behind some countries in Africa's clamour to assume title to land, I now proceed to defend the need to ensure that title to land is complemented with productive use of repossessed land.

Balancing Title to Land and Productivity

In this section, I argue for the importance of establishing balance between assuming title to land and ensuring that such land is used productively. I will show that merely assuming title to land without using it productively may not deliver the significant economic self-sufficiency that some countries in Africa are still yearning to attain following the attainment of political independence from colonial rule. In arguing thus, I will refer to the case of Zimbabwe's land "reform" programme in showing problems of giving primacy to the right of the indigenous people to attain title to land without necessarily complementing it with using it productively. This is not an indication of productivity deficiencies of indigenous farmers but perhaps deficiencies of some governments in Africa expressed through giving relative primacy to regaining title to land and giving marginal focus on provision of requisite funding and skills where they may be required. The intention is to ensure that title to land is not taken as an end in itself by countries in Africa that are thinking of embarking on land ownership transformation but as means of increasing levels of self-sufficiency through using it productively in future. I proceed to show why is it necessary for countries in Africa thinking of embarking or regaining title to land to think also of using that land productively.

In this connection, the clamour by countries in Africa to regain title to land could be primarily motivated by the economic benefits that accrue from its ownership and productive use. Countries in Africa might think that if they were especially to regain control of arable and mineral-rich lands that were confiscated from them, they may be able to enhance their economic potential. This could be rendered possible if the indigenous people assume title to land and use it more productively to the benefit of their respective economies. Such thinking appears credible especially if it is believable that some pre-colonial African countries were able to use sustainably and efficiently their land resource to produce enough to meet their internal needs as well as external trade requirements. In this light, the alleged mythical incompetence of the indigenous people of Africa to use their land and resources subsisting in them productively to produce enough for their needs and external trade can reasonably be disputed (Stoneman 1981: 128–129). In fact, it appears credible that, in some countries in Africa, colonial settlers felt threatened by competition that some indigenous farmers, for example, posed to them. As a result, there were moves to dispossess the indigenous people of their land and other resources thereby economically weakening them so that they would desperately submit themselves to cheap labour to the colonial settlers in order to earn meagre living (Stoneman 1981: 128–129). The move by some countries in Africa to regain title to land could reasonably be understood in context of attempts to ensure the indigenous people significantly and actively participate in using the land resource productively and contribute to development of their respective countries. This is intended to be a corrective to the problem of enduring colonial problem of exclusion of the indigenous people from meaningful economic activities. At least in theory, this has been the prime motivation behind the quest to regain title to land.

Though it is generally claimed that land "owned" by non-indigenous people and entities has been used productively over the years (*see* Moyo and Chambati 2013: 8), this does not totally discount the possibility that some land might have or is still being kept for speculative reasons thereby lying idle. Nevertheless, the overarching belief is that land "owned" by non-indigenous people and entities has generally been used productively thereby aiding countries in Africa's domestic and external requirements.

On the other hand, indigenous farmers have generally been conceived as incompetent and ineffectual users of land (Byamugisha 2014: 3). However, production levels between people of colonial extraction and entities, and indigenous people of Africa may expectedly be different given such variables as the quality of land and financial resources. In this light, considering that indigenous people of Africa have been managing to use land they have been confined to since colonial times somewhat productively, despite it being largely unsuitable for agricultural purposes, serves to give credence to the thinking that they will likely use repossessed land more productively thereby enhancing the economic statuses of their respective countries.

I urge countries in Africa to work towards ensuring putting this repossessed land to productive use. They may even have to surpass production levels of the previous land occupiers if they are to derive more benefits from the repossessed land. This is important because the success or failure of efforts to return title to land to the indigenous people of Africa is often measured in terms of how they could fare against production levels of previous land occupiers. This might appear to be an unfair standard of assessment of the abilities of indigenous farmers especially given that they may not have the necessary financial support, as is the case with land occupiers of a colonial extraction to draw maximum benefit from the repossessed land. However, it appears to be a plausible expectation that those countries in Africa who are thinking of repossessing land currently "owned" by non-indigenous people and entities to even use it more productively than is currently the case. This means that it might not be plausible for them to be content with merely regaining title to land for its own sake but to use it more productively. This seems not to be the case with some instances of land repossession in Africa. A good example is Zimbabwe that I proceed to focus on.

The intention is to draw some lessons on impressions one seems to get where regaining title to land seems to be given relative primacy to increasing production on the repossessed land. However, attaining this equilibrium has proved challenging given the general aversion especially by owners of capital who seem lethargic to fund indigenous farmers who are allocated the repossessed land. This has created impressions that the indigenous people may not put repossessed land to productive use. This could be a necessary learning curve as some countries in Africa think of embarking on land ownership transformations predicated on the objective of maximising production.

The Case of Zimbabwe's Land "Reform" Programme

The land reform programme in Zimbabwe stands out for two major issues that I discuss in detail below, one, its relatively violent, chaotic and forceful nature (Matondi 2012: 7; Lahiff, 2003: 3); two, its possibly unintended end, that is, widespread transitory underutilisation of repossessed arable land leading to significant food deficits and correspondingly a rise in importation of grains and foodstuffs (Pilossof 2008: 270–271). Such consequences of land repossession in Zimbabwe seems expected if one were to read critically into its designation as "The Fast Track Land Reform Programme (FTLRP)" (Moyo and Chambati 2013: 1). As I will argue, these two issues are strongly connected. Violence characterised land expropriation during the conquest of Zimbabwe and during its repossession by the indigenous people of Zimbabwe since 2000. This seems expected given force and coercion that accompanies expropriation. What appears to justify violence could be the fact that the ones who claim to have title to land are not prepared to surrender without resistance to those who want to wrestle it from them. Though violence against non-indigenous land "owners" during the land "reform" programme in Zimbabwe seems to have been given more prominence leading to the ostracisation of the country especially by the Euro-Western world, such condemnation seems not to have been advanced against the colonial conquest of land in Zimbabwe and Africa in general.

The indigenous people of Zimbabwe's supposedly "wrongful" repossession of land expropriated from them by colonial settlers have attracted sympathy from the dominant and mainline Euro-Western aligned media (*see* Chari 2013: 293; Moyo and Yeros 2013: 331). As Pilossof (2008: 271) argues:

> the increasingly violent nature of the invasions and chaotic manner in which they were carried out, supplied more than enough ammunition for those critical of the reforms. The loudest and shrillest of these voices were understandably the farmers themselves, who faced the very real prospect of losing everything they owned and had worked for. They were however joined by a sympathetic media in many parts of the world, particularly in Britain, the former colonial power. From the very beginning, the fate of the white farmers has had an unbelievably vast amount of representation in the British press.

Violence may not be the preferable way of gaining or regaining title to land not only because it brings a bad name to the country concerned but also because it violates the rights of those affected not to be psychologically and physically harmed.

The predominantly negative coverage of the land "reform" programme in Zimbabwe was however primarily premised on the violation of property rights of farmers of largely colonial extraction (Chari 2013: 309–310). The notion of property rights as it relates to the land that was initially expropriated from the indigenous people of Zimbabwe is a contentious one that ought not to be understood in simplistic terms. At this point, it might be necessary to imagine what the term "property rights" might mean. It might entail having certain entitlements or claims over a piece of land and what subsist in it. Raymond Talinbe Abdulai (2006: 8) defines property rights as "… rights of ownership and refer to the legal as well as the social relations among people in a society with respect to the ownership of things or resources. Thus, ownership of property defines the claim to rights, privileges and powers the owner of the property has as well as the duties such ownership imposes on him/her as the owner and other members of the society in relation to the property." In line with this idea of property rights, it becomes morally and legally incorrect for one to revoke forcibly one's property rights for, say, purposes of redistributing it to the landless indigenous people. The property "owner" ought to surrender openly and willingly title to land in exchange for a certain specified fee. In other words, there ought to be conditions for a willing-buyer, willing-seller scenario for property rights to change hands in a morally and legally acceptable way.

While the willing-buyer, willing-seller scenario has been spoken of in relation to how land ought to be changing hands in "post-colonial" Africa, curiously this is not spoken of the manner in which people of colonial extraction violated property rights of indigenous people of Africa through land expropriation. Yet, those enjoying the privilege of having title to land in the "postcolonial" era courtesy of constitutional provisions crafted and influenced by them seem to be oblivious of the way property rights were blatantly violated during the colonial era. This might point to the duplicity of the departing colonial governments in influencing constitutions of countries in Africa so that they protect the privileged status of land "owners" of a colonial extraction under the guise of property rights. Had property rights of the indigenous people of Africa been respected during the colonial episode, perhaps land expropriation might not have taken place. This means there will be no repossession to talk of and, by extension, the attendant moral and legal problems that it invokes. However, in order to curtail the indigenous people of Africa's repossession of land expropriated during the unjust wars of colonisation, respect of property rights has become the cornerstone of national constitutions in countries in Africa that previously were under direct colonial rule. This points to the politicisation of the concept "property rights" wherein it appears to mean different things when deployed in reference to land "owners" of colonial extraction and the indigenous people of Africa. As Moyo (2013: 29) avers, "focusing on the narrowly defined "human rights transgressions" that accompanied the FTLRP, using abstracted neoliberal good governance norms, the critics miss the important role that broad-based social mobilisation played in shaping state action towards accommodating a wide array of land demands."

Respect for property rights, not spoken of when the lands of the indigenous people of Africa were expropriated during unjust wars of colonisation (*see* Chari 2013: 309), has interestingly become the cornerstone of many national constitutions in Africa. In order to protect their privileged status gained during the colonial era through constitutional provisions, the departing colonial governments have emphasised the supremacy of constitutions over parliamentary supremacy (Ramose 2016: 96). In the presence of such constitutional provisions protecting property rights, it has become difficult for the indigenous people of Africa to repossess their land expropriated during colonisation. As a result, forceful repossession of land in violation of property rights as enshrined in constitutions is considered a viable option for the indigenous people of Africa. In the case of Zimbabwe, the Land Acquisition Act of 1992 was enacted in order to enable the repossession of land for the purposes of resettling the indigenous people. Such an Act faced contestations as it was seen as negating property rights enshrined in the Lancaster House constitution. Forceful repossession of land "owned" by people and entities of colonial extraction was pursued. This was seen as in violation of property rights. However, such a move was considered necessary in order to correct a colonial wrong. As Pilossof (2008: 273) rightly notes, "wholesale and widespread respect for property rights is not applicable to every situation, especially when the situation involves a colonial legacy that has not been adequately dealt with or resolved yet."

Besides its violent and forceful nature, another issue that stands out about the land "reform" in Zimbabwe is the untended significant and transitory decline in productivity levels on the farms, widespread hunger and rise in the importation of food and grains. These negative consequences of a necessary move to reverse asymmetrical land ownership between people and entities of a colonial extraction and the indigenous people (Moyo and Chambati 2013: 2); have been touted as indicators of the badness of such a programme. As a result, some countries in Africa that are thinking of a similar land ownership transformation are often advised to take note of how Zimbabwe has fallen from being a food and grain exporter into an importer of the same.

However, the narrative that commercial farmers of colonial extraction produced enough in the pre-land repossession period to justify labelling of Zimbabwe as the breadbasket of Southern Africa is contestable. To this effect, Sam Moyo (2010: 296; *see also* Moyo and Nyoni 2013: 195) states, "Zimbabwe had been an irregular food exporter to SADC countries until 1999, although South Africa, even under apartheid, has always been the dominant grain exporter." While I accept that things might not have gone the way the indigenous people of Zimbabwe wanted them to, I still defend the need to return land to the indigenous people who ought to use it productively. This is necessary because Zimbabwe's signs of failure in the form of transitory falling levels of productivity seem to have been used as evidence against its necessity (Moyo 2013: 31). As a result, detractors of land "reform" have often cited the example of Zimbabwe in attempts to dissuade those countries in Africa who may be tempted to pursue it in future. In this connection, violation of property rights was considered as behind Zimbabwe's dip in farm production and general economic performance (Pilossof 2008: 272).

However, the causes of the relatively poor show of Zimbabwe's land "reform" programme may not necessarily reside in the mere fact of transferring title to land from land "owners" of a colonial extraction to the indigenous people. It appears the government of Zimbabwe was ill prepared to give adequate financial backing and skill resource to some of those who were given land so that they could use it more productively.[2] Partly, this has brought Zimbabwe to a very difficult and untenable situation where they have turned from irregular grain exporters to importers of the same. The narrative then is to lay blame of whatever went wrong with the land "reform" programme on the government of Zimbabwe. However, this appears to be a too simplistic verdict. It appears this programme faced challenges of adequate funding both from local and external sources.

More fundamentally, lack of financial support to facilitate land redistribution from the erstwhile colonial powers as prescribed in the Lancaster House constitution, government and lending institutions (Matondi 2012: 1) could have contributed to the transitory decline in agricultural productivity. However, such declines appear expected as countries undergoing land redistribution reposition themselves for increased land use and production. This transition may have its setbacks that may be erroneously misread by detractors of land distribution as indicative of its lack of utility. As Moyo (2011b: 947) correctly notes, "extensive land redistribution is expected to alter the structure and orientation of agricultural

[2] However, it ought to be stated that a significant number of the indigenous people of Zimbabwe have the requisite skills and technical knowhow to use productively the repossessed land. What seems to be major challenges are allocating it to individuals and entities with requsite farming skills and sufficient funding necessary for use of repossessed land more productively.

production, including generating a transitional decline in output as new classes of farmers mobilise resources to establish themselves in relation to changing markets and state interventions."[3]

To this end, if this is a plausible assessment, it puts to question the common attribution of failure of the land "reform" programme and the general economy in Zimbabwe solely on indigenous farmers' productivity deficiencies. As Pilossof (2008: 272) argues, "this narrow and reductionist reading of the Zimbabwean situation has its limited merits, but more interestingly shows that this type of ahistorical reading of an economic implosion has its limitations." These limitations have not been noted especially by those who feel that this contested narrative accords to their preferred position that "violation" of property rights leads to economic decline for culprit countries.

Though the position of these reductionist detractors of the land "reform" programme has its problems, one need not lose sight of some failures on the part of the government of Zimbabwe to ensure adequate financial resources and skills are availed to beneficiaries so that they could use the land more productively. This is partly the basis of my contention that those who may be thinking of embarking on a similar programme in future could learn lessons from Zimbabwe. This is important if they are to ensure a future where productivity complements repossession of title to land. As I will argue in the next section, productive use of land for countries in Africa thinking of embarking on a land "reform" programme is necessary if they are to emerge successfully from a spectre of dependency on other countries concerning provision of grains and grains-related foodstuffs in future.

[3] A similar thesis was earlier made by Hans Bokermann (1975: 341–342) when he averred, "true, there can be no a priori certainty that efforts to achieve more justice of distribution will not affect competing aims, such as the increase of yields per hectare. But negative effects, if at all, are likely to be of short-run nature. A productivity comparison for an extended period before and after a reform shows that in the long run land reforms improve productivity."

Title to Land, Productivity and Dependency

In this section, I argue that when repossessed land is used productively, it is likely to reduce vulnerabilities of countries in Africa to dependency on other geopolitical centres and problems associated with it especially given their colonial history and the rhetoric to reverse it. This is a call for some level of self-sufficiency in the arena of food requirements. By calling for some level of self-sufficiency, I am not implying that countries in Africa need not at all depend on each other or other geopolitical centres in meeting some of their respective food requirements. Such total self-sufficiency appears largely impossible considering that countries may not have requisite conditions within their boundaries necessary for the successful production of certain grains and may lack the ability to produce all that they want. Such committed productive use of land could usher positive returns to these countries. However, I do not think that commitment to productive use of repossessed land could be taken as a necessary and enabling precondition for repossession. As I see it, it is a good thing for countries in Africa to do so if they are to improve their independence especially given the subsisting asymmetrical relations with their "former"[4] colonisers.

The rather common narrative shared especially among land "owners" of colonial extraction is their general demeaning assessment of the mettle of indigenous people of Africa in using land in ways that given them significant returns (*see* Moyo and Nyoni 2013: 195–196). This contestable narrative has been partly deployed as a basis for colonial dispossessions and appears to subsist to the present day. This is especially noticeable in overt and covert fears that repossession of land by the indigenous people will spell doom for their respective countries given their assumed incompetence. It appears such thinking has also made a mark on some indigenous people of Africa such that they share similar fears. As a result, it is necessary to debunk such notions of imposed self-doubt, if countries in Africa are to move seriously towards robust attempts at repossessing their land and put it to good use.

---

[4] The term "former" in reference to "colonisers" is used with caution given that hegemonic relations are still subsisting between them and countries in Africa.

Contrary to a common narrative that conceives land "owners" of colonial extraction as efficient users of land compared to the indigenous people of Africa, some countries in Africa seem to dispute it. In fact, they seem to blame some of these land "owners" for grossly underutilising it and at times holding on to it for speculative reasons. I take this indictment of land "owners" of colonial extraction as important in imagining a possible and more useful trajectory that countries in Africa could take in order to do better than the latter. This translates to a more robust programme to improve what the previous land "owners" were doing not so well in order to derive improved returns from it. This is necessary in order for these countries to cater for some of their needs as well as those of other countries. Repossession of land by countries in Africa ought to change their standing in the community of nations.

This demands control and efficient use of land in ways that enrich countries in Africa. Beyond the quest to create wealth for themselves, there is added premium in the form of some level of self-sufficiency necessary for a country to avoid being heavily dependent on others for its needs and wants. This is necessary given that some countries in Africa are still to emerge successfully from the colonial mode where they were considered as largely extractive industries and not as hubs that could also meaningfully add value to what they produce and resultantly generate more wealth for themselves. The imperative to be self-sufficient through effective use of land and resources that subsist in it has been the rhetoric of those countries in Africa that have or are thinking of repossessing land.

However, such a noble projection ought to be actualised. This is necessary in order to deliver changes that would give them a competitive urge through production of goods and services within the community of nations. This could aid them in their quest to attain meaningful independence. The point is any attempt to change the *status quo* ought to be disposed to improve on the capacity of countries in Africa to, first, be able to significantly cater for themselves and also partly contribute to the requirements of the community of nations. This could be a necessary attempt at lessening the asymmetrical relations between them and countries from other geopolitical centres especially in the area of economic performance. If this were taken seriously as part of the imperative to repossess land, then it could perhaps change perceptions for those who are still sceptical of such a programme and its utility for countries in Africa.

It appears scepticism concerning countries in Africa's capacity to maintain or raise levels of production on land they intent to repossess ought to be taken seriously by those concerned about the land question in Africa. The fear could be, because of their assumed inability to use land productively, these countries may plunge more into food deficits and be more dependent on external institutions and bodies to augment their requirements. However, what is often not stated is that food deficits are evident even in countries in Africa that are yet to embark on land repossession programmes, that is, countries that still have a predominant presence of land "owners" of colonial extraction. These deficits could be explained by what appears to be failure to utilise land productively to meet demand, lack of adequate funding for agricultural purposes, and natural catastrophes being experienced in these countries. Attempts at appropriating land underutilisation as consequent upon land repossession becomes debatable.

The starting point then would be how repossession of land could significantly change the prevailing land utilisation trajectory so that it could be used more productively. This is important, not only in attaining some level of sufficiency, but also to show those who are initially in doubt of indigenous people of Africa's mettle to use land even more productively that indeed they have such capacity through evidence of productive use. This then calls for a quick departure from the temporary setbacks of change in land ownership structure, that Moyo (2011b: 947) calls "transitional decline in output", as countries in Africa reposition themselves to increase outputs from repossessed land. Confidence building among those sceptical through productive use of repossessed land might be necessary in order for them to change their perceptions and perhaps lend moral and financial support to land repossession programmes in Africa. This will give countries in Africa the incentive to attain some level self-sufficiency that lessens their levels of dependency especially on other geopolitical centres for their food requirements.

Conclusion

In this chapter, I have sought to imagine how change in land ownership through repossession in countries in Africa could be taken more seriously if repossessed land is used more productively. This is important as countries in Africa seek to emerge from the present asymmetrical land ownership structure to one that is more egalitarian. As noted in the chapter, the tendency among those who might be thinking of repossessing land would be to consider it as an end in itself. I have, however, shown that this ought not be a plausible end especially when one considers that countries in Africa are generally facing food deficits partly due to underutilisation of arable land. Productive use of repossessed land becomes necessary. However, this is not to discount the importance of repossession of land as foundational issue in these countries' quest for some levels of self-sufficiency through its productive use. Fundamentally, if the motivation for countries in Africa to embark on land "reform" programmes is not only to regain title to their land, but also to use it more productively, then it is will be a noble undertaking that, in future, might enable them to meet their food requirements.

References

Abdulai, R. 2006. Is Land Title Registration the Answer to Insecure and Uncertain Property Rights in Sub-Saharan Africa? *RICS Research paper series* 6 (6): 1–29.

Adams, M., and J. Howell. 2001. Redistributive Land Reform in Southern Africa. *Natural Resource Perspectives* (64): 1–6.

Binswanger-Mkhize, H.P., C. Bourguignon, and R. van den Brink. 2009. Introduction and Summary. In *Agricultural Land Redistribution: Towards Greater Consensus*, ed. H.P. Binswanger-Mkhize, C. Bourguignon, and R. van den Brink, 3–41. Washington: The World Bank.

Bokermann, H. 1975. Land Reform in Developing Countries. *Intereconomics* 10 (11): 341–343.

Byamugisha, F.F.K. 2014. Introduction and Overview of Agricultural Land Redistribution and Land Administration Case Studies. In *Agricultural Land*

Redistribution and Land Administration in Sub-Saharan Africa: Case Studies of Recent Reforms, ed. F.F.K. Byamugisha, 1–16. Washington: The World Bank.
Chari, T. 2013. Media Framing of Land Reform in Zimbabwe. In *Land and Agrarian Reform in Zimbabwe Beyond White-Settler Capitalism*, ed. S. Moyo and W. Chambati, 291–330. Dakar: CODESRIA.
Cotula, L., C. Toulmin, and C. Hesse. 2004. *Land Tenure and Administration in Africa: Lessons of Experience and Emerging Issues*. Stevenage, Hertfordshire: SMI (Distribution Services) Ltd.
Mafeje, A. 1997. The National Question in Southern African Settler Societies. *Monograph Series* (6): 1–19.
Masaka, D. 2011. Zimbabwe's Land Contestations and Her Politico-Economic Crises: A Philosophical Dialogue. *Journal of Sustainable Development in Africa* 13 (1): 331–347.
Matondi, P.B. 2012. *Zimbabwe's Fast Track Land Reform*. London: Zed Books.
Moyo, S. 2010. The agrarian question and the developmental state in Southern Africa. In *Constructing a developmental state in South Africa: Potentials and Challenges*, ed. O. Edigheji, 285-314. Cape Town: HSRC Press.
———. 2011a. Land Concentration and Accumulation after Redistributive Reform in Post-Settler Zimbabwe. *Review of African Political Economy* 38 (128): 257–276.
———. 2011b. Changing Agrarian Relations after Redistributive Land Reform in Zimbabwe. *Journal of Peasant Studies* 38 (5): 939–966.
———. 2013. Land Reform and Redistribution in Zimbabwe Since 1980. In *Land and Agrarian Reform in Zimbabwe Beyond White-Settler Capitalism*, ed. S. Moyo and W. Chambati, 29–78. Dakar: CODESRIA.
Moyo, S., and W. Chambati. 2013. Introduction: Roots of the Fast Track Land Reform in Zimbabwe. In *Land and Agrarian Reform in Zimbabwe Beyond White-Settler Capitalism*, ed. S. Moyo and W. Chambati, 1–28. Dakar: CODESRIA.
Moyo, S., and N. Nyoni. 2013. Changing Agrarian Relations after Redistributive Land Reform in Zimbabwe. In *Land and Agrarian Reform in Zimbabwe Beyond White-Settler Capitalism*, ed. S. Moyo and W. Chambati, 195–250. Dakar: CODESRIA.
Moyo, S., and P. Yeros. 2013. The Zimbabwe Model: Radicalisation, Reform and Resistance. In *Land and Agrarian Reform in Zimbabwe Beyond White-Settler Capitalism*, ed. S. Moyo and W. Chambati, 331–358. CODESRIA: Dakar.

Moyo, S., P. Jha, and P. Yeros. 2013. The Classical Agrarian Question: Myth, Reality and Relevance Today. *Agrarian South: Journal of Political Economy* 2 (1): 93–119.

Pilossof, R. 2008. The Land Question (Un)Resolved: An Essay Review. *Historia* 53 (2): 270–279.

Quan, J., Tan, S. F. and Toulmin, C. 2004. Editors' Introduction. In *Land in Africa Market asset or secure livelihood? Proceedings and summary of conclusions from the Land in Africa Conference held in London November* 8–9, 2004, eds. J. Quan, S. F. Tan, and C. Toulmin, 3–14. London: Royal African Society.

Ramose, M. 2003. I Doubt, Therefore African Philosophy Exists. *South African Journal of Philosophy* 22 (2): 113–127.

Ramose, M.B. 2010. Learning Inspired Education. *Caribbean Journal of Philosophy (CJP)* 2 (1): 1–15.

———. 2016. Teacher and Student with a Critical Pan-Epistemic Orientation: An Ethical Necessity for Africanising the Educational Curriculum in Africa. *South African Journal of Philosophy* 35 (4): 546–555.

Stoneman, C. 1981. Agriculture. In *Zimbabwe's Inheritance*, ed. C. Stoneman, 127–150. London and Basingstoke: The College Press.

Toulmin, C. 2009. Securing Land and Property Rights in Sub-Saharan Africa: The Role of Local Institutions. *Land Use Policy* 26 (1): 10–19.

de Villiers, B. 2003. *Land Reform: Issues and Challenges: A Comparative Overview of Experiences in Zimbabwe, Namibia, South Africa and Australia.* Johannesburg: Konrad-Adenauer-Stiftung.

10

Is Land Reform the Last Step Towards Africans' Total Emancipation and True Empowerment?

Bernard Matolino

Introduction

In limiting my consideration, of the so-called land question to settler colonies of Southern Africa, I wish to pursue the emergence of land as an issue tied to the excesses of colonialism's disempowering and dispossession of the local populations (Nyandoro 2012). The response to these misadventures unfolded in several stages with the ultimate aim of returning stolen dignity, freedoms, and material property (principally the land) to their rightful owners. Yet the question that deserves an honest inquiry is how far along is the ordinary African path of freedoms? What has the fight for freedom presented and represented for the African? If the land question is tied closely to issues of freedom and redistribution of stolen resources, it must follow that this question must be addressed in tandem

B. Matolino (✉)
University of KwaZulu-Natal, Pietermaritzburg, South Africa
e-mail: matolinob@ukzn.ac.za

E. Masitera (ed.), *Philosophical Perspectives on Land Reform in Southern Africa*,
https://doi.org/10.1007/978-3-030-49705-7_10

with Southern Africa's achievements in securing true political freedom and true empowerment of the local people. I divide this chapter into four sections: the first section discusses land as a source of both dignity and economic empowerment, the second section locates the land issue within the broader political struggles for freedom, the third section gives an appraisal of the positionality of sub-Saharan Africa's political and economic global standing and what land redistribution can/cannot do, and the fourth section looks at land reform/redistribution in the history of structural failures of postcolonial African governments. These considerations, I hope, will show how far from ideal land redistribution is from solving anything other than presenting a facetious assurance of control, freedom, and empowerment.

The Land as a Source of Dignity and Economic Empowerment

Ideas of the fatherland, the motherland or the biblical Promised Land evoke strong feelings of attachment and affirmations of identity in people concerned with or closely related to those representations. Any individual's social identity is always tied to a place and a place is located on a piece of land (Bakare 1993). In Africa, ancestral land, the family's land or the clan's land also signifies the rootedness and connection to one's spiritual life. It is in/on one's land that you find family/ancestral graves, history, important spots including places of worship. For an African, particularly in her traditional set-up, home is not just a physical structure but the land and all extensions on it that are connected to the individual. The individual is at home when she is in that space which is both physically usable as well as spiritually affirming (ibid.). This connection is deep and fundamental and it should not be tempered with or disrupted without serious justification and consideration for its deleterious effect on the well-being of individuals and communities. Colonialism and apartheid disrupted the physical location of indigenous people either by displacing them or annexing the land. In most cases the indigenous people were moved to places that were less fertile or unproductive or were simply forced to leave (van Onselen 1976). This forced disruption had serious traumatizing effect on the affected people ranging from disruptions of familiarity, deprivation of sources of income, dislocation from places of birth, and disconnections from family, spiritual and ancestral ties (Bakare 1993). Where once people had felt whole and complete in the lands of their fathers, they were now shattered and dispersed all over with either little or nothing to affirm their existence as worthwhile. The taking away of the land or the confining of people to little unproductive land could only have left the affected people as strangers or foreigners in their own land. This process of cutting people off from their land and spiritual home ensured that they would be stripped of their identity and dignity as they now began to depend on alien spaces with no spiritual connections for their own sense-making. I need not overemphasize this point as I am sure that it is quite self-evident. To deprive anyone of her land is to essentially deprive dignity and self-respect due to her.

Additionally, in traditional societies and all of their approximations, land is the most important source of income affording its inhabitants the opportunity to earn a living. Not only do inhabitants use the land to farm produce that they will use for their own consumption, they also use that same produce either to trade or to provide for their future. The land is also necessary for their animals, which are a symbol of wealth, a source of security and inter-generational inheritance. To deprive such communities and individuals in those communities of the resource of land is to effectively kill off their source of livelihood. Again, I take this point to be too obvious such that it does not need any further emphasis.

However, what is important to articulate is how the combination of the deprivation of a people's dignity and the disruption of their source of income has an effect on those people. If the people's identity has been completely stripped and their ability to earn a living is taken away, then those people are turned into a state of perpetual dependence (Masaka 2011). They have to depend on the colonial master for their identity and they have to depend on the same master for their livelihood. This way, the colonial project becomes successful as it issues a new form of spiritual identity that is dependent on the dominant ideology favoured and promoted by the new land owner. The message, which is always Christian, urges the African to abandon her ties to the land and seek her salvation in the life to come, which ironically is not located in these spaces but an unzoned heaven. The African is also immediately impoverished and kept in that state for as long as she requires to sell her labour. This also is made possible by creation of centres of economic activity such as mines, cities, agricultural and industrial hubs where the African can only offer unskilled and semi-skilled hard labour (van Onselen 1976). She cannot claim any ownership of those zones and is unable to offer herself as an investor. She now lurks at the margins hoping to benefit from the generosity of the new owners of the means of production. As a worker she is made vulnerable to the vices of the market economy.

Needless to say this whole process of disempowerment, displacement and dependence is highly racialized with the white population benefitting and the black population suffering the outcomes. What this then leads to is making the land question, poverty, and matters of identity—black. These issues become black because the black person is the victim of this process and she is left in both material and spiritual dependence as a consequence of her identity having been systematically stripped away. The white population is sure of itself as productive members of society and as Christians who are authentically connected with God. The black population has to deal with the aspersions of blackness, the distortion of her religion and disruption of their source of stable income.

The history of Southern Africa, as a result of colonial encounters, bears testimony to this powerful disruption. The forced movement of indigenous people to make way for the white population, the creation of the so-called reserves ostensibly to keep black people in check and poverty, the phenomenon of migrant labour to support white-centred ownership are all too real (Thomas 2003, 695; Wuriga 2008, 5; Openshaw and Terry 2015, 73). All this was enabled by white minority rule that was recalcitrant and not prepared to cede anything to the black population. This resulted in struggles for freedom being waged, to varying degrees of armed engagement, in present-day Zimbabwe, Namibia, and South Africa. These countries were to gain political equality for the black citizens in, respectively, 1980, 1990, and 1994. However, this political freedom did not necessarily translate into economic restoration, empowerment, or equality. The economic differences have continued to varying degrees, probably leading to land expropriation/seizures in Zimbabwe. The aim, one can assume, was to give true meaning to freedom by ensuring that there is visible translation from politics to true freedom by taking the land from the population of land thieves/expropriators or whatever their identity may be.

It is quite hard to dispute or fight against such political moves. The land as the most visible and easily traceable aspect of conquest and displacement represents, probably, the last site of colonial injustice. That the land remains in the hands of the minority, while the majority are confined to landlessness, poverty, lack of access, and anger surely demands both redress and justice. Land redistribution becomes a matter of redress because there are people who can identify the times and places they were driven out by conquering settlers. Many, such as those of District Six in South Africa, do have memories of how they were violently evicted to make way for other aspirations. They live with both the hurt and distinct perception of the gravity of the injustice that was done to them, hence the call for justice. While the details of how the redress may best be done or how it would best meet conditions of restoration and justice are a matter beyond both my competence and the aim of this chapter. What must be observed, however, is that there is no denial that the colonial history responsible for this state of affairs was grossly unfair and something has to be done to restore both the dignity and earning capacity of the disenfranchised.

Politics, the Struggle for Freedom, and the Land

It is hardly surprising that the land is a political issue. It has to be, as it was at the centre of both the colonizing mission and the fight against that same mission. While colonialism was premised on some wrong-headed ideas, those ideas became visible in their operations in acquisition and expropriation of land. The land became the living theatre on which colonial ideas became real and their intentions were made all too visible. In fact some of the evidence of the violence of colonialism was grotesquely paraded in and on land issues (Thomas 2003). Even the mapping of towns and the spread of residences as distinguishing black from white neighbourhoods were done on land, with of course, beautiful spots kept for the white population and ordinary spots reserved for blacks. Hence the struggle for freedom was, on one hand, about ideas of equality, freedom, rights, race, and independence, but on the other hand it was about the social and economic empowerment of black/indigenous people. The latter could only be made real with either repossession or meaningful redistribution. Whatever the process was eventually going to be, it had to benefit the majority of the black, and unavoidably at the expense of the white minority.

The very idea that the process was going to be at the expense of a powerful minority group would in turn invoke questions of protection of minority rights, respect for rights to property, the legitimacy and fairness of legal instruments employed for either the actual or the suggested redistribution of the land, perceived threats to productivity, transfer of skills, and of course, blatant racism doubting the black person's capability to farm productively. On the other hand, land redistribution could be seen as the final step in the fight for freedom. What makes me believe that the issue of land reform is taken as a stage that follows on progressive accumulation of freedoms and claims against white minority rule is that rhetoric and visible action around it is intensified roughly two decades after the attainment of freedom. This is true of all three countries I rely on as examples: Namibia, South Africa, and Zimbabwe. While this observation is not meant to suggest that the issue of land only becomes real two decades into freedom, that timing may be significant in pointing us to other dynamics at play in relation to issues around the interpretation of the success of freedom. What is worth noting is that two decades into freedom, that is when a degree of disenchantment with the aims of the struggle for independence sets in. To demonstrate this disenchantment, I will assess two facets of the ordinary people's existence which exacerbate this disenchantment.

The first aspect is the economic exclusion of the majority of the black population. The creation of programmes that sought to promote a new black elite which is economically vibrant, connected, or successful was marred by accusations of corruption, political interference and connection, the creation of a small class of privileged black people, concentration of wealth in a few hands, and failure to meaningfully transform the lives of ordinary people. Life simply became harder and harder for ordinary people until, in the case of Zimbabwe, there was mass impoverishment. The promised economic transformation has not occurred for the masses as a firm majority has either been impoverished through joblessness or remain in fixed position of exclusion. Briefly, the attainment of independence or freedom, characterized by the end of white minority rule, has not led to the change in fortunes for the masses.

The second aspect has to do with how the goal of freedom has been just but a mirage. The case of Zimbabwe under the very personalized and brutal rule of Robert Mugabe is a fitting example. We could ask a number of questions about Mugabe's rule in an attempt to ascertain how it furthered any sense of freedom for the people. Whatever those questions are and whatever their answers could be, they ultimately point to a personal rule that was not always about land redistribution but opportunistically used that issue to retain power (see Windrich 2002). What can be said, then, is that land coincides with other issues such as intolerance to difference, reactions to possibilities of loss of power and Mugabe's own long rule (see Zimudzi 2002).

In the case of South Africa, a far less brutal but highly pernicious picture of nominal freedom of the masses emerges. While it is true that the black population is free from restrictions of pass laws, have free access to most parts of the country, have equality before the law, and can vote for any party they like, there has emerged serious social ills that directly undermine any meaningful interpretation of freedom. Public education, as universally acknowledged, has failed the black child in the most pathetic of ways. In actuality, public education has disempowered the black child through miseducation to a point of dysfunctional literacy. Life, on the streets, has become precarious as crime has taken a hold whose reverse is hard to imagine. South Africa continues to defend and hold the title of the most murders per day for any country not involved in official armed conflict. Access to social amenities such as good schools, best medical care, and even decent nutrition remains highly racialized. Access to courts is not for all as litigation costs are high which effectively denies the poor any opportunity to seek legal redress for their daily social victimization. Wealth remains firmly in the hands of white people, and the black people have gained the right to vote into power an avaricious black political elite. Corruption is rife, state-owned enterprises are running legendary losses, looting and bribery are the currency of new politics and business, and black economic empowerment programmes have been reduced to competitions for tenders and government connections (see Freund 2007). The state has failed both to empower ordinary people and give them a true meaning of freedom and equality (Ayittey 1998).

In the midst of all these failures, the issue of land emerges then as some kind of redress—an economic, political, and social justice issue that seeks to address the inequities of the past. While the couching of the land issue, in terms of redress, is undeniable and its urgency may be appreciated, the context in which it emerges is the most frightful. In the case of Zimbabwe, Robert Mugabe's urgency (or permission of the matter to be suddenly urgent) was against the backdrop of a restless urban citizenry, the emergence of an opposition political party that genuinely threatened his hold on power, and negative effects of imprudent economic decisions and management of the national fiscus. Politically, Mugabe pushed the land issue as a continuation of his fight for freedom by blaming the former colonial master for rescinding on promises of financing land redistribution or derailing the sponsorship of such redistribution. The matter became fully politicized with the remaining white farmers seen as evidence of the resilience and stubbornness of colonial excess. However, Mugabe's failures as a political head of a supposedly democratic and free country were to replicate themselves into land redistribution. All the dysfunctionality, corruption, lack of planning that characterized his rule became synonymous with land redistribution. Mugabe and his wife were to be the greatest beneficiaries of land grabs by redistributing several farms to themselves and their close family.

If we take, at a very general level, the histories of the liberation movements of Namibia, South Africa, and Zimbabwe, and were to ask what their victory against apartheid and colonialism has registered in terms of real benefits for the average black person, we might find the answer not to be positive. While there has been a nominal guaranteeing of political rights and freedoms, this has not translated into much tangible change of life. It has been a redress at the most conceptual of levels and it is a matter of discursive benefit that the majority of black people can refer to themselves as free. Since political freedom itself has not amounted to much except basic rights such as voting, freedom of movement, and other little obvious rights associated with basic civil liberties, we must inquire into what the land issue represents either as a continuation of rights acquisitions or political self-determination.

I think that the central question will be: Is the acquisition of land going to either work as a solution to already existing problems or work as an inspiration for future programmes that will inspire a new developmental and empowerment path? I am sure that proponents of land reform or redistribution genuinely hope and believe the answer to these questions must be in the affirmative. They will either take it to be a self-evident truth or they will take the issue of land to hold key leads to solving the problems that assail the black majority. I am convinced that neither option is going to work. The reason I am doubtful that land could work as a solution to our problem is based on that the real and taxing political problems that Africa is currently faced with do not originate from the land question. While a part of the land issue does contribute to political questions of redress of injustices of the past—that is only but a partial issue. There are, in my view, weightier political issues that deserve attention as they are responsible for the present decay. Let us return to the examples I cited above, of homegrown dictatorship; this political delinquency is self-inflicted and has done greater harm than any land issue. This delinquency when coupled with general mismanagement of state resources (which has become synonymous with the African bureaucracy), or habitual theft at a large scale, or uncompromising corruption, or dedicated looting of empowerment deals by a select few, or stinging buffoonery can be said to be responsible for reversing any political gain due to the African. In actual fact, this political delinquency has become the defining characteristic of politics and has managed to extend itself to affect other areas of human existence in distinctly negative ways. Politics itself has become toxic and its toxicity has been felt in all areas directly or indirectly connected to the shenanigans of political influence.

If land, then, is approached as a political issue, it is going to be affected by the same toxic characteristic that has become so visibly consistent with politics. If political freedom has been nothing but nominal, what can make the politicized land issue anything else? But the second proposed option is even more fraudulent than the political issue of land. When we think of land as a resource that holds promise for our future, we must be very explicit about what that promise is envisaged as and where precisely its benefits are going to emerge from. We must be able to explicate what land is capable of generating and where the effect of what is generated is going to be felt. We must show in clear detail how each square mile/acre/hectare, over and above being a political piece of pride—is actually going to do in empowering its owner and how that empowerment will be realized. This very consideration leads me to my next section in which I discuss what land cannot do for us in the globalized economy.

What Land Cannot Do

The argument I seek to make in this section proceeds from the realization that Africa is part of the global village. We are engaged in trade, negotiation, politicking and co-existence with the rest of the world. At times we co-operate with other parts of the world that are very far from us, and at times we compete with other parts of the world that are also very far from us. Our global networks or connections has a real impact on us. If we look at land as a resource that enables us to produce for purposes of trade and wealth generation, then we must understand land in its proper function. Land is a natural resource, not only does it give us a source of our geographic stand, it is just something that we were given. We did not invest any effort at all in having it. Just by facts of birth and positionality we lay claim to our land. Land, in itself, is a neutral natural endowment. It is us human beings who value it for different purposes in accord with standards we think appropriate for measuring worth. It is also us humans who invest in that land to make it profitable. A fallow piece of land in the middle of nowhere has intrinsic value just for being land. That intrinsic value is turned into some measurable and quantifiable value by either human speculation or human effort invested therein. It is not good enough that land is just land that people use. It has to be used to, at least, generate some income. Two obvious ways in which we can think of land as an asset that can be valued, and productively so, is in agriculture and real estate. Yet it is in this process of valuing land or turning it into a productive enterprise that things may begin to present a worrisome feature. If land is a natural resource, we might be encouraged to recall how we have used our other natural resources. A frank analysis will reveal that we have not used these resources to our greatest benefit. While nature or the gods have blessed this continent abundantly with the so-called mineral wealth, the reality of the matter is that such wealth is remembered for fuelling wars, banditry, looting, and death. Economically, our mineral wealth has not transformed lives of Africans in a demonstrably incontrovertible form. Even innocent wild animals have suffered our general incompetence as they are unnecessarily rendered vulnerable to poaching syndicates. If the species of rhinoceros that is natural to Africa were to be actually natural to Sweden or Denmark they would be sure of a poacher free environment, thanks to the diligence of the human residents of those places.

Land has not only to be understood in the context of how we have failed to utilize our (other) natural resources but also in relation to how we think we could leverage it to our advantage in the global arena. The plain fact is that whatever we produce from the land or whatever we do with it or on it, we must also think of it as an asset that can make us money. This is where the effect of the agricultural aspect of the land comes into question. While it is fact that in the settler colonies, there is some trade that happens with markets or consumers in the Northern hemisphere, thus earning the treasury hard currency, we must be open and detailed about how land reform of any form might have impact on these activities. For example, what models of continuity are proposed between large scale and highly specialized farming with any model of land reform? Particularly when that land reform's aim is not primarily aimed at commercialization or contributing to the national purse but at redressing past injustices through redistribution. While my point should not be confused with nonsensical racism that doubts the effectiveness or propensity of black people as commercial farmers, my worry is framed within simple and basic succession plans, keeping the momentum of present gains, and even advancing on present gains. Most of post-independence Africa has done quite badly with such plans. There could be a number of reasons why Africa has done badly in its post-colonial succession planning. Some of these reasons could be generated within Africa itself and others could be generated outside Africa. But whatever the reasons are, where land reform is proposed—do proponents of this reform understand reasons behind failures in other forms of reform? If they do, what do they think was responsible for those failures and how do they propose to avoid them with land reform? An interesting diversion is worth entertaining here. There could be an argument that can be made by those who might wish to place Africa's past failures on external causes. Such people, perhaps correctly too, might point out instances of foreign interference that led to Africa's failure to transform. They might even be able to point to instances where, historically, former colonial authorities and some other global superpower had a direct interest and need for sabotaging any transformation and empowerment agenda that different countries on the continent had. However, even if this were proven to be correct, what are proponents of land reform going to do differently to guarantee that land reform does not suffer the same fate as any other reform before it? Why would land reform not be subjected to manipulation so that its empowering effect is rendered meaningless or void by the same superpowers who have succeeded in derailing any transformation agenda? What would we do if they were to manipulate import rules of their own countries to exclude produce from African land reformists? This brings us back to the point that Africa is a generally weak global player that needs to think carefully about its own empowerment in the current global order. The truth of the matter is that Africa and Africans are vulnerable at various levels, land reform can effectively be sabotaged so that it is rendered a successful political programme of re-distribution but never a successful economic empowerment tool. While I may sound despairing, my intention is not to sow hopelessness but to invite reformists to think their plans through and be alert to all potential and real obstacles waiting on any land reform agenda.

Closely connected to the above point, what is also worth careful consideration in respect of viewing land as a resource that can generate income, is the very nature of land's viability depending on the favour of other factors. The productivity of the land, particularly in its agricultural usage, is not independent of other factors. Its productivity is entirely dependent on favourable weather patterns and/or climatic conditions. Recent and ongoing changes in weather patterns have had an adverse effect on sub-Saharan Africa. These changes directly threaten the agricultural productivity of this region and places severe strain on farmers as they are unable to plan their activities with the benefit of a pretty much regular and predictable weather pattern. They either have to bear long droughts interposed only by unproductive torrents and floods. If these unproductive patterns become the norm, as predicted, then farming will not only be rendered a precarious occupation but we could be a continent that is headed for insufficient agricultural output to even feed ourselves.

A final point under this section relates to the nature of land as a capital intensive venture. If my belief that redistribution must be meant to empower the black African population beyond mere ownership or any other associated political goal, then we must come to appreciate that a useful outcome would be one where land is used to generate wealth. However, in order to generate wealth land does require quite an intense amount of capital. If we look at the three countries chosen for discussion, the most suitable beneficiaries are the very poor who have no means of injecting the required capital into the land. If there was to be successful redistribution, these poor people would either have to depend on the goodwill of the private sector or efficiency of their government to provide them with the necessary capital that would give them a realistic chance to compete at the global level. It is hard to see how the private sector could even be willing to take a risk with unproven new farmers. In cases where it will, it would compromise the very goal of empowering these new land owners/users as they would find themselves either indebted to or in the trap of the so-called white monopoly capital. And if their ventures were to fail, as any business venture could, their only way out would be to surrender that land. Government itself has failed to be a source of comfort or promise to the disenfranchised black majority. How it would be able to find resources to make land capital investment a successful plan would be an absolutely amazing exception.

I hope the idea I am pursuing is clear. Land ownership, taking back our land, redistribution of our land in our own favour can never be the empowerment route some hope it to be. Redistributed land will be subjected to the vicissitudes of the same global forces that have rendered everything else about us way off the mark from our initial intentions. Land does not bring the sort of comfort and assurance we might hope it to be capable of. This is not to be taken to mean that refraining from land re-distribution will make the station of the African any better. Rather, the point is that the African is way down the line of mangled existence such that land re-distribution as a piecemeal empowerment political objective is not going to yield any result radically different from previous false starts of the road to development and freedom.

The Context of the Structural Failure of African Governments

In this last section I wish to spell out some detail of how land is implicated in the long-standing structural failures of the African government. One part of my argument is to show how that structural failure obtains and the other part is to show how land is already implicated in such failure.

If we look at the euphoria that accompanied the independence and freedom of Africa from the political tyranny of colonial masters, a very disturbing state of affairs emerges. The context in which our freedom emerges is simply one of ideological battle. We initially took this ideological battle to be not only an important aspect of organizing political life but also a necessary condition for development. The idea seems to have been that if we could get our ideological antenna to pick up the correct frequency everything else would also fall into place. The very same global forces that assail us today were partially responsible for driving us into making certain ideological commitments. With cessation of hostilities of the cold war and the breakup of the Soviet bloc we scurried around in search of new ideologies and plans. It was as if there was an empty ideological space that needed to be filled. Indeed that space was filled, in some cases, with disastrous advice and plans driven and sponsored by the IMF and the World Bank. True empowerment of the people was never really on the agenda that was underscored by a transformative ideology. Today, most of Africa looks to China to fill the ideological space that remains empty. Yet current evidence points to a cycle of indebtedness to the Chinese that would be almost impossible to break for those who are already in it and those who are being lured into it.

The biggest challenge, in my view, has been finding an appropriate developmental plan for the continent that is truly empowering and sticking with it to the end. But besides the global context that has clearly made it very hard for us to operate maximally and with discernible outcome, we have also tended to place our priorities in the wrong places. Bill Clinton once ran his campaign with the slogan "It's the economy, stupid" to show how he understood his job as primarily akin to a chief executive who has to make decisions that not only promote economic growth but make basic economic sense. He understood that the real power of his country and the empowerment of his people lay in economic success. Without decent jobs that secure a meaningful financial reward, citizens are deprived of opportunities to make choices they judge to be appropriate for their lives and aspirations. The economic factor is responsible for empowering citizens in ways that truly free them from the bondage of political rhetoric about some imagined gains that have to be made before they can lead decent lives. A growing economy means better educational facilities, better health facilities and job creation that free people from concentrating on the value of agriculture. The world is rapidly moving and changing in ways that Africa is not quite able to live up to. All these changes are authored by economically viable zones that have chosen to take responsibility for the direction of human life in ways that were not conceivable just 20 years ago.

Unfortunately, for Africa, prioritizing the economy has hardly been a feature of our governments. While there is a lot of talk about economic plans and targets on the continent, they always come to naught. Yet any African government must essentially understand itself in a business-like manner. For that is precisely what global economic interactions have become. With the exception of Rwanda in recent years, which other African country has deliberately sought to marshal all its resources towards development and growth? Not many, and if there is any growth that is registered it tends to be accidental and temporary. The reason why such growth tends to be temporary is simply because there is no thoroughgoing ideologically backed commitment to that growth and development (see Streak 1997).

An objection that can be raised at this point, in opposition to my position, would be that my way of proceeding is reductionist in a sense. It could be said that I have whittled all human development to markers of economic gains when in actual fact there are many routes to human development including the long hard road of political freedom. Alternatively, it could also be claimed that my argument is pessimistic without sufficient ground for that pessimism. Regarding the first objection, I would concede that while development is open to a number of interpretations, I find it unbearable to think of development that is incapable of attending to the most basic material needs of the people. Any idea of development that is unable to empower its people, which is unable to take its people out of material poverty and shame, is anything but development. Intellectual, political, or spiritual development that cannot guarantee that basic needs would be met, is a conman's idea of development. As for the second objection, it suffices to insist that a fair and unbiased assessment of what the majority of this continent have to endure on a daily basis, just to get by, is hardly flattering. If there is any pessimism, it is only because it proceeds from facts of existence that are so true of the silenced majority of this continent. Optimism on this continent is either ephemeral or sadly confused with the resilience of the majority.

The failure of many African countries, on the economic front, has left their citizens disempowered to fully realize their potential or to begin imagining other possible forms of life besides that of harsh poverty in a semi-dysfunctional environment. Any idea or programme of land redistribution will either have to boldly confront these realities and right them or it will find itself falling straight into the trap of all preceding transformation attempts.

I however think, as a second part of my argument in this section, that land is already implicated in Africa's failures. Land on its own is incapable of reversing any self-inflicted wounds. Land will not restore the dignity of Africans which they have been robbed by their governments' neglect, inefficiency, naiveté, or corruption. Even when land is directly restored to its previous owners in ways that seems to satisfy some requirement of justice, that would be just but a small step. A small step in a direction that leads nowhere because what is required is actually a reversal of a corrupt or dysfunctional system that has become synonymous with African frailties and failures. Cases of rampant corruption that characterize everyday existence in the former settler colonies could just as well become hallmarks of land redistribution. But land as an asset is vulnerable to abuse like any other natural asset has been. Land is also likely to be, like everything else before it, a source of false hopes and crushed dreams. A reorientation of creation and distribution of resources, in general, is what is needed. Such rethink will lead to a genuine empowerment of Africans in whatever area they choose. It will obviate the need to see ownership of a piece of land as a necessary condition for one's identity and empowerment. While there is nothing wrong with ownership of a piece of land, the reason for such ownership must always be clear and always aimed at improving the holistic experience of life by one who has such ownership. But with politicization of land, such ownership is likely to be added to all failures that have originated from the political source. The biggest problem is that if the land issue is left to be entirely determined by political processes, then it will be subject to the same political processes and outcomes as we have become familiar with.

Conclusion

My aim should not be interpreted as offering a defence against any suggestion of land reform. As I have maintained, land reform is necessary both as a form of redress of injustices of the past and as a promise of what it can do as a resource that may earn people a living. However, beyond the platitudes of approximating land to an ultimate political goal, there is need to think and plan very carefully how redistributed or even seized land will be used to build on already existing achievements of both a political and non-political nature. I have tried to argue that land, in itself, is a neutral resource that only becomes valuable because humans have assigned a value to it. That value may be commercial, economic, or political. Depending on what humans actually prioritize and what they want to see land being used for, such processes may spell either success or disaster for the very same people. In the three countries in Southern Africa I have chosen as examples of land reform projects, unless and until there is acknowledgement of what the political significance should be transformed into, land might just as well be another promise of political freedom that will become another "Not Yet Uhuru" moment. Thus the major thrust of my argument is that while political freedom is significant for its own purposes, there is also need to be mindful that rhetoric accompanying its celebration is not enough. The majority of the people are yet to taste the real benefits of that political freedom and it will take more than rhetoric of redistribution to truly empower the ordinary African.

References

Ayittey, G.B.N. 1998. *Africa in Chaos*. London: Macmillan Press Ltd.

Bakare, S. 1993. *My Right to Land in the Bible and in Zimbabwe: A Theology of Land in Zimbabwe*. Harare: Zimbabwe Council of Churches.

Freund, B. 2007. South Africa: The End of Apartheid and the Emergence of the 'BEE Elite'. *Review of African Political Economy* 114: 661–678.

Masaka, D. 2011. Zimbabwe's Land Contestations and Her Politico-Economic Crises: A Philosophical Dialogue. *Journal of Sustainable Development in Africa* 13 (1): 331–347.

Nyandoro, M. 2012. Zimbabwe's Land Struggles and Land Rights. Historical Perspectives: The Case of Gowe-Sanyati Irrigation. *Historia* 57 (2): 298–349.

Openshaw, K.S., and P.C.R. Terry. 2015. Zimbabwe's Odious Inheritance: Debt and Unequal Land Distribution. *McGill International Journal of Sustainable Development* 11 (1): 39–86.

Streak, J. 1997. The Counter-Counterrevolution in Development Theory on the Role of the State in Development: Inferences for South Africa? *Development Southern Africa* 14 (3): 307–325.

Thomas, N.H. 2003. Land Reform in Zimbabwe. *Third World Quarterly* 24 (4): 691–712.

Van Onselen, C. 1976. *Chibaro: African Mine Labour in Southern Rhodesia, 1900–1993*. London: Pluto Press.

Windrich, E. 2002. Then and Now: Reflections on How Mugabe Rules Zimbabwe. *Third World Quarterly* 23 (6): 1181–1188.

Wuriga, R. 2008. The Revolutionary Bond and Opposition Politics in Post-Independent Africa: The Case of Zimbabwe. *IKAMVA: International Journal of Social Science and Humanities* 2 (1): 1–36.

Zimudzi, T.B. 2002. Power Syndrome: Robert Mugabe and the Land Reform and Governance Crisis in Zimbabwe. *South African Historical Journal* 47 (1): 213–228.

Part III

Land Jurisprudence (and Justice Issues)

11

Integrating African Social Tenures through Rights Recognition in Land Reform

Christopher Allsobrook

Introduction

Over the past few years, public discourse on South African land reform has taken on alarm, since it symbolises failure to redress the racial injustices and inequalities of the apartheid era. Underwhelming transformation of the racial distribution of land possession over the past 25 years of democracy is blamed by government on the negotiated settlement on land rights, which is etched into our Constitution. The ruling ANC has decided that a constitutional amendment is needed to allow for expropriation of land without compensation (Marrian Merten, "#ANCdecides2017: Land expropriation without compensation makes grand entrance," *Daily Maverick*, 21 December 2017). But the Constitution already allows for expropriation at well below the market value for purposes of redress, which the state has not implemented (Lizeka Tandwa, "No willing buyer, willing seller in the Constitution—Albie

C. Allsobrook (✉)
Centre for Leadership Ethics in Africa, University of Fort Hare,
Alice, South Africa

E. Masitera (ed.), *Philosophical Perspectives on Land Reform in Southern Africa*,
https://doi.org/10.1007/978-3-030-49705-7_11

Sachs, *News24*, 30 May 2018). Such scapegoating is one example of many cases in which land reform discourse functions as ideology, narrowly focusing on a transfer of title deeds, neglecting reform of the underlying tenure system.

While politicians mobilise support with heated moral discourse regarding the race of land owners, the socially recognised tenure rights of most African community members are insecure under an enduring colonial system of land ownership, designed to protect exclusively owned, surveyed freehold title deeds. This system benefits elites, who are able to afford access to the system, at the expense of the poor.

South African land reform includes a complex set of problems of redistribution, restitution and tenure security, which depend on careful integration of segregated systems of land rights administration and governance. Land rights reform is overlooked by the blunt ideology of acquisition. Certainly, land reform begins, after careful planning, with acquisition of land. But what comes next? Just land reform cannot mean black ownership of colonial land rights. South African land reform calls for more than redistribution of title deeds from white to black hands. The state's legal and administrative systems of tenure management must be reformed to recognise, secure and enforce the social tenure rights of the excluded majority of Africans.

Stepping back from practical problems of political economy regarding the distribution and acquisition of land rights, this chapter in political theory examines how land rights are defined in public discourse and policy. The dominant narrow conception of land reform upheld by the state and by financial institutions functions ideologically to benefit elites. Maintaining the hegemonic Western tenure model of the registered title deed in official practices of land reform and land management, the state neglects its duty to secure, support or service living customary social tenure arrangements of over 60% of the population (Hornby et al. 2017, 7).

African subjects were displaced by colonialism not just from land but from their cultural heritage in land rights, that is, from common normative social practices of land rights recognition. Under indirect rule, African social tenure arrangements typically accorded to family lineages were collapsed into undifferentiated group rights administered by compliant ethnic tribal leaders. By relegating African land rights to secondary status and thereby maintaining a colonial divide between citizen and subject, land reform is captured by elites.

Under the colonial system of segregated land rights, inferior tenure security for land reform beneficiaries and rural subjects allows elite interests to dominate in communal trusteeship.

I first explain how land reform discourse in South Africa functions as ideology—in the press and in policy—maintaining a restrictive Western model of land rights which neglects social tenure security for African subjects. Against this ideological fetishism of the title deed, I draw on work by Michael Barry (2015) and Donna Hornby et al. (2017) to consider a more inclusive model of tenure, now accepted by the World Bank. This is conceived in terms of a visual metaphor as comprising a *continuum*, a constellation or a matrix of tenure arrangements (including formal/informal, Western/African, individual/communal, family/village etc.). But, if the inflexible registered title deed is too *tight*, or exclusively defined, for socially embedded, negotiable tenure arrangements, the problem with these accounts is that, in failing to account for relations of power, or authority, in recognition, the metaphor of a continuum is too *loose* or broadly defined to yield land rights. I thus propose and defend a defetishising theory of rights recognition that reconciles both challenges of definition, to better integrate land rights.

Segregated Land Rights in the Ideology of Land Acquisition

President Cyril Ramaphosa aimed to reassure the market on South Africa's land question with an article in London's *Financial* Times titled "This is no Land Grab" (reprinted *Business Day* 24 August 2018). He tries his best here to persuade investors with a reasonable explanation for Expropriation Without Compensation (EWC): most South Africans are still poor and unemployed, with inequality between blacks and whites "among the greatest obstacles to growth"—most devastatingly, "in ownership and access to land". He cites a World Bank report which finds unequal distribution of skills and land to be the main drivers of black poverty. So, "government has embarked on a programme of accelerated land reform," and, "South Africans are engaged in an intense debate over the prospect of expropriating land without compensation as one among several measures to achieve this reform".

But, is prohibition on EWC the reason why land reform has stalled? Former Constitutional Court judge Albie Sachs insists, in agreement with state legal adviser and land rights expert, Ngcukaitobi, as well as many others, that, "It's possible for the issue to be worked out by the courts to have prices well below the market value consistent with the Constitution." (Lizeka Tandwa, "No Willing Seller, Willing Buyer in the Constitution—Albie Sachs," *News 24*, 30 May 2018). Admitting that "the current clause in the Constitution dealing with property rights does not necessarily prohibit such a measure," Ramaphosa maintains, "an amendment would provide certainty and clarity". The release of the final report of his land advisory panel on 28 July 2019, at last, provides such clarity. It specifies that EWC may be used as a targeted approach in limited cases, where land rights are weak, such as, "abandoned land; hopelessly indebted land; land held purely for speculative purposes; land held by state entities and not utilised; land obtained through criminal activity; land already occupied and used by labour tenants and former labour tenants; informal settlement areas; inner city buildings with absentee landlords; land donations (as a form of expropriation without compensation); and farm equity schemes." (Claudi Mailovich, "Presidential Land Advisory Panel Delivers Final Report," *Business Day* 28 July 2019). This bundle of instances surely cannot constitute the obstacle to South African land reform. The problems go deeper than sensational EWC.

The ANC's policy message on EWC is confusing because of the need to send two different messages to different audiences. On the one hand, the party sends out a populist message that the challenge of land reform is so extensive that the current Constitution must be amended for the state to deal with it. On the other hand, investors are assured that only very limited changes will be made to the law. But the scope for redistribution allowed by the proposed amendment is much smaller than the scale of the problems cited to support such amendment.

Such moderate circumstances for EWC are not sufficient to explain the slow pace of reform. Moreover, as I go on to argue, land reform extends far deeper than the transfer of tenure: it includes reform of the legal and administrative systems by which the state recognises tenure.

Ramaphosa alludes to underlying problems of tenure security and support in his assurances to investors that, "SA has learned from the experiences of other countries" (i.e. Zimbabwe). This strategic intervention is no "assault on the private ownership of property". On the contrary, he argues, these proposals will ensure that the rights of all South Africans are strengthened. Stressing "substance" over "soundbites", aware of the limits of expropriation, he frames land acquisition as a means not to weaken but to *reinforce* property rights. He assures investors that EWC is just "one element of a broader programme of land reform that seeks to ensure that all citizens can have their land rights recognised, whether they live in communal areas, informal settlements or on commercial farms... For land reform to succeed," he argues, "it is essential that support is given to beneficiaries." As these remarks reveal, in the context of poor protection of property for the poor, EWC is a red herring.

Many land experts and political analysts regard the ANC's policy on EWC as an ideological smokescreen, which scapegoats the Constitution for failures related to corruption, incompetence and incapacity (Simon Hull "On the necessity of mechanisms for expropriating land without compensation," *Daily Maverick*, 11 June 2018). Raymond Suttner dismisses the turn to EWC as "hype without a plan" (Raymond Suttner, "'Expropriation without compensation'—Where is the plan for addressing reform?" *Daily Maverick*, 6 August 2018).

Public discourse on EWC is ideological to the extent that (1) moral discourse of post-apartheid land acquisition shifts responsibility for (2) failure to secure and support the social tenure rights of the poor. "Social tenure" is communally recognised off-register tenure, including a wide range of land tenure systems found in different parts of the country, such as informal settlements, inner city buildings, rural communal systems, land reform projects etc. Most people occupy land or dwellings in these areas under a very different kind of property regime to that recognised by the state. These are often termed social or off-register tenures.

Ruth Hall ("PLAAS's Professor Ruth Hall on Land, and What you Should—and Shouldn't—Worry About," *Daily Maverick*, 29 March 2018) claims, along with weak support for black farmers and land reform beneficiaries in land reform, "there has been no policy direction, no political leadership, almost no budgetary allocation, massive mismanagement, institutional incapacity and corruption." Redistribution, moreover, "has been captured by elite interests."

"The state buys farms and gives them to those who are politically connected." Beneficiaries are made to farm collectively on marginal or failed commercial farms without support or they are forced into exploitative partnerships. The theoretical basis used by state officials for land reform, explains Simon Hull, relies on fetishisation of colonial concepts of ownership and titling (Hull "Necessity"). Land reform functions ideologically to sustain tenure apartheid. Arguments for the transfer of ownership of title deeds to land from white to black owners have implicitly accepted the reproduction of the colonial and apartheid forms of ownership, which marginalise the socially recognised and communally negotiated social tenures of the majority of the population to the detriment of the most vulnerable members of society.

Fetishism of the Western title deed is often reproduced in public discourse on land reform. Distancing the ANC from the EFF's radical platform for nationalisation, Enoch Godongwana (Natasha Marrian, "ANC will not nationalise land and has no designs on people's homes" *Business Day*, 1 August 2018) insists that EWC reinforces property rights: "We are going to give you title deeds. We are not nationalising the land of this country." While it upholds the hegemony of the Western title deed, however, the government supports segregated and inferior colonial tenure rights in land reform programmes and fails to secure social tenure for African subjects.

The ANC government's reluctance and lack of political will to tackle segregated land tenure is evident in its promise to traditional leaders that their land, as the Minister for Cooperative Governance and Traditional Affairs (COGTA), Zweli Mkhize put it, "is safe from being expropriated for purposes of restitution, as it would be 'meaningless'" (Zweli Mkhize, "White Fear, Black Anger: why getting the land issue right is so important" 2 July 2018). Ramaphosa, Mkhize and other senior ANC leaders have gone out of their way to reassure traditional leaders of this. Zulu King Goodwill Zwelithini warns that anyone who touches his Ingonyama Trust (comprising a third of Kwa-Zulu Natal) is declaring war against the

Zulu nation. Mkhize makes it clear that communal land will not be expropriated. But, as Marianne Merten argues, "by excluding communal land from the current EWC deliberations, the ANC not only entered into an elite pact with traditional leaders, but also agreed to the effective continuation of Bantustan boundaries." (Marianne Merten, "Bantustan boundaries, alive and well in modern South Africa," *Daily Maverick*, 12 July 2018). This leaves 18 million rural residents without the security of tenure provided for all citizens in Section 25(6) of the Constitution. This land is owned by tribal councils the majority of which fail to meet legislated democratic requirements. In investment deals, they have sole authority to sign agreements in respect of communal land. Their subjects, treated as tenants, not owners, are precluded from opting out (ibid.).

Public discourse and policy on land reform function ideologically to benefit elites, (1) in overly narrow focus on the morality of land expropriation, (2) in blaming the Constitution for stalled reform, and (3) by reproducing colonial conceptions of segregated tenure. The post-apartheid state takes for granted Western norms such as individual title deeds and large-scale commercial agriculture. While most of the population is strongly influenced by off-register tenure arrangements under conditions of chieftaincy or informality, policy and legal frameworks privilege the title deed above these, rendering invisible the ways in which most people access tenure and livelihoods (Hornby et al. 2017, 4). The state fails to secure social tenure for those in communal areas, in former homelands, for farm labourers and tenants, for tenants in informal settlements and for beneficiaries of housing and land reform.

A total of 17,439 million ha have been transferred from white ownership since 1994, which is equal to 21% of the 82,759 million ha of farmland in freehold in South Africa (Wandile Sihlobo and Tinashe Kapuya, "Special Report: The Truth about Land Ownership in South Africa", *Rand Daily Mail*, 23 July 2018). Much of the land restored or redistributed is held by groups of beneficiaries, in private, through collective institutions such as Communal Property Associations (CPAs) or trusts. Government has not exerted proper oversight of these institutions, many are dysfunctional, and the tenure security of members is often weak (ibid., 5). Disjuncture between socially and officially recognised land rights leaves social tenure insecure for most of the African population (ibid., 7), left in poverty traps in under-serviced, risky, investment-averse locations. This disjuncture between the communally recognised social tenures of the African majority and the form of the registered title deed imposed by the Western legal and administrative property system fosters corruption and elite capture, playing on gaps between living normative practices and the law. In official policy and practice, there is need to reform the theoretical basis for land reform, so as to accommodate a broader range of land rights at various levels. Off-register rights and tenure systems must also be protected.

By maintaining segregated land rights, as Kepe and Hall (2018) argue—i.e. by exclusively securing title deeds under the official state apparatus to the neglect of other social tenures—"land reform perpetuates the colonial present". The political ideologies of the ANC and EFF, and in official state law and practice—perpetuate colonial and apartheid ideologies of land tenure and finance capital. Land reform has perversely kept control of the land and the means of production in the hands of whites, corporate capital and black elites (Kepe and Hall 2018). The state takes for granted private title deeds as the preferred standard for land tenure and large-scale commercial agriculture for productive efficiency. African subjects are effectively not trusted with ownership or democratic decision-making in governance. Customary subjects, farm dwellers and reform beneficiaries—mostly, blacks—hold insecure land rights and they are often beholden to the state and whites for their use of the land as "partners" (Kepe and Hall 2018).

In their arguments for expropriation of "unproductive" land, both the ANC and the EFF appeal to Locke's principle of property (mixing labour and soil into commodity form).[1] In doing so, they unwittingly promote the colonial ideology of *terra nullius*, used to justify dispossession (Boisen 2017). But communal, pastoral land stands at risk of expropriation for "low productivity". Use of colonial standards for assessing "productive

[1] The justification of land taken by colonialists in South Africa (and elsewhere, including Australia and the USA) was grounded in the principle of *terra nullius*, that is, that the land was "empty"—i.e. not already owned. Such "emptiness" was indeed predicated on criteria of cultivation: land was owned once you had worked on it. These cultivation norms were defined by European standards and excluded indigenous migratory patterns. Likewise, such colonial norms are re-imposed by criteria proposed to expropriate "unproductive" land.

use" of farmland therefore forces claimants into collective ownership as captive junior partners and labour tenants for "strategic partners" in large-scale commercial agricultural operations, where they exercise little control and seldom benefit financially, working, for below minimum wage, as tenants on their own land (Kepe and Hall 2018, 7).

The EFF advocates state ownership of the land and the ANC actively practices this in its land acquisition strategy, as the landlord for dependent reform and housing beneficiaries and for traditional rural communities. This perpetuates the colonial ideology of trusteeship, or custodianship, which assumes rule of the capable on behalf of incapable blacks, for their improvement (Allsobrook and Boisen 2017), alongside a segregated system of tenure for secure, private, enforced and serviced white land. On the basis of trusteeship, custodians of the land are given wide discretion over communal land, and the state restricts tenure rights for the beneficiaries of land and housing reform. The rights of individuals and families are thereby amalgamated under the identity of a "tribe" whose decisions may better be imposed.

Thus, the state reproduces colonial concepts and patterns of land tenure not only in land administration and governance but, perversely, in land reform. The High-Level Panel Parliamentary Report on Land Reform (2017) singles out two main kinds of problems in land reform: (1) Failures in redistribution and restitution, with the latter overloading and suffocating the former, and (2) Denial of land rights and dispossession (202). The state is failing to redress dispossession and to protect the vulnerable rights of the poor. There is overlap between these two problems (203), in that no secure rights are issued to land reform beneficiaries, who acquire their land as tenants of the state with conditional use rights. Those who receive redistributed land should be owners, not excluded with risky rights of land tenure from access to credit, while starved of government support, subsidies, tools and training (50). Investment is negatively impacted by the insecure tenure of customary or group-based social land tenure, which is aggravated by its inferior status. "Land redistribution is not sustainable without secure tenure… protected and enforceable by way of accessible, effective remedies." (230).

For land acquired in reform, no secure tenure rights are issued. Beneficiaries are issued "conditional land use rights" or leases which secure neither the land, nor state support, nor access to credit to develop it. In redistribution, colonial and apartheid ideologies of "proper farming" are still promoted, which prioritise large-scale, capital-and-technology intensive commercial farming, in allocation and funding, over more inclusive redistribution. This forces claimants into strategic partnerships (235). Thus, the Western ideal of large-scale commercial agriculture narrows land reform and makes it vulnerable to elite capture (207).

Behind the ideology of expropriation, administration of social tenure is not just segregated; it has disintegrated. EWC will be a time and skills intensive process, likely to put near impossible demands on state expertise and support. Land reform cannot proceed without accurate, efficient land records, or coherent planning, monitoring and support for reform beneficiaries. The state cannot secure, administer or enforce rights of tenure it does not recognise. But the Commission on Restitution of Land Rights and the Departments of Rural Development and Land Reform struggle with low funding, poor coordination, high turnover, vacancies, acting managers, inexperienced, poorly trained, under-qualified personnel, instability, poor institutional memory, fraud, corruption and incoherent administration. Matters which reach Land Claims Court are easily contested due to inadequate preparation, research and documentation. In this context, "Rebuilding the state, rather than rewriting the Constitution may be more effective to address land," (Cartwright 2018, 12). Thus, land reform ideology not only typically reproduces segregated patterns of colonial tenure; it also masks the withering away of the capacity of the state to secure rights of tenure for the poor.

From Land Ideology to Social Tenure Security, Administration and Governance

The problem of tenure in South Africa is grounded in the mismatch between registered title and the wide array of alternative tenure (Hornby et al. 2017, 23). Apartheid's segregated systems of tenure rights leave a distinctive effect on the physical geography of the country. This is visibly evident as one drives through the patchwork landscape between the former South African border region and Ciskei, from vast pastures, fields and bushveld to the densely clustered villages sprawled on top of overgrazed hills. It is estimated that over one third of housing beneficiaries (between 1.1 m and 1.4 m) do not have title deeds, so they cannot transfer or inherit title or access bonds. Forced removals generate mushrooming informal settlements (Sune Payne and Leila Dougan, "Dweller Evictions, the Heart of Farm Darkness," *Daily Maverick*, 10 July 2018). Overcoming these legacies of segregation depends on recognition and integration of social tenure and long-term tenancy. The Western legal framework of private property proves a poor fit for most African families.

Noah Schermbrucker et al. argue that we need to fundamentally reconsider the norms, standards and regulations which govern title provision, since they are largely dysfunctional for the urban and rural poor; by "recognising the logic of informality with special powers to fast-track processes like title provision," with, "the onus placed on inclusion within formal structures," and, "relaxation of current land use management standards" (Noah Schermbrucker et al., "Hundreds of thousands of home-owners do not have title deeds," *Ground Up*, 6 June 2017). Insecure social tenure raises credit risk and shuts out investment. But the paradox is that, in opening up social tenure to capital, with formal recognition, tenants are vulnerable to distressed sales.

Ideological fetishisation of title deeds for recognition of land tenure has gripped investors and politicians since the 1930s. Titling was re-popularised in the late 1990s by Hernandes De Soto's *The Mystery of Capital*, which argues that capitalism can work for the poor by formalising their rights in considerable assets in houses, land and small businesses. Their "dead capital" can't be traded or leveraged unless legal and administrative systems recognise it. This ideology of fungible commodification, capitalist penetration of public assets and property-owning democracy has been proved wrong time and again, in costly, failed titling projects. The true mystery of capital is why this ideology continues to hold sway in the face of the evidence. Private ownership is seldom appropriate for poor people (Barry 2015, 7).

Formalising social tenure in an integrated system of title deeds has been tried at huge expense around the world and failed. Awarding titles to individuals renders insecure the tenure of women and tenants in male-headed households. Capital typically fails to materialise, with banks more likely to consider strong business plans for venture investment than title deeds (Wiley 2018, 19). The tax base also falls short, if it does not force the poor to sell (Sjaastad and Cousins 2009, 4). Tenure security depends not on the substitution of social tenure for formal title deeds, but, rather, on integration of social tenure with the formal system. To integrate in official recognition a continuum of overlapping types and uses, we need to make major readjustments to existing dominant formal frameworks (Cousins et al. 2005, 2).

Strengthening existing social tenure—for informal, vulnerable occupants—is preferable to imposing titling. Statutory recognition of rural communities as collective owners of their lands is increasingly accepted, expanding and substantial, with state laws now recognising customary tenure in over 78% of Africa (Wiley 2018, 7). Tenure reform can include confirmation of *de facto* land rights. Hence, the World Bank revised its individual tenure policy in 1975, recognising that communal tenure systems can be a more cost-effective way to increase security and provide a limited base for land transactions (Adams et al. 1999, 10).

Segregation of tenure in South Africa raises the problem in land reform of how to integrate the politics and culture that permeate social tenure, to support social practices with widespread legitimacy. Better security for social tenure arrangements—even without title deeds—can help to prevent forced evictions, to facilitate transfer, in inheritance or sales, to reduce property disputes and to include a wider base for taxes and services. Tenure reform is needed to provide a legal basis for decision-making about common resources, to prevent exploitation by local administrators and traditional leaders (ibid., 18). Legislation is needed to clarify governance over social tenure, to ensure equitable allocation of benefits and sustainable environmental management in development initiatives. Parameters of decision-making must be regulated and monitored, for agents who act on behalf of a community, to ensure transparency and democratic accountability and to minimise scope for abuse (21).

Tenure terminology privileges formal, registered title over customary or informal tenure but social tenure is seldom disorganised and chaotic; it is often complex, organised and regulated, and the formal and informal often interact and influence one another (Hornby et al. 2017, 9). Informal processes worked out on the ground tend to produce rules and systems over time regarding socially accepted codes of practice for acquiring and maintaining rights to land. To protect the socially recognised rights of the majority of citizens to use and access of land, it is essential that tenure terminology be expanded to incorporate these informal social tenures. Systematic land reform depends on the recognition of existing normative patterns of tenure which are neglected by the current cadastral system based on surveyed freehold title deeds.

The dominance of the current formal conception of property is so strong in South Africa that the state and the private sector only recognise registered titles fitting legal categories recognised by the deeds registry as valid property rights. Informal social tenures, which are recognised by most communities in the country, are not protected, recognised, supported or valued. This absence of recognition results in severe disjunctions between the normative values that inform the law and the normative practices that inform local practices (ibid., 10).

To extend official recognition to a wider range of tenure options than the registered title deed, that is, to off-register, social tenure, Michael Barry advocates use of the metaphor of a "continuum of land tenure rights". He stresses that the tenure continuum is a metaphor and not a theory and takes pains to argue that it does not presume hierarchy, evolution or incremental upgrading of tenure toward Western norms of private ownership (2015, v). Since it is a minimalist metaphor, he claims, it accommodates a range of ideologies and theories.

Barry acknowledges the value of a range of theories of property—relating to identity, personhood, bundles of rights and webs of interest—but he prefers the metaphor of a "constellation of interests" to account for a complex range of land tenure systems and interests one may recognise in a unit of land (vi). He emphasises the importance in land reform of recognising and building on working tenure systems. Following Peters (2006), he maintains a distinction between three main sub-systems: (1) ideology (i.e. positions stakeholders have about development and land tenure systems, e.g. socialist or liberal), (2) law (institutional property laws, linked to rules of authority), and (3) actual relations of tenure pertaining to a relevant property. These levels may differ markedly (29). But, how do all these sub-systems fit on a continuum? The problem with Barry's minimalist metaphor is that it is too accommodating for such definition. The range of options these sub-systems does not imply a straight line from custom to registry. If the state must be required to secure a broader range of tenure, limits must be set between social practices and authority.

Whereas the registered title derived from Western law allows exclusive use and sale, or transfer, customary tenure allows shared use and ownership. It is typically derived from African customary law, that is, regulated by values and principles informed by customs.

Customary tenure often involves negotiation, local mediation and social investment. Land resource rights are embedded in a range of social relationships and units, including households and kinship networks and communities, which adapt through bloodline and historical continuity to new external challenges over time (Hornby et al. 2017, 18). The authors of *Untitled* (ibid.) argue that the metaphor of a tenure continuum is too simplistic to account for the complexity of tenure arrangements, composed of degrees of elements of each extreme. Some customary systems show strong formality and many official title deeds are inaccurate. They therefore favour the concept of a *matrix* of multidimensional factors, which, for instance, compare different *sources of authority* with corresponding *tenure rights and access* (21).

As Christian Lund (2002) argues, struggles over property are as much about the scope and constitution of authority as they are about access to resources. This underscores the limitations of the metaphor of a tenure continuum: its accommodation of a wide range of tenure arrangements is too loose to distinguish legitimate tenure rights from social relations of domination, exploitation or abuse. Legitimate land rights rely on authoritative recognition. One may acknowledge Barry's claim that, "classical legal and philosophical theories of property are ill-equipped to handle the present complexity of land tenure" (14). But to work with complexity and to determine a useful "template for action in all land management challenges", we need to limit astrological accommodation of a "constellation of interests" (8).

Pauline Peters argues that the metaphor of the land continuum privileges negotiability and flexibility in "socially embedded" tenure to the neglect of accounting for power and authority. Privileging negotiation in communal consensus, for instance, overestimates the ability of all to influence what constitutes tradition and to lay down the norms for access to shared resources. Land tenure problems in Africa over the past century have involved the denial of property in land of individuals and families through the construction and reproduction of "customary" communal tenure (Peters 2013, 538). The consent, benefits and interests of community members and families are thus amalgamated under tribal identities and traditional leaders. A single representative may thereby be pressured to sell out benefits to the group, at a substantial discount to the overall cost, in exchange for individual, private benefit. Moreover, what counts as "consensus" often favours the interests of more powerful members, who are able to persuade others and mobilise support with authority or control of resources.

Since it is not regarded as property, communal tenure rights are often poorly enforced (546). Most land threatened by corporate land grabs is under weaker customary social tenure (548). Segregation between customary tenure and formal land administration leaves customary tenure insecure (Kingwill 2005, 49). Officials often conflate the rights of chieftaincy with rights of users and occupiers of land. The state needs to establish institutional, administrative and legal tenure measures to recognise the tenure arrangements of the excluded, invisible, unofficial, extra-legal, marginalised poor majority (Hornby et al. 2017, 130).

Integration of our divided tenure systems depends on working with customary practices and recognised local authorities, but, as Ntsebeza argues, land reform must include the review of authoritarian structures dominated by hereditary chiefs and headmen, and establishment of democratic and popularly accountable structures over rural communal land (Ntsebeza 2003, 70). Legislative reform is needed to ensure residents are consulted before decisions are made about the land and to ensure that ownership by property holders is distinguished from governance and administration by local authorities (72). Land reform requires distinctive criteria a spectral metaphor cannot capture in order to establish legitimate rights of tenure.

A Theory of Rights Recognition, to Integrate South African Tenure in Land Reform

Barry's metaphor of a constellations of land interests can guide integration of social tenure and formal tenure in South African land reform. But we need more than a metaphor. While exclusive recognition of the hegemonic Western model of registered ownership is too tight to accommodate the social tenure arrangements of the African majority in this country, not all tenure arrangements on the continuum are fit for formal recognition as tenure rights. The flexibility of Barry's continuum metaphor to accommodate a diverse of social tenure practices also strains against coherence and equity concerns. Land reform cannot recognise all socially embedded tenure forms; it must also reform, constrain and limit. The principles of recognition and adaptation offer alternatives to titling within the framework of an incremental, progressive approach to securing tenure over time (Hornby et al. 2017, 35). Integration of land rights in a coherent framework requires a theory of land rights recognition that accommodates social tenure with reference to moral and political criteria of legitimacy.

The first section of this chapter detailed instances where public land reform discourse and policy function ideologically to benefit elite interests at the expense of the poor. I argued that a narrow moralistic focus on the transfer of land ownership from whites to blacks masks the reproduction of colonial forms tenure and distracts from state incapacity to recognise and secure the social tenures of dependent communal, customary and informal tenants.

Furthermore, the narrow conception of tenure in terms of hegemonic Western norms such as the title deed, and of productivity in terms of large-scale commercial agriculture, works in favour of power and money. Fetishism of Western concepts of ownership sustains a colonial system of segregated tenure and indirect rule that outsources the social tenure of African households to governance by communal trusteeship, which is often vulnerable to weak systems of accountability and to elite capture.

These examples are ideological in the classic sense that they concern a set of ideas (such as property) whose self-subsistent appearance mystifies underlying social and material conditions which people reproduce to the benefit of elites, at the expense of their interests. Peters identifies such a mechanism in land reform as fetishism, explaining that neoliberal economic logic fetishises and naturalises property ownership as the only vehicle that ensures a market in land which guarantees individual incentives to produce and improve income. This narrow focus of market economies on privatisation in the dominant ideology of ownership neglects the creative productivity of hybrid public-private land rights and practices (2006, 97–98). Challenging this fetishism of property marketisation requires more than recognition of "social embeddedness" or "complexity" in a "constellation" of tenure rights (100). As explained in "Segregated Land Rights in the Ideology of Land Acquisition" section, legitimate authority is needed to secure land rights. To qualify as rights, social tenure arrangements must satisfy definite normative criteria of legitimacy.

An account of land rights is thus needed which (1) accommodates social tenure arrangements presently excluded by fetishism of registered private ownership but which (2) sets limits of legitimate authority for rights of social tenure. The contours of such an account of tenure are well established in rights recognition theory. Rights recognition theory is defetishising to the extent that it traces rights back to their basis in underlying customary practices of recognition, which may otherwise remain obscure in the ideological fetishism of formal representation. The normative warrant of established principles is traced back to its moral justification and customary recognition, evident in socially accepted conforming conduct and official support.

On the basis of rights recognition theory, Rex Martin (2013) defines a successful or active right as one which, (1) is justified by critical moral standards, (2) has some sort of significant social recognition, (3) has official recognition in law and in the action of courts, (4) is maintained primarily by conforming conduct, and, if need be, (5) is officially protected through oversight, enforcement, regulation and support by government. In essence, to qualify as rights, tenure arrangements depend on both social and official recognition.

One may presume that we establish rules of justice by social convention out of concern for our common interest or the common good. The political and legal principles and rules which guide our conduct are immanent in historical process. For rights to guide conduct, they must be moral, socially established, recognised and maintained. What it means to have a right is that it is recognised by a community, with social, moral and political authority (Martin 2013, 5). Without *authoritative recognition*, no set of social practices can qualify as a right. The problem with South Africa's segregated tenure system, at present, is that authority in social tenure is neither adequately regulated nor accountable to state institutions to yield rights.

Land rights, including title deeds, depend on social and official recognition. But social tenure is not officially recognised by the state. As Gerald Gaus (2006) explains, a right is a moral claim involving, (1) a power, (2) recognition by others or society, as (3) contributing to a common good. Unless a right is recognised, we do not have good reason to ascribe it to anyone. The concept of a right implies the concept of a correlative duty and one cannot have a duty that is not recognised as such. We only have rights if rational others recognise the correlative duties they entail. Furthermore, a right is also a power, that is, it represents an authority. Without social recognition, no authority exists; and without authority, rights cannot regulate social action. These vectors—authority and social recognition—are interdependent.

South Africa's Western tenure framework of individual property ownership accommodates customary African social tenure patterns by collapsing the details of household and kinship tenure into the general communal ownership of a defined group under a leader, who acts on behalf of the trust, essentially as if she were the individual holder of a freehold trust. Thus, the chief is made an effective rights holder, whose subjects lose their own rights to common resources. This gives chiefs much stronger rights than they hold under a customary principle of African leadership: *inkosi yinkosi ngabantu* ("a chief is a chief through other people) (Hornby et al. 2017, 410). Land rights at present are not conceptually grounded in customary recognition. This mismatch between law and common practice fosters a culture of illegality, unaccountability and systematic abuse of the formal system, which excludes most citizens.

I have framed the South African "Land Question" as a problem grounded in the restrictive ideological fetishism of title deeds to the exclusion of social tenure. Failure of the state to recognise social tenure sustains the colonial present for the African majority, who live under informal or customary social tenure arrangements with little support from the state. Colonial conceptions of tenure, trusteeship and productivity are reproduced in land reform for beneficiaries, who are kept dependant on the state as tenants, locked out of capital, expected to manage large farms without adequate state support, or pressured into a collective to front strategic partners the state subsidises to produce exports. Since the dominant theoretical conceptual basis of tenure in state policy does not recognise and accommodate African tenure practices, a colonial system of indirect rule is reproduced, even in land reform. Beyond a narrow conception of land reform as the expropriation and transfer of freehold title deeds, we need to decolonise the underlying system of land rights recognition and management.

At present, most socially recognised land tenure in South Africa is not officially secured. It is held in *de facto* possession and in insecure, off-register tenure, which the state neglects to recognise, secure and enforce, due to its restrictive, prescriptive framework for protecting property rights. Barry's alternative conception of tenure has been discussed, which considers tenure in broader terms, to accommodate a wider range of tenure arrangements. However, I have argued the metaphor of a "constellation" of tenure on a continuum, which Barry puts forward is too accommodating to define political limits for land reform along interdependent vectors of social recognition and official authority. Without *authoritative* recognition, social tenure arrangements cannot qualify as rights which a state may be obliged to secure.

Whereas our segregated tenure system in South Africa currently prescribes an overly restrictive concept of land rights, rights recognition theory accommodates a plural register of recognised customary norms, by tracing land rights back to their recognition. The normative basis of land rights is predicated on their recognition in customary normative social practices.

This theoretical basis provides for a defetishising account of land rights beyond individual ownership of freehold title deeds. But rights recognition theory also prescribes moral and political limits of authority to ensure socially recognised customary practices are legitimate. Social tenure cannot be said to yield rights unless it satisfies such stipulative political criteria. For this reason, I suggest, a full-fledged land rights recognition theory is needed, such as I have sketched out, which accounts not only for the *range* of tenure forms included by Barry's metaphor of a tenure constellation on a continuum but also for the *authority* to enforce them.

References

Adams, Martin, Ben Cousins, and Siyabulela Manona. 1999. Land Tenure Reform and Economic Development in Rural South Africa. *Overseas Development Working Paper 125*.

Allsobrook, C., and Boisen, C. 2017. "Two Types of Trusteeship in South Africa: from subjugation to segregation", *Politikon 44*(2): 265–285.

Barry, M. 2015. *Property Theory, Metaphors and the Continuum of Land Rights*. Nairobi: UN-Habitat.

Boisen, C 2017 "From land dispossession to land restitution: European land rights in South Africa", *Settler Colonial Studies 7*(3): 321–339.

Cartwright, K. 2018. DRDLR Staff Capacity, Competence and Corruption. *Land Knowledge Base: Occasional Paper*. Phuhlisani NPC.

Cousins, Ben, Tessa Cousins, Donna Hornby, Rosalie Kingwill, Lauren Royston, and Warren Smit. 2005. Will Formalising Property Rights Reduce Poverty in South Africa's "Second Economy"? Questioning the Mythologies of Hernando de Soto. *PLAAS Policy Brief 18*.

Gaus, G. 2006. The Rights Recognition Thesis: Defending and Extending Green. In *TH Green: Ethics, Metaphysics and Political Philosophy*, ed. Maria Dimova-Cookson and W.J. Mander. Oxford: Oxford University Press.

Hall, Ruth. 2018. PLAAS's Professor Ruth Hall on Land, and What You Should—and Shouldn't—Worry About. *Daily Maverick*, 29 March. https://www.dailymaverick.co.za/article/2018-03-29-the-interview-plaass-professor-ruth-hall-on-land-and-what-you-should-and-shouldnt-worry-about/.

Hornby, Donna, Rosalie Kingwill, Lauren Royston, and Ben Cousins, eds. 2017. *Untitled: Securing Land Tenure in Urban and Rural South Africa*. Pietermaritzburg: UKZN Press.

Hull, Simon. 2018. On the Necessity of, and Mechanisms for, Expropriating Land Without Compensation. *Daily Maverick*, 11 June. https://www.dailymaverick.co.za/article/2018-06-11-on-the-necessity-of-and-mechanisms-for-expropriating-land-without-compensation/.

Kepe, Thembela, and Ruth Hall. 2018. Land Redistribution in South Africa: Towards Decolonisation or Recolonisation? *Politikon* 45 (1): 128–137.

Kingwill, R. 2005. *Options for Developmental Land Administration Systems in the Context of Communal Tenure Situations; and Implications for Service Delivery*. AFRA.

Mailovich, Claudi. 2019. Presidential Land Advisory Panel Delivers Final Report. *Business Day*, 28 July. https://www.businesslive.co.za/bd/national/2019-07-28-presidential-land-advisory-panel-delivers-final-report/.

Marrian, Natasha. 2018. ANC Will Not Nationalise Land and Has No Designs on People's Houses. *Business Day*, 01 August. https://www.businesslive.co.za/bd/national/2018-08-01-anc-will-not-nationalise-land-and-has-no-designs-on-peoples-houses/.

Martin, R. 2013. Human Rights and the Social Recognition Thesis. *Journal of Social Philosophy* 44 (1): 1–21.

Merten, Marianne. 2018. Bantustan Boundaries, Alive and Well in Modern South Africa. *Daily Maverick*, 12 July. https://www.dailymaverick.co.za/article/2018-07-12-bantustan-boundaries-alive-and-well-in-modern-south-africa/.

Mkhize, Zweli. 2018. White Fear, Black Anger: Zweli Mkhize on Why Getting the Land Issue Right is So Important. *Business Day*, 02 July. https://www.businesslive.co.za/bd/national/2018-07-02-white-fear-black-zweli-mkhize-on-why-getting-the-land-issue-right-is-so-important/.

Ntsebeza, Lungisile. 2003. Land Rights and Democratisation: Rural Tenure Reform in South Africa's Former Bantustans. *Transformation* 52: 68–95.

Payne, Sune, and Leila Dougan. 2018. Dweller Evictions, the Heart of Farm Darkness. *Daily Maverick*, 10 July. https://www.dailymaverick.co.za/article/2018-07-10-dweller-evictions-the-heart-of-farm-darkness/.

Peters, P. 2002. The Limits of Negotiability: Security, Equity and Class Formation in Africa's land systems. In K. Juul, & C. Lund (eds.), *Negotiating Property in Africa*, 45–66. Portsmouth: Heinemann

Peters, P. 2006. Beyond Embeddedness: A Challenge Raised by a Comparison of the Struggles Over Land in Africa and Post-socialist Countries. In *Changing Properties of Property*, ed. Franz von Benda-Beckmann, Keebet von Benda-Beckmann, and Melanie Wiber. Berghann Books.

———. 2013. Land Appropriation, Surplus People and a Battle over Visions of Agrarian Futures in Africa. *Journal of Peasant Studies* 40 (3): 537.

Ramaphosa, C. 2018. This is No Land Grab. *Business Day*, 24 August. https://www.businesslive.co.za/bd/opinion/2018-08-24-exclusive-this-is-no-land-grab-writes-cyril-ramaphosa/.

Report of the High-level South African Parliamentary Panel on the Assessment of Key Legislation and the Acceleration of Fundamental Change. 2017. https://www.parliament.gov.za/storage/app/media/Pages/2017/october/High_Level_Panel/HLP_Report/HLP_report.pdf.

Schermbrucker, Noah, Victoria Mdzanga, and Christine Botha. 2017. Hundreds of Thousands of Homeowners Do Not have Title Deeds. *Ground Up*, 6 June. https://www.groundup.org.za/article/hundreds-thousands-homeowners-do-not-have-title-deeds/.

Sjaastad, Espen, and Ben Cousins. 2009. Formalisation of Land Rights in the South: An Overview. *Land Use Policy* 26 (1): 1–56.

Suttner, Raymond. 2018. Expropriation Without Compensation—Where is the Plan for Addressing Land Reform? *Daily Maverick*, 06 August. https://www.dailymaverick.co.za/article/2018-08-06-expropriation-without-compensation-where-is-the-plan-for-addressing-land-reform/

Tandwa, Lizeka. 2018. No Willing Buyer, Willing Seller in the Constitution. *News 24*, 31 May. https://www.news24.com/SouthAfrica/News/no-willing-buyer-willing-seller-in-the-constitution-albie-sachs-20170530

Wiley, L. 2018. Collective Land Ownership in the 21st Century: Overview of Global Trends. *Land* 7 (2): 68.

12

Land Reform and Redistribution as Environmental Justice Frameworks for Post-colonial Africa

Munamato Chemhuru

Introduction

Land reform and redistribution are necessary frameworks for post-colonial Africa's quest for equality, justice as well as social and economic development through agrarian reform.[1] However, from this discourse, the central question that has not been taken seriously is whether land reform and redistribution exercises and programmes in post-colonial Africa take into account, and solve questions around environmental

[1] The terms *land reform* and *agrarian reform* are sometimes misunderstood to mean the same. However, *land reform* should be understood as being more focussed on the broader land policies aimed at addressing land structures and inequalities in society, while *agrarian reform* should be understood to refer to agricultural reform in order to increase productivity. In this chapter, I will therefore be more specifically focussed on land reform as it broadly precedes and implicitly informs agrarian reform. (*See also*, Moyo 2011, 494).

M. Chemhuru (✉)
Katholische Universität Eichstätt-Ingolstadt, Eichstatt, Germany

Great Zimbabwe University, Masvingo, Zimbabwe

University of Johannesburg, Johannesburg, South Africa

E. Masitera (ed.), *Philosophical Perspectives on Land Reform in Southern Africa*,
https://doi.org/10.1007/978-3-030-49705-7_12

justice in Africa? This question ought to be critically addressed because "environmental practices and policies affect different groups of people differently, and environmental benefits and burdens are often distributed in ways that are unjust" (Figueroa and Mills 2001, 426). In this chapter, I seek to interrogate the notion of land reform and redistribution in post-colonial Africa by focussing on an underexplored perspective of environmental justice which is implicit within the discourse of land reform and redistribution. Yet it has not received much attention in much of the discourse of land reform and redistribution in Africa.

My response to the question of whether land reform and redistribution are a necessity for post-colonial Africa is in the affirmative considering that "land remains a basic source of livelihood of the majority of southern *Africans*[2] and is key to the development of agriculture, tourism, mining housing and industry" (Moyo 2007, 60). I provide various reasons why land reform and redistribution ought to be taken as viable frameworks for achieving environmental justice in post-colonial Africa. At the same time, I interrogate various reasons that have so far been espoused in order to justify why land reform and redistribution programmes in post-colonial Africa are seen as retrogressive and in violation of other people's fundamental human and property rights. As I have already observed, questions "of how to equitably share or distribute the benefits and burdens of environmental or climate change remain unresolved in much of contemporary environmental ethical thinking" (Chemhuru 2019, 30). This is why I seek to contextualise them within the discourse of the land question and assess plausible ways in which land reform and redistribution could be understood to satisfy the quest for environmental justice.

Generally discourse on the land question in post-colonial Africa is more focussed on the extent to which land reform and redistribution could be executed without necessarily violating fundamental human and property rights like what has been the case for Zimbabwe's 2000 *fast track* land reform and redistribution. However, less attention is paid to the questions around exploring plausible ways to achieve environmental justice for the post-colonial African condition. Although Sam Moyo is not focussing on environmental justice, he comes close to this view as he

[2] I have made my own emphasis because I think that this view is applicable to the rest of Africa and not specific to southern Africa.

argues that "the land question is not only an agrarian issue but also a critical social question" In this work, I therefore explore some different perspectives to the land reform and redistribution by focussing on novel and underexplored questions around the environmental justice import of land reform and redistribution in post-colonial Africa.

First, I give a background to the colonial and post-colonial land policies that were introduced by the white settler colonial governments which in the end violated fundamental human and property rights of the indigenous African people. I then analyse the issues that have mostly been raised as a result of attempts to reform and redistribute the land in post-colonial Africa. In the end, I propose that environmental justice in Africa can only be realised within the context of a robust land reform and redistribution framework in post-colonial Africa.

Colonial and Post-colonial Land Policies and Injustice in Africa

The land question and other problems associated with it in contemporary Africa such as dispossession, land imbalances, poverty and environmental injustice could all be attributed to the Berlin conference of 1884–1885. It is at this conference that owing to Africa's vastness in terms of size, favourable climatic conditions and natural resources, it became a prime target for European countries such as Germany, Belgium, Spain, Italy, Portugal and Great Britain. These countries agreed on rules of how to partition the African continent amongst themselves in order to avoid clash of interests as they competed for Africa's natural resources without being at war with each other.

In particular, the most basic natural resource which was at the core of the decision to partition the African continent was the land. After the Berlin conference regulated European colonisation of Africa, the indigenous African populations were dispossessed in terms of their land. As a result of the advent of colonialism, indigenous African populations have suffered dispossession from their land. The land formed part and parcel of their basic property, basic right and a largely agrarian source of livelihood. As Simon Mawondo sees it, "the process of dispossession was legitimated by a series of pieces of legislation, which sought to entrench white privileges and to bring the Africans under colonial control. In this process Africans were denied rights to own land in the most agriculturally productive parts of the country" (Mawondo 2008, 7). Yet, land remains the most basic form of property for any household management. Although I do not agree with Aristotle's conception of human nature where he justifies slavery within his ancient Greek society, in his spirited criticism of Plato's communitarian view of property in the *Politics*, he confirms the centrality of land towards the safeguarding of human well-being and property rights (*See*, Aristotle, Part III-VIII).

The colonial and post-colonial land policies developed in most African countries were, and some still remain, contrary to the distributive conception of justice expressed in Aristotle's *Nicomachean Ethics, Book V* where in one sense, justice involves equals getting equal shares (of whatever is being distributed) and unequals unequal shares. The patterns of land distribution during and after the colonisation of Africa show the extent to which land dispossessions violated human rights to property as well as how it contributed to social injustice. This explains why Lawrence Tshuma comes to the conclusion that the colonial land tenure systems were *A Matter of (In)justice*[3] (1997). Because of the injustice that has been bred by the advent of colonialism and the extent to which it has contributed to the dispossession of land among the indigenous people of Africa, land has become the centre of most African indigenous black people's struggles and movements in both the colonial and post-colonial Africa.

In view of the social injustice that had been caused by the land dispossessions in the rest of Africa, struggles for liberation and repossession of land characterised the better part of the mid and late twentieth century in Africa. Mawondo argues that "a deep sense of injustice caused by the inequalities and deliberate dispossession of Africans by the white settler regimes was amongst the fundamental causes of the liberation struggle in Zimbabwe [*and many other African countries*[4]]" (Mawondo 2008, 7). Although Mawondo is more focussed on Zimbabwe, the story of the

---

[3] This is with reference to the title and argument of Lawrence Tshuma's book.

[4] My additional point and emphasis.

fight for injustice that was caused by land dispossession is not simply a Zimbabwean story. It is an African story that was started by Kwame Nkrumah in Ghana in 1957.

In an opinion written for *Bulawayo24news*, Terence Simbi argues that "the liberation war against white minority rule's black political formations were all created on the [principle] of repossessing and redistributing land to the black indigenous population as their formation basis" (Simbi 2019, 23 April). However, there has been little progress in this quest for justice in light of the land question. Writing on *The Land Question in Southern Africa*, Moyo argues;

> The principal land question facing Southern Africa is that little progress has been achieved in the implementation of agrarian reform. The enduring challenge is to redress colonially driven and post-independent unequal land ownership, discriminatory land use regulations and insecure land tenure systems which marginalise the majority of rural and urban populations. (Moyo 2007, 60)

This view could best be authenticated by some of the events unfolding in Africa's post-colonial era such as land repossession and redistribution, formation of alternative political parties, protests and demonstrations over land inequalities.

In post-colonial Africa, some of the main political formations emerge such as Zimbabwe Unity Movement (ZUM) (1989) and the Movement for Democratic Change (MDC) (1999) in Zimbabwe as well as Economic Freedom Fighters (EFF) (2013) in South Africa. These *opposition*[5] political parties have all been formed as alternative political formations intended to revisit the unresolved land question in the two respective countries, Zimbabwe and South Africa. This explains why in Zimbabwe, owing to growing pressure from ZUM and most specifically the MDC and veterans of the liberation struggle, the Zimbabwe African National Union (ZANU PF) government rushed to execute what has come to be

[5] I use this term under protest. I do not necessarily believe that an alternative political party is an opposition political party in the strongest sense. Although these alternative political formations could at times have opposing views to those of the ruling parties, they at times could be in consensus with the ruling parties.

known as the Fast Track Land Reform and Redistribution Program (FTLRRP) at the advent of the new millennium. In South Africa, the BBC reports that the relentless focus of the EFF on inequality and failure of the ANC to redistribute the land from the white minority to the black majority could be responsible for the diminishing support for the ANC (BBC News). This is why the ANC is now in the midst of exploring possibilities for compulsory land repossession without compensation in order to give it to the majority black population in need of land. Pascah Mungwini argues that "the recent student protests under the 'Rhodes must fall' campaign are a reminder of the unfinished historical and humanistic project of independence in (South) Africa" (Mungwini 2018, 123). A similar view is also expressed by Moyo as he argues that "the land question in South Africa remains unresolved partly because of its gradualistic approach to land reform, but largely because the peasant question is underestimated by official policy and denied by intellectuals and civic society" (Moyo 2007, 60).

Struggles for the repossession of land are therefore taken as serious matters of injustice around the land question. Considering that after the advent of colonialism in Africa, the indigenous African populations were resettled in dry and unbearable climatic conditions. As a result they have received the greatest amount in terms of environmental or climatic burdens compared to the colonial white settle farmers who on the other hand enjoyed the benefits thereof. For example, indigenous local communities in Mozambique, South Africa and Zimbabwe residing closer to the Great Limpopo Transfrontier Park continue to suffer the burdens of human-wildlife conflict owing to their proximity to wildlife. This is why Patrick Tom argues that "colonialism is partly to blame for the current conflicts between local communities and animal wildlife" (Tom 2008, 86). So, as long as these conflicts are unresolved, it may be difficult to conceptualise environmental justice within such communities. This challenges us to rethink of a land reform and redistribution approach that could take into account the quest for environmental justice.

However the bulk of the literature on land reform and redistribution in Africa has tended to be more focussed on issues such as the questions to do with violation of human and property rights. Yet there remain a largely underexplored area of environmental justice within the quest for land reform and redistribution. In most cases, discourse on the land reform and redistribution has been largely considered from anthropocentric and anthropogenic perspectives as they have tended to focus on the extent to which only indigenous African people have been affected by the land dispossessions. However, an environmental justice framework demands that there ought to be an equitable redistribution of the benefits and burdens of climate change.

Issues from Post-colonial Land Reform and Redistribution in Africa

Generally, issues on the various programmes of land reform and redistribution in post-colonial Africa have been centred on the quest for access, equality, social justice and the need to uphold human and property rights. To confirm the centrality of natural resources to conceptions of environmental justice, in a 2014 report, the United Nations Development Program observed that "in sub-Saharan Africa, the natural resource sector is arguably the largest driver of environmental justice claims and actions" (UNDP 2014, 17). This is why land reform and redistribution, as key aspects of agrarian reforms (Moyo 2011, 494), have been on the agenda of most post-colonial African governments after attaining their independence. According to Sam Moyo, "agrarian reform entails transforming the role of various agrarian classes in struggles for development and democratization, towards equitable land ownership and social relations of production, and developing the agricultural production forces to enhance food security, livelihoods and accumulation of capital" (Moyo 2011, 494). While Moyo's view cannot be overemphasised, at the same time, these agrarian reforms raise fundamental questions of justice and human rights in Africa because of the way land and agrarian reforms have been handled from the colonial period to date. As long as these key aspects of land and agrarian reform are not addressed, it becomes difficult to have an acceptable view of environmental justice that is acceptable to people belonging to different social and economic classes where others have access to means of production while others do not have, and at the same time in a situation where those without access to land or with limited access to it suffer disproportionate impacts from environmental burdens.

In post-colonial Africa, the questions of human rights violations and justice with regards to the land question are paradoxical in nature. In Africa, prior to colonialism, originally the land belonged to the indigenous black people. After Africa's conquest, land, especially the most productive and fertile parts, ceased to belong to these indigenous black people. For argument's sake, some may want to claim that some parts of the land were unoccupied and virgin when it was first occupied by the white settler farmers. However, this argument is flawed because it is now evident that indigenous black people were pushed to the less productive soils of the countryside where the majority continue to live up to the present day. Interestingly, the *natural*[6] land that was taken by the white colonial settlers may have been in its natural state and at the time of occupation, unsuitable for farming until it was developed through various infrastructural and other developments by the white settler farmers. This view therefore poses a challenge for the redistribution of such land in terms of whether it should take into account and/or ignore the developments that would have taken place. Accordingly, following this kind of thinking based on John Locke's labour theory of land, one might be persuaded to look at the land reform and redistributive measures to be contrary to principles of human rights and social justice. For example, according to Locke:

> Though the earth and all inferior creatures be common to all men, yet every man has a "property" in his own "person." This nobody has any right to but himself. The "labour" of his body and the "work" of his hands, we may say, are properly his. Whatsoever, then, he removes out of the state that Nature hath provided and left it in, he hath mixed his labour with it, and joined to it something that is his own, and thereby makes it his property. (Locke 1823, 115)

[6] As I have already stated, this view that the land taken by the white settlers was in its state of nature is contested.

In a way, this kind of argument might be appealed to in order to justify reasons why the white minority farmers in post-colonial Africa could continue to claim ownership of the land that they naturally found and developed through their labour. However, some might argue that such land rightfully belonged to the indigenous people who were forcibly removed from it. This would therefore make Locke's theory to be inapplicable.

As a result, the notions of social injustice and human rights in post-colonial Africa have often been appealed to without properly contextualising them within the context of the land question and environmental justice in Africa. Except for the incidences of violence which characterised Zimbabwe's land reform and redistribution after the year 2000, the idea and practice of repossessing land and redistributing it to the minority indigenous population remains noble if the quest for environmental justice is to be achieved in Africa. In the following section, I provide several reasons why land reform and redistribution are precursors to the attainment of a sound conception of environmental justice in Africa.

Achieving Environmental Justice through Land Reform and Redistribution

In the light of the critical issues raised in the post-colonial era with reference to land reform and redistribution such as the violation of human and property rights, injustice and sometimes violence, one therefore wonders how best environmental justice could be reasonably achieved. In this section, I seek to find plausible ways in which environmental justice could be attained through the twin processes of land reform and redistribution in Africa. This approach resonates well with John Rawls's principles of social justice where "justice as fairness applies to the basic structure of society" (Rawls 1971, 229). Accordingly, my working understanding of environmental justice is informed by the quest for equitable sharing and distribution of benefits and burdens of environmental or climate change. This view is basically captured by a definition given by the American Environmental Protection Agency (EPA) where:

> Environmental Justice is the fair treatment and meaningful involvement of all people regardless of race, colour, national origin, culture, education, or income with respect to the development, implementation, and enforcement of environmental laws, regulations, and policies. Fair Treatment means that no group of people, including racial, ethnic, or socioeconomic groups, should bear a disproportionate share of the negative environmental consequences resulting from industrial, municipal, and commercial operations or the execution of federal, state, local, and tribal environmental programs and policies. Meaningful Involvement means that: (1) potentially affected community residents have an appropriate opportunity to participate in decisions about a proposed activity that will affect their environment and/or health; (2) the public's contribution can influence the regulatory agency's decision; (3) the concerns of all participants involved will be considered in the decision-making process; and (4) the decision makers seek out and facilitate the involvement of those potentially affected. (EPA 2008)

In light of this understanding of environmental justice, and considering, for example, the traditional land imbalances that were created by colonial land policies in Africa, one wonders how, for example, *fairness* could be meaningfully achieved in the quest for environmental justice if one considers the plight of the indigenous African communities living in the countryside compared to their counterparts in the urban environment and even worse still if we compare the plight of those in the less developed countries with those living in the first word countries.

As I have already alluded to in the previous sections, a fascinating fact about African countries is that, with the exception of Ethiopia, they are all former colonies of some of the most developed countries in the global North such as Britain, Germany, France, the Netherlands, Italy and Portugal. Yet these African countries still remain within the global South and being less developed compared to their counterparts in the global North. Colonialism has helped to widen the gap between the global North and the global South. Through colonialism, indigenous African populations have been dispossessed of their land such that it has become very difficult for them to contribute to economic production and development yet they receive the greatest amount of environmental effects from climate change and global warming owing to the effects of industrialisation in the global North as well as the effects of pollution from Western-owned transnational companies which continue to explore the vast mineral and other resources in Africa because they own such resources, including the land. This is what prompts Margaret Ssebunya, Stephen Nkansah Morgan and Beatrice Okyere-Manu to see the need to "challenge the social, political and economic inequalities that make people of a particular class (usually the lower class) suffer the negative impacts of environmental degradation caused by the avaricious-driven behaviours and attitudes of others (usually the wealthy)" (Ssebunya et al. 2019, 176). Accordingly, this is why I argue that unless land reform and redistribution is properly executed, environmental injustice will continue to be mostly felt by the greater populace residing in these African countries who do not have access to the means of production, which is the land. This is why I have argued elsewhere against "unpersuasive global environmental practices that support inequitable distribution of environmental benefits and burdens" (Chemhuru 2019, 32). In this context, one such practice is the distribution of natural resources such as the land.

It is difficult to think how African indigenous communities with limited or no access to land could meaningfully contribute to environmental justice or how they could be meaningfully involved in the environmental decision making processes. For example, most African indigenous people rely on subsistence farming and wildlife animals for their livelihood. Yet environmental justice demands that all people be meaningfully involved towards development, implementation and enforcement of environmental laws, regulations and policies. This is why Patrick Tom thinks that "it would be unfair to the rural communities, if they do not receive environmental *goods* and receive only environmental bads" (Tom 2008, 94). Central to my argument here is the notion of whether the previously colonised African communities ought to have duties towards climate change mitigation, which in itself is an important ingredient of environmental justice. Also, it is a problem to imagine whether such communities ought to be considered to be at par with the other industrialised and developed economies in the global North so that they can all be *meaningfully involved* in the quest for environmental justice. Also, from a distributive approach to environmental justice, it would be unfair to meaningfully involve *all people regardless of race, colour, national origin, culture, education or income* towards enforcing environmental laws and regulations yet the most basic natural resource, the land is unfairly distributed in the first place. Interestingly, the UNDP admits that "at its core, environmental justice is bout legal transformations aimed at curbing abuses of power that result in the poor and vulnerable suffering disproportionate impacts in pollution and lacking equal opportunity to access and benefit from natural resources" (UNDP 2014, 17). From this view, what needs to be addressed first are the legal frameworks surrounding issues of access to, and the disproportionate burdens of environmental impact on people with limited access to natural resources, especially the land.

The above dilemmas arise because the approaches and conditions to land ownership are not fair in the first place. Although Rawls is not so much focussed on the land question in particular, he would want us to imagine a social system which should also take into account the problem of distributive justice like what presently transpires between those with access to land vis-à-vis those without access to it. According to Rawls,

> The social system is to be designed so that the resulting distribution is just however things turn out. To achieve this end it is necessary to set the social and economic process within the surroundings of suitable political and legal institutions. Without an appropriate scheme of these background institutions the outcome of the distributive process will not be just. (Rawls 1971, 243)

Following Rawls's view, it therefore becomes difficult to imagine possibilities for equitable distribution and sharing of the benefits and burdens of environmental justice and climate change without first considering the fair redistribution of natural resources like land which is most basic. A land reform and redistribution programme based on the distributive approach to justice therefore becomes a necessary condition for the realisation of environmental justice in Africa.

The kind of framework for environmental justice which I propose here is one that also takes into account the basic principles of justice such as fairness and equity in the distribution of land or natural resources. Following Rawls's principles of justice, first there is need for some certain minimum standards of fairness or equality that ought to be satisfied first before realising justice (Rawls 1971, 15). For example, the evident social, political and economic disparities between communities in the global North and the global South demands that land in post-colonial Africa be redistributed in a way that achieves justice to the indigenous populations. According to Rawls, injustice "is simply inequalities that are not to the benefit of all" (Rawls 1971, 54). Similarly, in order that environmental justice could be attained, certain standards of fairness in terms of land possession, ownership and use ought to be fair first such that there are no inequalities with regards to the land.

Also, from the American Environmental Protection Agency (EPA)'s understanding of environmental justice it is a problem to think of how *meaningful involvement* in the quest for environmental justice could be done with the landless yet they are obliged to contribute to environmental justice. In situations where the land belongs to the minority, like what is the case in African post-colonial countries without robust land reform and redistribution programmes, it becomes difficult to contribute to environmental justice through meaningfully involving everyone with respect to the development, implementation and enforcement of environmental laws, regulations and policies. Alternatively, Aristotle offers a distributive perspective to justice which could also be taken to reasonably inform a conception of environmental justice in post-colonial Africa. For Aristotle;

> There must be the same *equality* [i.e.: the same ratio] between the persons and the things: as the things are to one another, so must the persons be. For if the persons be not equal, their shares will not be equal; and this is the same of disputes and accusations, when people who are equal do not receive equal shares, or even persons who are not equal receive equal shares. (Aristotle, NE 1906, 145)

Following this view, a reasonable conception of environmental justice would be one that meaningfully involves all individuals who are equal in terms of possession and access to land. At the same time, it would be unfair to think of distributing environmental justice or benefits and burdens equally among people who are unequal in terms of possession.

In much of Africa, environmental justice issues are closely connected to issues on race, sex, class and poverty. It is such that land ownership patterns have often been modelled by disparities in race, sex, class and gender. Similarly, concerns for environmental justice ought to consider and address such ownership patterns in accordance with race, sex, class and poverty. According to the UNDP 2014 Report,

> In South Africa, environmental justice is often seen an extension of the nation's revolutionary anti-apartheid struggle. Apartheid era policies had created various forms of environmental injustice related to control over land and natural resources, lack of access to environmental services, and disproportionate impacts from industrial toxicity. Many of the structural causes of these injustices have remained in the post-apartheid era, owing to underlying systemic dynamics connected to the nature of resource governance, and the long-standing legacy of toxics from heavy industry, such as mercury poisoning of workers and communities, health impacts from asbestos mining, and waste dumping next to poorer townships. (UNDP 2014, 18)

From this view, if land ownership patterns are unfairly distributed in accordance with discriminatory policies such as apartheid, environmental injustice will also continue to affect the landless, poor and black communities of Africa. I therefore argue that in order to meaningfully conceptualise environmental justice in Africa, these unresolved issues from apartheid and colonialism ought to be addressed first. This could perhaps satisfy the UNDP's understanding of environmental justice as an emerging development discipline that should as well contribute towards fighting injustice, poverty and inequality (UNDP 2014, 3).

The fact that one does not have the land, or access to it, means that there can be no fair treatment of all people. For example, landless individuals cannot meaningfully participate in decisions about how to sustainably use the land and its resources in a way that promotes environmental and human wellbeing and the interests of future generations. This is because some of these issues do not make sense to them. It is for this reason that an indigenous African community with no access to land for animal ranching may not understand it when they are being discouraged from hunting wild animals for meat and other purposes. This is why it becomes necessary for post-colonial African governments to institute land reform and redistribution as a viable framework for achieving environmental justice.

Conclusion

It is now evident that African countries need to weigh the benefits and burdens of land reform and redistribution first before the quest for environmental justice. At the same time, environmental justice demands that everyone participates towards decisions about activities that have a bearing on the environment and ultimately their wellbeing. What I have attempted to do here is to explore reasonable ways by which environmental justice could be achieved by addressing the land question in Africa. Although I do not intend to be understood as implying that land reform and redistribution naturally lead to environmental justice, I seek to propose an environmental justice framework that is premised on first addressing the land question.

Acknowledgments The author wishes to thank the Alexander von Humboldt Foundation for the generous support of my research fellowship under which this chapter was written.

References

Aristotle. 1906. *The Nicomachean Ethics*. Trans. F. H. Peters. London: Kegan Paul.

B.B.C. News. 2019. *South Africa's Radical Agenda Setter*. https://bbc.in/2VgQa2r.

Chemhuru, M. 2019. The Paradox of Global Environmental Justice: Appealing to the Distributive Justice Framework for the Global South. *South African Journal of Philosophy* 38 (1): 30–39.

Environmental Protection Agency (EPA). (2008). Environmental Justice: Learn about Environmental Justice. http://www.epa.gov/environmentaljustice/learn-about-environmental-justice.

Figueroa, R., and C. Mills. 2001. Environmental Justice. In *A Companion to Environmental Philosophy*, ed. Dale Jamieson, 426–438. Malden: Blackwell Publishers.
Locke, J. 1823. *Two Treatises of Government*. http://www.yorku.ca/comninel/courses/3025pdf/Locke.pdf.
Mawondo, S. 2008. Search of Social Justice: Reconciliation and the Land Question in Zimbabwe. In *The Struggle After the Struggle: A Zimbabwean Philosophical Study 1*, ed. David Kaulemu, 7–20. Washington, DC: The Council for Research in Values and Philosophy.
Moyo, S. 2007. The Land Question in Southern Africa: A Comparative Review. In *The Land Question in South Africa: The Challenge of Transformation and Redistribution*, ed. Lungusile Ntsebeza and Ruth Hall, 60–86. Cape Town: Human Sciences Research Council.
———. 2011. Three Decades of Agrarian reform in Zimbabwe. *Journal of Peasant Studies* 38 (3): 493–531.
Mungwini, P. 2018. The Question of Recentring Africa: Thoughts and Issues from the Global South. In *Decolonisation, Africanisation and the Philosophy Curriculum*, ed. Edwin Etieyibo, 115–128. New York: Routledge.
Rawls, J. 1971. *A Theory of Justice*. Cambridge, MA: Harvard University Press.
Simbi, T. 2019. Whites Score Big Against Blacks—Land Compensation. https://bulawayo24.com/index-id-opinion-sc-columnist-byo-161113.html.
Ssebunya, M., S.N. Morgan, and B.D. Okyere-Manu. 2019. Environmental Justice: Towards and African Perspective. In *African Environmental Ethics: A Critical Reader*, ed. Munamato Chemhuru, 175–189. Cham: Springer.
Tom, P. 2008. Rethinking Wildlife Conservation in Zimbabwe. In *The Struggle After the Struggle: A Zimbabwean Philosophical Study 1*, ed. David Kaulemu, 85–98. Washington, DC: The Council for Research in Values and Philosophy.
Tshuma, L. 1997. *A Matter of (In)Justice: Law, State, and the Agrarian Question in Zimbabwe*. Harare: SAPES.
UNDP. 2014. *Environmental Justice> Comparative Experiences in Legal Empowerment*. https://www.undp.org/content/dam/undp/library/Democratic%20Governance/Access%20to%20Justice%20and%20Rule%20of%20Law/Environmental-Justice-Comparative-Experiences.pdf.

13

Individual Justice in Land Redistribution: Appropriating Some Ideas from the Capability Approach

Erasmus Masitera

Introduction

In this work I respond to the following questions: Which capability functionings are violated in disorderly land redistribution? And in what ways does the Capability Approach (C.A.) advance the cause of (individual) justice within the land redistribution?

My thinking in this chapter is guided by redistribution experiences that have occurred in some African states. Of concern is the violation of human rights that have occurred and, in some instances, continue to occur; the violated human rights came through violence, displacement, exploitation, assaults, marginalisation, land expropriation and appropriation, among others. One may relate this experience to the Zimbabwean land redistribution of the year 2000 onwards. In the redistribution mentioned, certain individuals' functionings were violated I relate the

E. Masitera (✉)
University of Johannesburg, Johannesburg, South Africa

E. Masitera (ed.), *Philosophical Perspectives on Land Reform in Southern Africa*,
https://doi.org/10.1007/978-3-030-49705-7_13

resulting violations to other disorderly land redistributions that have occurred and may occur in the Southern African region. By functionings, I mean the state of living (beings) and the activities (doings) that one may engage in to realise one's goals. In this chapter, I will expose the loss of functionings on the part of the general populace, though more emphasis may be placed on former farm owners, farm workers as well as the resettled individuals. As regards violated functionings, I group these as social, political and economic functionings. I note the following violations:

1. Being safe
2. Being healthy and being well nourished
3. Being involved in community life and being respected
4. Working

It is important to state that the violation of functionings constitutes injustice through impinging on the achievement of individual well-being and personal goals. With that in mind, the chapter also focuses on advocating for an objective good way of living that would assist individuals to realise desirable goals. In this way, my argument moves away from positions that generalise values and interests as belonging to the community, which Daka (2006) and Masaka (2011) argue for. In that regard, I recognise the pertinence of the C.A. approach, which advocates objective justice. By objective, I mean a view that proffers a system that "leads individuals to be able to act (and live) in ways that they wish, as well as to achieve such objectively desirable functionings as participating in the life of one's community" (Bilchitz 2017, 205).

This means a system that promotes access to basic goods for all and beyond that pays attention to other individual needs, especially for the naturally less endowed so that they could live life with dignity. The foregoing view is opposed to the property rights theory, which concerns itself with the individual's claim to a property, but which is not concerned much with the individual being and activity in achieving valuable goals. In addition, my view, which is modelled on the C.A. perspective (presented above), can be contrasted to the historical (and related entitlement) theories, which are concerned more with the patterns of transactions towards (in)justice than the individual's state of life and way of achieving own goals. I argue that important as these theories (rights, resources and entitlement) may be, they ignore and are unconcerned with the kind of life that individuals ought to live, which the C.A. makes sense of. I intend to argue for land redistribution from this C.A. point of view.

In presenting the C.A. on land redistribution, I also recognise that Daka (2006), Scalet and Schmidtz (2010) and Bhatasara (2011) make inputs into African land redistribution from the C.A. point of view. I note here that in the arguments forwarded by these scholars, they note the importance of human agency on the part of the black communities (Daka 2006) and women in terms of gender equality (Bhatasara 2011), and the importance of entitlement relations attained through trade, production, labour and inheriting, especially for white land owners (Scalet and Schmidtz 2010). These observations touch on the fundamental issues that are at play in the land reform and distribution debate, such as freedom, eliminating poverty, bettering livelihoods or well-being, albeit limited to particular groups, such as women, blacks and whites. The chapter goes on to prioritise the individual functionings in a more inclusive and comprehensive way, a point the mentioned scholars have not cared to tackle.

In the ensuing discussion, I will follow and elaborate on Sen's (1999a) perspective on functionings and the relation to individual well-being. Note that Sen does not specify any relevant functionings, but leaves that to democratic bodies to decide. In that regard, one of my contributions in this chapter is to identify functionings that former landowners and new landowners are at danger of losing when land redistribution is disorderly. I draw these functionings from literature, in which the losses and violated rights in the affected populations in states that underwent disorderly land redistribution are recounted. As a response to the functionings loss, I propose and advocate for democracy. The democracy I present is premised on political freedoms, economic freedoms, social opportunities, transparent guarantees and protective securities (capability freedoms). These freedoms, I argue, are achievable through individuals' active advocating for the establishment and realisation of the freedoms. Individuals are in this sense responsible for establishing political and social systems that respond to individuals realising their well-being (functionings).

To successfully present my position, this chapter will firstly define the concept Capability Approach, at the same time revealing the importance of capability and functionings; I will also contrast C.A. with some common ethical approaches that have been used to critique land reform. Second, I will make a detailed account of functionings lost through disorderly land redistributions. Third, I will focus on examining the importance of democracy in land redistribution. Fourth, the chapter will present objections to the proposition of using C.A. on land redistribution, to which I will respond. And lastly, the chapter will have a conclusion.

Understanding the Capability Approach

The Capability Approach is concerned with assessing the quality of life that individuals are leading (Bilchitz 2017, 204). Additionally, the Capability Approach is a normative framework that endeavours to engender an objectively good kind of life that individuals ought to live (Sen 1999a). The kind of life referred to is that life in which individuals flourish and well-being is realised.

The foregoing definition of this approach is based on Amartya Sen's conception of the term capability. In concocting the definition and term, Sen considers the diversity of both individual humans and the many social and political variables or factors in which they operate. The diversity and the various factors raise complex normative questions concerning justice and equality. Sen uses the term 'capability perspective', which takes human functioning as its normative core. Human functioning entails focusing on expanding human capabilities in society (Sen 1999a, 1) to enable its members to lead lives they have reason to value and choose on their own (Chavez 2015, 21). Or as Nussbaum (2011 17) puts it, the framework is concerned with what opportunities and freedoms are available for people to be self-determining and self-defining. In order for humans to function or lead lives they have reason to value, the C.A. argues that there is need for social, political and economic activities to interact with one another in order to realise their capabilities (opportunities and choices to live lives the way they value). In fact, the conditions in which individuals can convert different social, political and economic resources for their own benefit is the major concern of the C.A. framework. The interaction of these different human facets is referred to as the 'beings' and 'doings'. The discussion about beings and doings is concerned with the states of living and the activities of individuals. That is, what kind of life do individuals lead and in what activities are they involved in order to pursue their own way of life. Both these may be briefly summarised as individual choice and expanded opportunities.

C.A. is thus to be understood as both (1) a framework[1] that evaluates the quality of life that individuals lead in society and the opportunities they have there, as well as (2) a social theory of justice (Sen 1979, 218–219, 1999a, 55; Watene 2010, 5; Nussbaum 2011, 18; Kukathas 2013, 198; Poli 2015, 106). The kind or quality of life that individuals are expected to live is premised on access to social, political and economic opportunities and the freedom to make choices concerning the kind of life they have reason to value. It is from this perspective that different philosophers such as Robeyns (2016), Chavez (2015, 21) and Pedersen (2015, 1, 6–7) understand C.A. as a theory of justice interested in understanding individuals' capabilities and how these capabilities can be promoted, enhanced and developed in society. The framework in this sense is more concerned about the social, political and economic opportunities available to each person rather than about the welfare of people in society generally.

In order to promote and enhance human capabilities, is necessary to understand the social reality in which humans find themselves with the intention of bringing about change in cases where the social circumstances inhibit human well-being. As an evaluative framework, the C.A. attempts to understand the social, economic and political environments that include the institutional arrangements and policies in which humans operate. These are important in as much as they have a bearing on and contribute significantly to people's realisation or non-realisation of their capabilities (Sen 1999a, 38). The idea behind this is that institutional arrangements either expand or restrict the freedoms and choices that individuals may have (Little 2010, 41; Nussbaum 2011, 21). In this sense then, the C.A. is an appropriate framework for evaluating concrete social circumstances by enquiring how institutional arrangements,

[1] C.A. according to Sen does not have a well-developed and even agreed-upon theory of justice as is the case with Nussbaum. Despite this difference, advocates of the framework agree on some expectations that advance human capabilities.

policies and practices in any given country promote or inhibit individual *functionings*. Besides evaluating, the C.A. also proposes ideas and design policies with the aim of changing social systems towards the expected 'good'. The main idea is that the human functioning is promoted; more concretely, the C.A. aims at promoting human dignity.

The idea of human functioning and well-being is prioritised by the C.A. over other human facets, such as resources, needs, interests and entitlements. The main reason for placing human well-being and functioning at the centre of human activities is that humans are considered as *ends-in-themselves*, whereas resources, needs and entitlements are means to achieving human ends. In this sense, the C.A. reflects on the freedom humans have in order to choose one way of life among many other possibilities, that is, C.A. questions what goods or resources do to humans (Sen 1979, 218–219). In the end, the conclusion reached is that resources, needs and entitlements are instruments for human well-being. Moreover, by arguing in this way, the C.A.'s conception of justice focuses on humans and the conditions in which they live, rather than on the establishment of just institutions (as is the case with an entitlement or resource-based approach).

For Sen, understanding the individual's beings and doings is central to realising how they are affected by their environment rather than focusing and speculating (hypothesising) on actions and outcomes about social arrangements, such as income levels and access to resources and commodities (Sen 2009, 8–10; Kukathas 2013, 198). Moreover, Sen thinks that the other conceptions of justice are too restricted since they are not universally applicable but are partial in application and provoke serious disagreements in society (Kukathas 2013, 19); since, the other conceptions of justice concentrate on one or other aspects of justice and not on how the individual functions in society. For Sen (2009, 77) the concern should rather be on advancing human justice in society through mitigating injustice that impinges negatively on human functioning.

Furthermore, the C.A. starts from already known and existing positions, that is, the framework recognises that people know what they want and are aware of their positions in society, their abilities and weaknesses and how to use this knowledge to better their living standards. This is unlike Rawls' theory of justice, which argues for the betterment of people's lives from a hypothetical position of resource redistribution. However, the C.A. does not ultimately reject the relevance of the ideas advanced by Rawls' and Nozick's theories. C.A. theorists maintain that other theories of justice are necessary in as much as they reveal the importance of what resources, entitlements and property rights do to humans. The argument is that while resources or commodities are necessary in assisting humans to realise their ends, these resources are not *ends-in-themselves.*

The C.A. is a people-centred theory because it emphasises the moral importance of humans and their freedom to pursue their own goals and ambitions. The Capability Approach (C.A.) or Human Development Theory (HDT) is a conception of justice that has inspired a new way of understanding the role of humans in the world and especially their role in institutions in which they live and operate. More importantly, the C.A. conceives human beings as ends rather than as means to a good life. According to Ntibagirirwa (2014) and Watene (2010, 1), before 1990 there was an emphasis on Gross Domestic Product (GDP) and developing human capital instead of a human-centred understanding. The C.A. places human beings at the centre of all human activities, and it concedes that human beings are intrinsically responsible for shaping their lives around them for their own good. For this reasons, functionings become very important. I shall now focus on functionings, before assessing functionings that are in danger of being violated during unordered land redistribution.

Functionings

The accepted definition of functioning is that it refers to achieved ways of life (beings/states of living) and different activities (doings/activities) that people engage in. *Functionings* are the 'various things' that a person may value to be and want to do (Sen 1999a, 75). They are realised achievements and fulfilled expectations. Being and doing are directly related to the state of living, which is what a person can do and be. The things that one values are both mental and physical. This means that *functionings* are the states of living that people value and have reason to value, such as pursuing certain activities (doing) and living (being) a kind of life; in fact, functioning is being involved in actions that are self-expressive. The ability to function depends on social conditions, which either enhance or hinder people's participation in life of society. Conversely, social conditions[2] have an effect on the degree and extent of mental and physical participation of an individual in the life of society. According to Wells (2019), *functionings* are equal to inputs that are necessary for individuals operating in society to achieve their well-being. The inputs or states or conditions of living or *functionings* are of value if and only if an individual could convert them to achieve their own ends.

Robeyns (2016) develops this argument by saying that *functionings* are the "available alternatives" that people have. These available alternatives are present in the context of social norms, personal status and the physical environment, that is, resources available for use (in the case of this chapter, land). Examples of 'being' *functionings* include, but are not limited to, being safe, well nourished (health), literate, free from disease, involved in community life and respected (Alkire 2010, 18–21; Robeyns 2016; Hick 2012, 2). 'Doing' *functionings* include, but are not limited to, travelling, taking care of someone, working, voting, taking part in different forms of social life such as helping others and debating (Robeyns 2016). It is necessary to mention that *functionings* are always interrelated; they work together to bring about human flourishing or well-being. I should mention here that Amartya Sen does not list the functionings, except to mention that being health and being nourished are the essential functionings that humans ought to have to flourish. The list provided above is an elaboration on Sen's perspective, which says, each democratic community chooses functionings that it deems necessary for individual well-being. In addition, I note that functionings that are closely associated with land as a resource are being safe, being healthy, working, being involved in community life and being respected; the interaction among these is necessary in promoting the well-being of individuals.

In my perspective, when these functionings are respected, individuals can convert their abilities, opportunities and resources to achieve their

[2] These include the political, social and economic guarantees that promote individual freedoms to choose and live lives of their own choice.

goals. When this is the case, justice is achieved; yet when functioning is hindered, injustice occurs and individuals will fail to achieve their goals. In conjunction with my forgoing perspective, ordered land distributions epitomise respecting individuals and at the same time falls within the democratic systems. In democracy, there is the setting up of systems that respect, listen and respond to the needs of individuals or groups—in short there is the promotion of human dignity by respecting people's choices. The opposite is true for undemocratic systems and in the same vein, disorderly land redistributions. Disorderly land redistribution accounts for violation of human dignity (hindered functionings). I shall now focus on functionings violated during disorderly land redistributions.

Functionings Violated by Disorderly Land Redistributions

In this section of the chapter, I critically analyse four functionings that are at danger of being violated through disorderly land redistribution. Note that undemocratic systems (disorderly land redistributions) infringe on individuals' freedom and ability to select, combine and convert opportunities and resources for the individuals' own good. Disorderly land distributions promote injustice. Having said that, I now turn to the functionings that are and can be violated during disorderly land redistributions.

Being Safe

This functioning has an expansive description. Being safe include having a secure means to realise the minimum expectations to basic ends. In a broader understanding this includes protection from different forms of abuse, i.e. political, social and economic abuses. The abuses are mostly expressed through exploitation, discrimination, manipulation, exclusion and perpetual fear, among others. The existence of these abuses shows that livelihood security, security of physical space, promotion of individual safety, and financial security are violated (Rao 2019, 72).

Livelihood security refers to the sanctity attached to the means that promote and protect an individual's source of living. In the case of land, this refers to the instrumental means by which land assists individuals to realise the goals they consider valuable. Land is conceptualised as the source of income, food, shelter, a form of status (through ownership); in this sense, land is a source of empowerment, self-improvement and self-actualisation. It is appropriate to say that land is a means to avoid humiliating livelihoods in that without food or income one is bound to develop feelings of exclusion, that is, not fitting into society, thus not connecting with others. Over and above, individuals are susceptible to abuse if they have no land ownership on which they rely for other means of survival. One may make reference to the expropriations that occurred at the onset of colonial occupations whereby natives who were dispossessed of their lands became slaves and became other means of cheap labour to the settlers (Van Onselen 1976, 91). The same occurs if expropriation of land is to happen today, it will create vulnerable individuals among current landowners, farm workers and even among new landowners who are hastily resettled without proper planning and means of support. This implies that individuals will be deprived of the right to ownership of land and even to use it for the betterment of their own lives.

Being safe also refers to security of physical space assured through the right to ownership. Right to ownership is connected to guaranteeing individual security and safety from interference from the state and other individuals without due diligence. In other words, proprietorship is guaranteed together with the associated rights, such as unwarranted search, forced removal and seizure of property. Rao (2019, 77) adds that right to ownership accords one with physical and psychological comfort and assurance; in this way, abuse is guarded against. Interference hinders individuals from engaging in activities that are beneficial to the individual and it impedes on the well-being of an individual.

Furthermore, I think that whenever there are these guarantees, a sense of belonging, respect and recognition is constructed. In instances where there is disorderly land distribution, there will be the abuse of rights, such as non-recognition of ownership rights, as well as physical and psychological abuse (Shaw 2003; Mlambo and Chitando 2015, 14); individuals have been victimised, discriminated and unjustly lost property. There has been rights abuse, which have culminated in dehumanising living conditions and loss of freedom.

Another aspect that is worth reflecting on in the functioning of being safe is financial security. The idea expressed in financial security is that land is a (re)source of income. Individuals engage in different activities on land, activities such as tourism, mining, industrial and agricultural activities. As such, land provides individuals with opportunities to work, and employ others as workers, in this way land becomes a source of income. Apart from that, land ownership can be used as financial security in the sense that individuals may use the land for speculative purposes (Rao 2019, 78) and as a collateral security for funding (Obeng-Odoom 2012, 162–163). Land in this sense is of value to which individuals may turn whenever the need arises. In addition to the stated, land ownership is a financial security when it is used as collateral, whereby individuals access loans from banks. These financial uses cease when disorderly land reforms and redistributions occur.

The functioning of being safe is essential in as much as it assures individuals the autonomy to decide and act in a way that fulfils their dreams within the confines of what is considered societal good. Making autonomous decisions can be equated to individual liberty, free will, rationality and sovereignty (Dworkin 2007, 443). These are all important when it comes to the question of allotting personal responsibility and obligations for decisions and actions. Yet, this is abrogated in disorderly land redistributions.

Being Healthy and Being Nourished

The gift of life is central to the argument behind this functioning. Life ought to be lived and lived well; beyond this, Sen (1999a, 30) insists that individuals have to live long lives by avoiding escapable deaths that shorten life. The same argument is supported by Nussbaum (2000, 3–4, 2012, 8) when she discusses that human life ought to be "live(d) to the end of a human life of normal length; not dying prematurely, or before one's life is so reduced as to be not worth living". I think the foregoing views are foundational to the idea of life as the prominent functioning. I reach this conclusion on the basis that without life, there is no need to elaborate on all the other functionings.

Further to the pertinence of human existence as the foundation of functioning, there is the view that life is supported by being healthy and being well-nourished. Among the causes of human suffering and premature deaths (especially in Africa) is failure to access means to survival, such as food, which is a fundamental basic human need. From food humans derive different nutrients that are useful to their bodies and ensure long life; and thus, reducing the chances of dying prematurely from hunger and lack of nutrients. Considering this fact, land becomes an important resource. The importance is that land nurtures plants from which humans draw the necessities or the basic nutrients for their survival. Land becomes a vehicle through which human well-being is realised, especially in achieving individual bodily needs (nourishments). The ethical issue of responsibility, that is, duty to avoid illness/disease and avoidable death through the provision of food. It is the responsibility of individuals owning land to provide food for themselves and those who have no access to land. The responsibility is twofold, that is, to the individual themselves and to the community. This also means maximum utilisation of land for agricultural activities and ensuring a healthy society.

Apart from the stated, being in a healthy state strengthens one's position in society in the sense that being healthy boosts self-confidence, self-actualisation and inevitably increases one's participation in community social life. In addition, Nussbaum (2011) postulates that a healthy being is capable of reproducing; the reproduction is in the form of sexual reproduction, that is, regenerating the human species. Yet, at the same time, the reproduction may also be in the form of non-sexual activities, which involve art and other laborious activities. Involvement in these activities ensures that an individual uses his/her energy in the production of something that is admirable and acceptable to the person and community. As a way of augmenting Nussbaum's perception, I note Lötter (2008, 11, 17) who argues that being healthy leads to personal growth and development. Personal growth and development are products of good mental growth and physical growth (Lötter 2008, 17). Whereas mental growth and physical growth are reflective of being healthy. The significance of the argument presented by the noted philosophers is that being healthy reduces the chances of social exclusion, while increases social inclusion. An individual's well-being is enhanced through being healthy, a healthy state necessarily avoids humiliating conditions of being malnutritioned and developing poor mental health, which results in the exclusion of an individual. Social inclusion includes participation in social activities of one's community. This is essential for the well-being of an individual.

From the above presentation, it seems as if being healthy is only dependent on land agrarian production. A close analysis of the foregoing arguments also points to the issue of societal systems that necessitate being healthy. I will briefly discuss conditions that also contribute to the individual well-being, apart from those already stated. There are certain living conditions that enhance being healthy, including having access to healthcare (Sachikonye 2012, 238; Mutopo et al. 2014, 56), such as access to facilities such as dispensaries, clinics and hospitals that are adequately equipped. Access to healthcare assists individuals in improving their failing health, and generally maintaining society in healthy conditions through outreaches and notifications on how to keep healthy. Other social conditions that contribute to individual health are inclusive social arrangements. In my mind, I have societies that are democratic, societies that are non-racist/non-tribalistic, societies that are non-partisan, to mention a few. In such communities, individuals are accepted, respected and allowed to become who they want to be, but within the expectations of the society's conception of good. More importantly, individuals living in such non-marginalising communities avoid living in degrading and humiliating conditions that push them into mental sickness and inevitably personal underdevelopment (Lötter 2008).

In this part of the chapter, I reflect on the functioning of being healthy and nourished within disorderly land redistribution, by using as point of reference Zimbabwe's year 2000 land redistribution. The land redistribution has been dubbed as fast-tracked (Masitera 2017), and *jambanja* (unplanned/haphazard) (Dube 2018). In the different cases mentioned, the land redistribution was disorderly, unprecedented and unplanned. It disrupted farming activities and, in some cases, was violent resulting in loss of life. The disruptions and deaths that occurred denote the hindrances to the expectations of being healthy and living a long life. First, disruptions occurred through land invasions which caused stoppages to production of food (Masaka 2011, 341), thus reducing nutritious output. Resultantly, food shortages followed and continued to be experienced to this day. Closely connected, the economy of Zimbabwe shrank (Hanke and Kwok 2009).

Second, the deaths that occurred during the expropriations marked the end of human life through brutality. Such deaths could be avoided, had there been proper planning and consultation on land redistribution. Third, as for the new settlers there was no infrastructure provision in the new settlements (Sachikonye 2012, 238; Mutopo et al. 2014, 56). Infrastructure provision would include the provision of healthcare facilities in the new settlements that happen to be subdivided former largescale farms. The absence of healthcare facilities meant the absence of health enhancing facilities to assist people to recover, regain and maintain their health, with the result that poor health occurred. An unhealthy person in most cases excludes himself from others, as such social exclusion is imposed upon them mostly by themselves, mostly rather than by society. The non-involvement of individuals in community activities is detrimental to social cohesion and general social building.

Being Involved in Community Life and Being Respected

This functioning denotes the nature of humans, that is, humans are naturally social animals (Aristotle's *Nicomachean Ethics*, 1134a26–1134b2). As such, humans strengthen the social bonds by interacting, connecting and affiliating with others. These characteristics show the human ability to live with and live towards others. The importance of this functioning is that it reveals the pertinence of being in relation with others, especially by the fact that as humans we accidentally belong to a community. A community that we do not choose to belong to, in that regard. Wells (2019) argues that the nature of relationships within a community ought to extend "across class or ethnic divisions"; that is, relationships ought to go beyond the confines of political, economic and religious divides.

Communities are essential in as much as they help individuals to connect with others (normally beyond the family connections) and it also offers individuals protection. Protection of freedom is the major issue here. In this regard, the freedom of assembly, association, conscience, participation in community and individual activities, among others, is guaranteed. Having these guarantees assures individuals of respect and recognition. As members of the human race, it is a way of reducing abuse and exploitation, which is the case when the opposite exists. This social acceptance also assures that non-humiliating environments exist for all; such a situation satisfies individuals to live meaningful lives and flourish at the same time (Dillion 1997, 226). In addition, there is a sense in which equal treatment and dignity for all are honoured.

In communities that have experienced disorderly land redistributions, abuses have been frequent. Participation in one's community has been limited. Mlambo and Chitando (2015) note that a particular political party has dominated activities (social and political) and has limited movement of non-members into particular resettled lands. There is a danger that disorderly land redistribution may have the same result in other places, thus depriving people the freedom to choose how to live.

Working

By working, I mean a form of employment (occupation) by which individuals seek means of surviving and satisfying their desires, and occupying time by being productive. There are various forms of employment, such as self-employment, permanent employment and part-time employment. Considering these forms of employment, land as a resource is utilised by different individuals for diverse human activities, which range from agricultural activities, mining, industrial and tourism activities. In these activities, individuals occupy themselves as self-employed, permanently employed or employed on a part-time basis. Through employment, individuals self-actualise and self-improve themselves, in a sense employment offers empowers individuals; more importantly they become productive. This is the case in highly stratified societies as well in societies that have capitalistic tendencies. In such communities, individuals who are unemployed are discriminated and castigated against; working thus offers an economic and social empowering tool to individuals.

Land expropriation thus disrupts human functioning by occupying themselves for their own good. Land expropriation hinders the activity of self-actualisation, empowerment and fulfilling of individual desires. This applies to both the employer and employees who survive agricultural activities. An existential case is that of Zimbabwe's Fast Track Land Reform Programme of 2000 whereby several individuals lost farms that were productive. On these farms, the farmers and their employees lost their livelihoods and or their well-being (Shaw 2003). Most relied on the farms for their survival, for meeting their needs and even for them to avoid embarrassing human situations connected to being unemployed. While the forgoing case is limited to farmers, the same may be applied to other activities, such as mining, tourism and industrial activities disrupted by disorderly land redistribution and reform. The productivity of individuals or groups of people is hindered whenever land redistribution is disorderly.

Enhancing *Functionings*: The Role of Democracy

C.A. theory strongly suggests that there is a strong connection between human flourishing and living conditions in evaluating the kind of life that individuals have reason to choose. The framework also recognises the importance of democratic values in establishing a well-functioning society, as Glassman and Patton (2014, 1353) have observed. Moreover, the C.A. perspective that places importance on the interaction of liberal, social, political and economic activities finds fulfilment in the practice of democracy. C.A. does not depart from the traditional understanding of democracy and democratic principles. In that sense, the C.A. argues for the importance of participation of citizens, recognition and respect for individual reasoning and argument, pluralism and accountability.

A single and universally agreed definition of democracy is elusive, although recognising it in action is not. Democracy is a complex system of governance that has to reconcile competing claims; but it is noteworthy that it is not simply majority rule (Sen 1999b, 10); but a system that holds government responsible, accountable and responsive to its citizens (Sen 1999b, 11; Glassman and Patton 2014, 1353). To limit democracy to majority rule is simply appeal to the mechanical condition of 'part' of the expectations of democracy in practice. Appealing to majority rule is tantamount to creating partial policies and practices that are exclusive in nature, especially of the minority. As a complex system of expectations, democracy involves participation, expression and support for citizens' views so that they form values and priorities, both individually and as a group (Sen 1999b, 10–11; Nussbaum 2000, 103). Participation brings with it the idea of rational deliberation among members of society, such that the concept of pluralism of ideas and values is safeguarded (Rawls 1993, 384; Nussbaum 2000, 103).

Rational deliberation involves examination of individual principles and judgments as well as application of these for the good of all. In this sense, the liberties and freedoms of people are promoted and safeguarded. Furthermore, the participation and expression of the citizens' will, and government compliance conform to the idea that government should be accountable, responsive and responsible to its citizens. Some of the liberties and freedoms that citizens expect to enjoy include, but are not limited to, freedom of assembly and association (political parties and trade unions among others), freedom of expression, freedom of conscience (criticising and scrutinising authority), freedom to acquire and exchange property and the freedom to vote and stand for political office (Sen 1999a, 38). Additionally, there is need for guarantees of security and transparency that guard against abject poverty among citizens and prevent corruption, citizen abuse and financial irregularities on the part of administrators and governors. Democracy guarantees removal of hindrances to liberties and freedoms, such as censorship of press, arbitrary arrest, forced associations, political interference in economic relations and indoctrination. In short, democracy is an open system that aims at advancing people's freedoms, be they social, political and economic, and is achievable through the promulgation of policies that are people-oriented (Sen 1999b, 8). Democracy promotes social, economic and political security, while enhancing the individual's capacity to choose their own ways of life according to their own values in a society that they formulate.

In relation to capability development, democracy thus has a major role to play, especially in promoting people-oriented policies of value to them. To this end, Sen (1999b, 8) avers that defective policies and practices are linked to economic failure, mostly because of non-democratic institutions. Democratic institutions, he maintains, have appropriate policies aimed at the prevention of suffering, degradation, deprivation and inhuman conditions among the citizenry. An open system in this sense refers to a government that listens and actively responds to the needs of its community and individual citizens, which is not the case in most non-democratic countries where the needs of the general populace are routinely ignored. This point brings us back to the importance of C.A., which I mentioned earlier, namely that C.A. is concerned with individual justice. This means that the individual realises the kind of life they ought to lead without hindrances from the community at large. In other words, democracy is a people-oriented system that promotes different facets of human existence and well-being, which include, economic, political and social liberties enabling people to lead lives of their choice. In other words, democratic systems are interested in promoting the individual good within circumstances that are agreeable to all members of the community. The good and well-being of the individual leads in turn to the good and well-being of the whole community.

On the other hand, disorderly land redistribution is the direct opposite of democratic principles, in particular, the abrogation of human dignity, and thwarting rights and other liberties that are instrumentally necessary for individuals to lead a good life of their choice. Disorderly land redistribution leads to curtailment of freedoms, abductions, expropriations, marginalisation and exploitation that hinder people's participation in the life of their community and cause poverty and deprivation. Such a situation makes individuals to fail in choosing the kind of life they may deem important for their own living. Notably, disorderly land redistributions impinge negatively on the ability of individuals to be safe, to be healthy and nourished, and affect their ability to work and to participate meaningfully in their community's activities. Despite this, the C.A. further argues that individuals and groups have to act so as to bring about change, or to improve their living conditions (Sen 2009, 19; Robeyns 2016, 1; Ntibagirirwa 2014, 271–272). Sen (1999a, xvi–xvii, 191) and Alkire (2010, 207) agree in saying that humans are agents of their own freedom by being actively involved in removing iniquities and deprivation. Following from this, it is prudent to say that individuals have to actively involve themselves in the war against deprivations and exploiting circumstances. Furthermore, the individuals ought to be responsible for setting up democratic institutions that would in turn respond positively to their demands. This is a task that individuals living in compromised areas have to do, which include redistributed lands.

Objections to the Capability Approach of Land Redistribution

In this section, I will present some objections that may be levelled against the proposition I have forwarded. I will only mention and respond to two objections that I think have a strong basis in countering the approach that I have proposed.

The first objection relates to the idea of a systematic orderly land redistribution. This objection takes a historical approach to understanding land distribution in Africa as a whole. The historical argument contends that African land was expropriated from its original owners at colonisation. The argument also contends that European colonisers used chicanery and fraudulent means to claim the locals' lands (Greenberg 2007, 1406; Wuriga 2008, 7). The argument also notes that gross rights abuses of various forms followed the colonisation of African countries. Abuses such as forced labour on white farms, annexation of land and property, arbitrary arrests and forced taxes (Ranger 1967, 122–123; Van Onselen 1976, 91; Wuriga 2008, 8; Openshaw and Terry 2015, 74–75). It is apparent that the colonial land distributions were skewed in favour of the colonisers and that the situation continued after the attainment of independence. There was exclusion of the African. Considering this, one asks why the contemporary African should be expected to be prudent in terms of redistributing land in an inclusive and considerate manner.

My response to the objection is that, contemporary political theory and practice urge people to be tolerant of one another and that violence towards one another is destructive rather than constructive. Beyond that, contemporary society has mechanisms of correcting past offensives, considering that some of the injustices are (inter)generational crimes, it is difficult to address them as if they were committed by current generations (Perez 2011, 155; Perez 2012, 40–90). However, Mawondo (2008), Alexander (2014) and Powers and Proctor (2015) hold that intergenerational rectifications are the most ideal in building contemporary societies. Their argument is that certain injustices transcend generations and the effects cannot be limited only to individuals or a generation. The effects of injustices are sometimes present even in contemporary societies. In such circumstances, I think that it is important to find a civil way of correcting the past injustices, rather than retaliating through violent land expropriations that may result in exclusion of others. Rather, a more inclusive approach to the redistribution would assist in healing, correcting and reorganising society so that every individual is included. In saying this, I agree with Powers and Proctor (2015, 2–3) who argue that inclusive ways of correcting past injustices repairs, restores and rehabilitates the victims, while also addressing inequalities that exist in society. I, therefore, see the C.A. as an ideal approach in closing the gap created by skewed land redistributions, since it focuses on the individual, especially by suggesting the conditions that are conducive for individual advancement and realising their full potential.

The second objection that can be levelled against my proposal is that C.A. is a foreign approach, since it does not relate to the communitarian nature of African societies. That is, the C.A. is excessively individualistic in that it places more emphasis on individual well-being and individual freedom than on communal values (Wells 2019). Furthermore, the C.A. does not assess how individual freedoms might affect others. My response to this criticism is that individuals have reason to value certain kinds of life and this includes ethical evaluations from which they can make reasonable decisions that not do impinge negatively on others. In a sense, this is a consideration for living in a community. In addition, the same ideas are somewhat contained in the idea of democracy, whereby individuals are encouraged to make decisions that are in line with promoting inclusivity and focusing on oneself and others. These are not necessarily views equal to communitarian thinking, but I note there is a semblance of similarities and these can be applied to African systems as well.

Conclusion

In this chapter, I have established that disorderly land redistributions are tantamount to impinging negatively on individuals' well-being. Disorderly land redistributions are closely connected to undemocratic approaches to distribution of resources. I have established that human *functionings* (in the form of being safe, healthy and well-nourished, involved in community life and respected, and working) are violated. I arrive at this conclusion through evaluating the experiences emanating from particular disorderly land redistributions from the C.A. framework, which argues and urges for democracy as a societal expectation. As a prescription to the violations, and in line with the expectations of the C.A., I advance that democracy ought to be appropriated into the discussion and practice of land redistribution. In advocating for democracy that individuals drive towards, fight for and that respond to their needs. I also highlight that through democracy, individual well-being is respected and achieved, and the same ought to happen in redistributed lands.

References

Alexander, S.G. 2014. The Complexities of Land Reparations. *Law and Social Inquiry: The Journal of the American Bar Foundation* 39: 1–28.

Alkire, S. 2010. Instrumental Freedoms and Human Capabilities. In *Capabilities, Power, and Institution: Towards a More Critical Development Ethics*, ed. S.L. Esquith and F. Gifford. Philadelphia, PA: Pennsylvania University Press.

Bhatasara, S. 2011. Women, Land and Poverty in Zimbabwe: Deconstructing the Impacts of the Fast Track Land Reform Programme. *Journal of Sustainable Development in Africa* 13 (1): 316–330.

Bilchitz, D. 2017. Whom Do Rights Protect? In *Jurisprudence in an African Context*, ed. D. Bilchitz, T. Metz, and O. Oyowe. Cape Town: Oxford University Press.

Chavez, E.A.A. 2015. Which Way Out of Poverty? The Human Capital versus Human Capabilities Approach. *MASKANA* 6 (1): 19–25.

Daka, L. 2006. *Towards A Human Empowerment Approach to Justice: An Appropriation of Amartya Sen's Capability Approach, With Particular Reference to the Zimbabwe Land Reform*. PhD Thesis. Boston College, Chestnut Hill, MA.

Dillion, R.S. 1997. Self-respect: Moral, Emotional. *Political Ethics* 107 (2): 226–249.

Dube, E. 2018. The Search for Justice and Peace: Reflections on the Jambanja Discourse as an Articulation of Justice Foreshadowing Peace. In *Power in Contemporary Zimbabwe*, ed. E. Masitera and F. Sibanda. London: Routledge.

Dworkin, R. 2007. *Autonomy. A Companion to Contemporary Political Philosophy*. Edited by R. E. Goodin, P. Pettit, and T. Pogge. Malden: Blackwell Publishing.

Glassman, M., and R. Patton. 2014. Capability through Participatory Democracy: Sen, Freire, and Dewey. *Educational Philosophy and Theory* 46 (12): 1–13.

Greenberg, D. 2007. *Stroud's Judicial Dictionary of Words and Phrases*. Vol 2. Edited by D. Greenberg. London: Sweet and Maxwell.

Hanke S. H, Kwok A. K. F. (2009). On the Measurement of Zimbabwe's Hyperinflation. *CATO Journal* 29 (3): 353–364

Hick, R. 2012. The Capability Approach: Insights for a New Poverty Focus. *Journal of Social Policy.* 41 (2): 291–308.

Kukathas, C. 2013. On Sen on Comparative Justice. *Critical Review of International Social and Political Philosophy* 16 (2): 196–204.

Little, D. 2010. Institutions, Inequality, and Well-Being: Distributive Determinants of Capabilities Realization. In *Capabilities, Power, and Institution: Towards a More Critical Development Ethics*, ed. S.L. Esquith and F. Gifford. Philadelphia, PA: Pennsylvania University Press.

Lötter, H. 2008. *When I needed a Neighbor were You There? Christians and the Challenge of Poverty*. Wellington: Lex Verbi.

Masaka, D. 2011. Zimbabwe's Land Contestations and Her Politico-Economic Crises: A Philosophical Dialogue. *Journal of Sustainable Development in Africa* 13 (1): 331–347.

Masitera, E. 2017. Dilemmas and Controversies Surrounding the Land Debacle in Zimbabwe: Appropriating Some Ideas from the Shona *Unhu (Ubuntu)* Justice. In *The African Conundrum: Rethinking the Trajectories of Historical,*

Cultural, Philosophical and Development Experiences of Africa, ed. M. Mawere, T.R. Mubaya, and J. Mukusha, 267–286. Mankon: Langaa Research and Publishing C I G.

Mawondo, S. 2008. In Search of Social Justice: Reconciliation and the Land Question in Zimbabwe. In *The Struggle After Struggle: Zimbabwean Philosophical Studies 1*, ed. D. Kaulemu. Washington, DC: The Council for Research in Values and Philosophy.

Mlambo, O.B., and E. Chitando. 2015. "Blair, Keep Your England, and Let Me Keep My Zimbabwe": Examining the Relationship of Physical Space and Political Order in Zimbabwe's Land Redistribution Programme (2000–2008). *The Journal of Pan African Studies* 8 (8): 8–26.

Mutopo, P., J. Manjengwa, and M. Chiweshe. 2014. Shifting Gender Dimensions and Rural Livelihoods after Zimbabwe's Fast-Track Land Reform Programme. *Agrarian South: Journal of Political Economy* 3 (1): 46–61.

Ntibagirirwa, S. 2014. *Philosophical Premises for African Economic Development: Sen's Capability Approach*. Thesis No. 7. Globalethics.net, Geneva.

Nussbaum, M. 2000. *Women and Human Development: The Capability Approach*. Cambridge: Cambridge University Press.

———. 2011. *Creating Capabilities: The Human Development Approach*. Cambridge, MA: Belknap Press.

———. 2012. Creating Capabilities: The Human Development Approach. Accessed 11 August 2019. https://apps.ufs.ac.za/media/dl/userfiles/documents/News/2012_12/2012_12_10_Martha_Nussbaum_UFS_December_2012.pdf.

Obeng–Odoom. (2012). Land Reform in Africa: Theory, Practice and Outcome. *Habitat International* (36): 161–170.

Openshaw, K.S., and P.C.R. Terry. 2015. Zimbabwe's Odious Inheritance: Debt and Unequal Land Distribution. *McGill International Journal of Sustainable Development* 11 (1): 39–86.

Pedersen, L.-P. (2015). *Kant and Well-Being: Exploring Kant's Moral Philosophy from the Perspective of the Capabilities Approach*. M.A. Thesis. University of Oslo, Oslo.

Perez, N. 2011. On Compensation and Return: 'Can The Continuing Injustice Argument' for Compensating for Historical Injustices Justify Compensation for such Injustices of the Return of Property. *Journal of Applied Philosophy* 28 (2): 151–168.

———. 2012. *Freedom from Past Injustices: A Critical Evaluation of Claims for Intergenerational Reparations*. Edinburgh: Edinburgh University Press.

Poli, R. 2015. The Implicity Future Orientation of the Capability Approach. *Futures* 71: 105–113. https://doi.org/10.1016/j.futures.2015.03.002.
Powers, K.L., and K. Proctor. 2015. Victim's Justice in the Aftermath of Political Violence: Why Do Countries Award Reparations. *Foreign Policy Analysis* 13: 1–24.
Ranger, T.O. 1967. *Revolt in Southern Rhodesia 1896–1897*. London: Heinemann.
Rao, J. 2019. A 'Capability Approach' to Understanding Loses Arising Out of the Compulsory Acquisition of Land in India. *Land Use Policy* 82: 70–82.
Rawls, J. 1993. *Political Liberalism*. New York: Columbia University Press.
Robeyns, I. 2016. The Capability Approach. *Stanford Encyclopedia of Philosophy*. plato.stanford.edu/entries/capability-approach.
Sachikonye, L.M. 2012. From 'Growth with Equity' to 'Fast-Track' Reform: Zimbabwe's Land Question. *Review of African Political Economy* 30 (96): 227–240.
Scalet, S., and D. Schmidtz. 2010. Famine, Poverty, and Property Rights. In *Amartya Sen*, 170–190. Cambridge: Cambridge University Press.
Sen, A. 1979. Equality of What? In *The Tanner Lecture on Human Value*. Stanford: Stanford University.
———. 1999a. *Development as Freedom*. Oxford: Oxford University Press.
———. 1999b. Democracy as a Universal Value. *Journal of Democracy* 10 (3): 3–17.
———. 2009. *The Idea of Justice*. London: Allen Lane.
Shaw, W.H. 2003. They Stole Our Land: Debating the Expropriation of White Farms in Zimbabwe. *The Journal of Modern African Studies* 41 (1): 75–89.
Van Onselen, C. 1976. *Chibaro: African Mine Labour in Southern Rhodesia, 1900–1933*. London: Pluto Press.
Watene, K.P.M. 2010. *Strengthening the Capability Approach: The Foundations of the Capability Approach, with Insights from Two Challenges*. University of St Andrews.
Wells, T. 2019. Sen's Capability Approach. Internet Encyclopedia of Philosophy. https://www.iep.utm.edu/sen-cap/#SH3a.
Wuriga, R. 2008. The Revolutionary Bond and Opposition Politics in Post-Independent Africa: The Case of Zimbabwe. *IKAMVA: International Journal of Social Science and Humanities* 2 (1): 1–36.

Part IV

African Ethics and/on Land Reform and Redistribution

14

Towards a Critical Ethic of Land in the Southern African Context

Mark Rathbone and Anné Hendrik Verhoef

Introduction

In a previous series of articles,[1] Rathbone and Verhoef argued that the failure of land reform in Southern Africa can be ascribed to the deadlock in the opposing groups' ontologies of land[2]. On the one hand land is understood as mere economic function—a position held for example by commercial farmers who see land as means to provide food security. They

[1] See Rathbone and Verhoef 2015 on the need for alternative ontologies of land in the Southern African context, and Verhoef and Rathbone 2015 on examples of such alternative ontologies. These articles were preceded by an article on the relation between violence and modernity (Rathbone and Verhoef 2012), and an article on economic justice (Verhoef and Rathbone 2013), which laid the groundwork for our articles on land in 2015.

[2] Land refers to much more than farms or physical ground (demarcated areas). It is also associated with oppression and colonial control of geographical space and people perpetuated by the Natives Land Act of 1913, amongst other (Rathbone and Verhoef 2015). In terms of the crisis of land in Southern Africa, the concept of land is often described in three categories: "white commercial rural areas, former reserves and urban areas" (Hendricks et al. 2013:1). These categories are all included within our broad understanding and definition of land.

M. Rathbone (✉)
Faculty of Economic and Management Sciences, North-West University, Potchefstroom, South Africa
e-mail: mark.rathbone@nwu.ac.za

E. Masitera (ed.), *Philosophical Perspectives on Land Reform in Southern Africa*,
https://doi.org/10.1007/978-3-030-49705-7_14

will argue typically against subsistence agriculture which does not explore the full potential of land. On the other hand, land is understood as that which gives people their dignity, integrity and identity, and links them to their history, ancestors and culture. We argued that both these ontologies of land need to be questioned and that a more complex, rather than reductionist, ontology should be developed. We criticised both ontologies and proposed that a more dialogical and complex perspective should be developed. We proposed that some alternative ontologies—e.g. from common religious perspectives—must inform this dialogue and development of a new more complex and non-reductive ontology of land.

In this chapter we want to build on this earlier work and position of us, but we also want to overcome some of its shortcomings we identified since then. We realise that reference to ontology is inherently problematic. The subject/object dichotomy embedded in the quest for understanding reality may lead to subversive views and hierarchies. Further, the assumption that inaccessibility of the hermeneutics of the other can be bridged and accessed is experienced as offensive and even patronising by oppressed communities. It runs the risk of simply continuing the colonial obsession of observing, codifying and controlling the colonised through European eyes (Said 1994: 276). It also reflects the obsessions of European culture to name and control the other e.g. Orientalism (Said 1995). Culture is a crucial aspect to be considered in the hermeneutics of land, but in order to respect the culture of the other, asks that one do not simply assume that it can be described and named through observation.

A different approach than bridging the cultural and functionalist understandings of land through dialogue (as we argued earlier) is needed.

The relationship between culture and hermeneutics is evident in Mda's and Locke's reductionist views of land. On closer scrutiny it is clear that the issue of land is far more complex and cannot be understood in reductionist means, because the view of the other remains inaccessible from the

A. H. Verhoef
Faculty of Humanities, School of Philosophy, North-West University, Potchefstroom, South Africa
e-mail: anne.verhoef@nwu.ac.za

perspective of ontology. Finally, we acknowledge that dialogue (and even the possible development of a new more complex ontology of land) without action is superficial. It remains insensitive for the immediate need of land of previously oppressed communities. The ontological approach to land remains stuck within these dilemmas. On the other hand, a clear ethical criteria for action is crucial for land reform and land redistribution in Southern Africa. Such ethical criteria should accentuate the need for accountability and responsibility in terms of the history and the future sustainability of society as a whole. Such ethics must be inclusive of the need for justice (especially in the case of landless and exploited citizens), but also for social, economic and political stability for a sustainable future for all citizens in South Africa (or Southern Africa, due to our interdependence on food security). Such a critical ethical approach to land has therefore the potential to overcome the dilemmas the ontological approach was stuck in, but it needs to be carefully developed.

In developing a critical ethic of land in the Southern African context, we will bring into conversation an African cultural perspective on land (Mda's novel) and a Western perspective (Locke's private ownership). However, we do not thereby want to generalise or simplify this complex issue of culture and traditional school of thoughts. We rather develop in this chapter an example of an African understanding of land from Mda's novel *The Heart of Redness* (2000),[3] and a more Western understanding of land from the work of John Locke[4] to show that culture is crucial in the land debate. Culture is not essentialist but rather complex and should be critically scrutinised because of possible embedded reductions. What we add then in this chapter as a unique contribution to our earlier work (and hopefully to the scholarship on land), the notion of developing a critical ethic of land. Our previous argument was for a more dialogical ontology where a 'functionalist' and 'cultural/identity' ontology of land acknowl-

[3] Of course Zakes Mda does not represent "the African" understanding of land. He (Zanemvula Kizito Gatyeni Mda) writes as an African (born 1948 in Herschel in the Eastern Cape, South Africa) about isiXhosa people's understanding of land. This represents thus just one culture within "the African" perspective—"There are many different ways of being African" (Mda 2018d: 205–215) remains a complex and dynamic issue.

[4] As with Zakes Mda, John Locke does not represent the whole tradition—in this case the Western. It is rather the case that his work was very influential in the Western tradition and especially on understanding land (private property).

edges the value of both and alter and enrich each other. A critical ethic of land further this exploration and process by arguing for some definitive goals or norms within this debate. It is not only critical as being self-aware and evaluative of one's own reductionist views, but by putting forth the critical aspects of sustainability and 'life-giving', as an ethic of land. In other words, it argues critically against destructive forms of reductionist views of land and at the same time develop the importance of sustainability and complexity associated with land. It critically reflects on injustices of the past, on historical and traditional (strongly cultural) notions of land and how it affects us, but also critical reflects on the future, on the life-giving potential of land. It aims to formulate how important the notion of sustainability is in a possible non-reductionist, complex, inter-cultural and more just notion of land.

Our argument is that land is never understood in objective and/or neutral terms. Land is interpreted. Land has a history. It locates us (or others), grounds us, belongs to us (or not), gives us life, and forms us. There are political, economic, cultural, historical, psychological, philosophical, esthetical, agricultural, personal, communal, factual, mystical and many other perspectives (or ways of understanding) land. Land is a complex, multifaceted and rich notion. The ontology of land—what land really is—is thus a crucial question to ask.[5] Any simplified way of answering this question may be guilty of reducing land to something it is ironically not. At the same time, one should be aware of only a theoretical understanding of land and forgetting the urgency of our existential relation of land—especially for those who are landless, hungry and desperate. An ethic of land is an urgent matter and must deal with the structures of what land essentially is, with that which is implied in the very definition of land, but in a very practical matter that is focussed on redressing the injustices of the past. To develop such a critical ethic of land will thus be based on a specific understanding of land. This understanding of the

[5] Braidotti's definition of ontology is used here. She says that ontology is "the branch of metaphysics that deals with the structure of that which essentially is, or that which is implied in the very definition of an entity…" (2011: 123). She wants to reject the essentialist notion in her argument for an ontological basis of sexual difference and rather redefine it as an open-ended one. We follow this open-endedness of ontology she argues for, without moving to a complete relativistic notion of land.

'essential structures' of land (as an ontology) may be prone to be a reductionist notion of land, and therefore we will argue for a more open-ended 'hermeneutic of land'. This is our starting point for developing a critical ethic of land. We will first look at Mda's understanding of land, and then Locke's. Thereafter we will develop some aspects of what we think might be an appropriate and much needed critical ethic of land within the Southern African context.

The Heart of Redness

Zakes Mda's novel, *The Heart of Redness*, tells the story of the prophet Nongqawuse that lays bare an understanding of land that is inextricably part of the Xhosa tradition. Nongqawuse's relation to the land is crucial. Mda explains that "the landscape is paramount among the environmental factors that determine the emotional and spiritual development of my characters and ultimately their sense of identity" (Mda 2018c: 43). Mda's description of the "Eastern Cape as being 'replete with memory and trauma' may also be applied to the entire country, containing as it does so many memories and stories of a traumatic past" (Jacobs 2018: 9). The novel illustrates that tradition can become dangerous and destructive if it is the singular view on land.[6]

However, it will be argued that the story of Nongqawuse is far more complex and can also be viewed as emancipatory and as a protest against white oppression. It is in this regard that a similar, but older African story needs to be taken account of here.

Nearly three centuries ago, in the area surrounding the mouth of the Congo River, a Congolese girl, Kimpa Vita, was baptised as Béatrice, and started to make appearances as a prophetess.[7] She claimed divine inter-

[6] Of course this is a fictional work and the question may arise how much authority should be given to such a work in this context. One should keep however in mind that Mda's "fictional and non-fictional writings (further) reveals him to be in the imaginative space of constant border-crossing, between text and intertexts, written and oral narratives, conventional reality and 'magical' African reality, self and other" (Jacobs 2018: 11).

[7] The development of Southern African Black Theology is traced back to Bosch (1979: 220–221) to this story of Kimpa Vita.

vention in which the spirit of St Anthony took possession of her. She sold all her possessions and fiercely attacked the Roman Catholic Church. She forbad her followers to keep to the RCC's rituals and to possess symbolic instruments like the crucifixes. She taught that Christ appeared as a black man and that the apostles were black. She taught that Christ identifies himself with the Africans and with their suffering by the hands of the white colonial powers. She believed that Christ will restore the Congolese Kingdom and that he will create a paradise on earth. After a couple of years, Kimpa/Béatrice was arrested and burnt at the stake.

The similarity between Béatrice's message and that of Nongqawuse was that both were protest movements against white oppression.[8] In a very similar way the story of Nongqawuse resists the coercion of "missionary theology" that subdues the people and reveals an understanding of land that delves deep into the sacredness and identity of people (Saayman 1991). Nongqawuse's and Béatrice's stories share on many levels similarities, but the fundamental need of emancipation from the colonial powers, is central. This need is not symbolic, but physical, intimately connected to identity and land.

The Heart of Redness was first published in 2000 as a fictional work wherein Mda links the events of the 1850s in kwaXhosa (the land of Xhosa) with events in the late 1990s in the area known as the Transkei (called the Eastern Cape now). All these events are based on real happenings[9] and in both events (1850s and 2000s), the land is at stake for the Xhosa people. In the 1850s the Xhosa prophet Nongqawuse prophesised that "if the people killed all their cattle and set all their granaries alight, the spirits would rise from the dead and drive all the white people into the sea" (Mda 2000: 86–87). This prophecy split the amaXhosa into believers and unbelievers and led to devastating consequences for the entire nation. In the late 1990s plans were mooted to build a casino in kwaXhosa which promised to bring development, but also threatening to

[8] Béatrice's message became the message of Black Theology: both were protest movements against white oppression. The name Black Theology came later and found its first expression in the 1970s at a seminar on Black Theology at Roodepoort (1971) (Bosch 1979: 220–221).

[9] Mda explains in an interview about his work that "a lot of my work is informed by history. It is an interpretation of what occurred in the past into fiction. Imagination intervenes in the re-creation of that past as historical characters interact freely with fictional characters" (Mda 2018a: 96).

destroy amaXhosa heritage and land. This split the amaXhosa again into groups for development and those against it—mimicking and revitalising the original split of believers and unbelievers of the 1850s.

The prophecy of Nongqawuse is a historical fact. Mda says her prophecies "arose out of the spiritual and material anguish of the amaXhosa people" (2000: 283). The idea behind her prophecy was that a major sacrifice would encourage the ancestors to act on behalf of the amaXhosa and swept the white people into the sea so that they will not be able to over them (Mda 2000: 125). The majority of the amaXhosa became believers and they killed their cattle and burnt their crops. This left them with disease, starvation and (still) with the English colonialists. It made the amaXhosa a nearly distinct nation, pacified to such an extent that the British centralised their power and authority in the region. The prophecy had devastating and destructive consequences. The believers saw the unbelievers as traitors and even burnt their crops and houses, and killed their cattle: "What choice do we have? Kill the andGogotya! Destroy their crops! Kill their cattle! Burn their houses!" (Mda 2000: 123).[10]

Why would people do such a destructive thing to their land and to themselves? Mda encapsulates the underlying need of the amaXhosa to get rid of their colonisers, to get their land back, very well in the novel. The land is not just something they can let go of. It is deeply connected with who they are as amaXhosa. Mda tells for example of the "sacred waters of the Keiskamma River" (2000: 19), of the wild fig tree that knows all secrets "for it is directly linked to the ancestors ... who planted it more than hundred years ago" (2000: 40), of the stone piles at the crossroads where you add a stone "for protection of the ancestors for a safe journey" (2000: 121), and of "our rivers and our ocean" for those who belong there (2000: 231). The title of the novel refers to the redness of the ground—the red ochre which symbolises to not be civilised: "those who have not seen the light and who still smear themselves with red ochre" (2000: 61). The red ochre was applied by girls "on their bodies to beautify themselves" (2000: 90), but it got a negative connection within

[10] On page 129 Mda illustrate this clash between the believers and unbelievers very dramatically with one twin brother who burns down his twin brother's house and the confrontation between them.

the divide between believers and unbelievers as being “backwards”, about “African traditions” in contrast to “civilised people” (2000: 184). The heart of redness as the title suggest reflects on this centrality of African tradition and identity—with its strong connection to land and its redness—that is something positive (a celebration of the mystical or sacred connection of land with previous generations), but also as something negative: “The curse of redness!” (2000: 184) that became destructive with the huge following Nongqawuse had, and their deeds, according to Mda.

Mda’s novel helps one to understand that when the hermeneutics of land is determined by tradition and culture it can have very positive and negative results. Positively it contributes to value the land as sacred, respecting it, living in harmony with it—snakes are for example not killed because they are seen as lucky totems. Negatively it can however lead to the destruction of land and it potential life-giving capacity—e.g. with the killing of cattle, burning of fields and houses. The “curse of redness” is the destructive force that tradition can have over one understanding of land, and eventually how one relates to it.

Such a view of land, based on the dominance of tradition, is not restricted to the amaXhosa. There are many other examples of other nations and tribes that connect, value and relate to land predominantly and determinatively through their tradition, heritage and religion. The problem is that in many of these cases it is infused with colonial exploitation. Tradition and religion is used to justify control of the land and people for the enrichment of the coloniser. Interesting enough one hear in Mda’s novel the Englishman Dalton say: “This is my land. I belong here. It is the land of my forefathers” (2000: 160) and then later on to fellow Englishmen: “The Afrikaner is more reliable than your chaps. He belongs to the soil. He is of Africa. Even when he is unhappy with the present situation he will not go anywhere. He cannot go anywhere” (2000: 160). It is clear that tradition and racial stereotypes are used to justify colonisation. A critical ethic of land is important to rectify this colonial injustice.[11] In this case the story and prophecy of Nongqawuse is

[11] Mda will argue the injustice of racial stereotyping should also be addresses—see his “Justify the Enemy: Becoming Human in South Africa” (2018b: 30–40). Our focus is however on justice about land specifically.

a powerful discourse of resistance to beliefs and systems of control that enable the coloniser to take control of the wealth of the amaXhosa. We argue for a critical approach towards oppressive narratives must dismantle the colonial hermeneutics. To explore the impact of European culture on the views of land in Southern Africa we turn now to John Locke.

Culture, Tradition and Land in European Society: John Locke

Land, Ownership and Colonialism

The relationship between culture and land can also be seen in European culture and hermeneutics of land. European hermeneutics of land can be traced back to the work of John Locke who developed a functional understanding of land based on the role of labour. It has to be added immediately that this is not the only view of land in European societies. The obvious alternative is Marxism that follows a holistic and communitarian view of land. However, the prevalence of individualism and private ownership of property is associated with thinkers like Locke. His view of land that is also closely related to economics—land is used to produce goods for consumption and trade. Locke's functional perspective accentuates production and the optimal use of land that supports food security above tradition. The problem is that the optimal use of land usually goes hand in hand with science and technological developments that may be harmful to the environment. Another problem is that the presumption that vacant or land that is not used for production can be accessed by colonisers supports injustice.

The darker side of the functional view of land is the association between colonialism, modernism and capitalism. The principles envisioned by Locke seems to provide justification for taking control of the land of others. Mignolo (2007: 155) notes that "….the link between modernity and colonialism as the 'darker side' of modernity (a European narrative) or coloniality. Coloniality highlights the fact that modernity developed as a function of the engagement between European and non-European peoples, cultures and communities". In other words, the modern view (that severs the link between land and people) was the foundation for the creation of methods to control geographical spaces for the economic benefit of Europeans—'...hidden behind the rhetoric of modernity, human lives became expendable to the benefit of increasing wealth and such expendability was justified by the naturalisation of the racial ranking of human beings'" (Mignolo 2007: 157). This had direct impact on legislative processes on the private ownership of property.

Rathbone and Verhoef (2015) note that the 'darker side' of modernity and the perceived superiority of certain races as envisioned by Europeans is seen in international law and the notion of jus gentium (rights of people and nations) of Francisco de Vitoria (fifteenth century). According to this, European and non-Europeans are on the same level of humanity, but non-Europeans were 'sort of childish and needed guidance and protection' by Europeans (Mignolo 2007: 164) Thus there is a difference between Europeans and non-Europeans on an ontological and epistemological level that function as rational binaries that establishing a hierarchy of human beings. These binaries that function in colonial discourse can be in the legislation in South Africa during apartheid that legitimised forced removal and relocation of people based on race. It is also present in the novel of Mda that highlight the destructive aspect of the cattle killing, without viewing the importance of it as an act defiance and resistance that is the basis for restorative justice and land reform.

Today the influence of modernism can be seen in globalisation and deterritorialisation that has a major effect on the hermeneutics of land (Tomlinson 1999). Globalisation and urbanisation is the movement to construct standardised spaces for mainly functional reasons e.g. airport terminal buildings. Identity is open and not limited to a particular space or place. The global space is the main concern and accessibility across cultural differences. This movement can be viewed as a new form of cultural imperialism on the one hand and relativism on the other. Cultural imperialism is closely linked to the connection between modernism and Wester culture. Relativism focusses on the dislocation of the individual or community from a particular geographical space.

Although these views that can be traced to Locke and seems to support colonialism and globalisation it has also come under criticism. Locke's theory has come under scrutiny in terms of the logic of his hermeneutics of land as stated by Diedericks (2018). She notes that Day (1966: 212) rejects the idea of ownership of labour as irrational because labour is an activity and not something to be owned. Mautner (1982: 260) questioned the idea that the combination of labour and land is the basis for ownership—"*...if he were to take water from a well and throw that water in a lake, will all the water in the lake also be his?*" Another problem is the role of employees that labour on the land of the land owner. This creates a contradiction. The individualistic view of ownership has also received wide scrutiny from cultural criticist.

It is clear that Locke's hermeneutics of land is not without problems and that its possible support of colonialism is based on logic that is susceptible to critique. However, it does also offer a positive dimension to a critical ethic of land in the South African context and the question of the redistribution of land without compensation. This is specifically important in terms of the right to ownership of property and sustainable economics. The functional view of land advanced by Locke focusses on land from the perspective of production, economics and providing food security for the citizens of a country. This can be viewed as a European form of enclosed identity that accentuated the functional and economic aspect of land because the relationship between labour and land is the basis of ownership. Private ownership of property is an important aspect of European culture that underpins liberty. Economics is therefore linked to these functional hermeneutics because labour and production has the benefit of producing goods for trade.

From this perspective the land is a crucial aspect for the functioning of society. Therefore, private ownership of property like land must be protected. This is done by enshrining private ownership in law that highlights the juridical dimension of the hermeneutics of land. Although these views may be understood as European it does not mean it has no role to play in the South African context. As was the case with the story of Nongqawuse a more nuanced and in-depth exploration of Locke's hermeneutics of land is required in the development of a critical ethic of land. Conversely, Rathbone and Verhoef (2015) underlines that the decolonial strategy can be perceived as the "lighter side" of modernity because it is a perspective that emphasises the subject as the epistemological starting point who writes his/her own narrative and history.

Land and Sustainability

Locke made a distinction between common ownership and private ownership of property (Diedericks 2018). According to Locke, God gave the earth to all men [*sic*] in common and also the ability to use the earth to "....the advantage of their life and convenience" (Locke 1823: 115). Individual ownership is directly linked to labour. Labour is viewed as the most basic individual ownership—"property in his person" (1823: 116). Hence, each individual owns "...the labour of his body and work of his hands" (Locke 1823: 116). Locke (1823: 12) states that "a man [*sic*] owns whatever land he tills, plants, improves, cultivates, and can use the products of so much is his property". In this way a distinction is made between individual and common ownership. The strength of this hermeneutic of land is that culture challenges views of land that does not use this scarce resource optimally and may therefore endanger food security. This emphasises the focus that Locke placed on the needs of society and the flourishing of citizens. This focus on society is clear from the "provisions" that Locke included in his hermeneutics of land. These provisions include the following: spoliation; subsistence; and sufficiency.

Locke (1823: 17) notes that the *spoliation or the no-waste provision* focusses on "...use in a beneficial way before it spoils; anything beyond this is more than his share and belongs to others" because nothing was "made by God for man to spoil or destroy" (Locke 1823: 117). Therefore, the allocation of land must be based on the ability to cultivate the land. This principle is important because it limits waste as an offence against the common law of nature. Locke (1823: 120) states that when people "... gather so much into their possession that it perished without being properly used, they committed an offence against the common law of nature and is liable for punishment." The implication is that if land is vacant and not used it is to the detriment of society. This provision must be understood in conjunction with subsistence or care of others and sufficiency.

Further, at no time may land be used by individuals without consideration of others and charity because assisting with the survival of others is crucial for a healthy and sustainable society (Locke 1823: 115). To be cared for is also a basic social right of members of a society. This provision accentuates that narcissistic or excessive individualism is denounced by Locke. This can be seen in the sufficiency provision that highlights that that self-care is paramount because this individual responsibility alleviates strain on the resources of society to care for others (Locke 1823: 117).

The main aim of the provisions of Locke's hermeneutics of land is to highlight the socio-ethical aspect of his theory. Land is mainly at the service of social harmony and sustainability. The moment land is used for personal enrichment at the expense of other citizens it become an immoral practice. The annexation of land for the benefit of colonial exploits is in direct contradiction of Locke's theory. At the same time land redistribution that lead to famine or economic decay undermines the socio-ethical aspect of land as an important foundation of a flourishing society.

Critical Ethic of Land

A critical ethic of land is based on the premise that culture does impact on the hermeneutic of land; vice versa, geographical space does also impact on culture (e.g. the redness of the soil in Mda's novel). Although there is a relationship between land and culture that leads to diverse views on land (e.g. tradition in the case of Nongqawuse and functionality in the case of Locke); it is imperative that any hermeneutic of land must support a sustainable future. Therefore, a critical ethic of land is paramount. Such a critical ethics must accentuate responsibility and accountability in its execution because sustainability is not singular or neutral. Diverse views on sustainability are in many cases in a state of tension (e.g. the need for justice of the landless and functionality).

In the article of Lucas Ledwaba, *The land: SA's unifying and divisive issue* (2019), that reports on the land hearings held across the country in 2018, it is evident that people have an "unmatched love and connection to the land" (Ledwaba 2019: 15). People have "lived through the horrors of apartheid's land dispossession and displacement policies" and hoped that the first democratic elections will be "the return of the land" (Ledwaba 2019: 15). People were also "violated by big business in the form of mining companies" (Ledwaba 2019: 15). The problem is that people do not see eye to eye on the hermeneutics of land and this can sometimes end in emotional and violent outbursts causing more rifts between people. Like the suggestion by some participants in the hearings that redistribution of land will lead to food insecurity because "black people had no capacity to use and own land productively" is not only irresponsible, it is demeaning and offensive (Ledwaba 2019: 15).

The danger of reducing sustainability to singular views is that it can lead to the further polarisation and politicisation of the issue of land. For example, radical identity politics infused with populism of organisations like Black Land First (BLF) limits engagement between people and the ethics of responsibility and accountability. Reductionism can become a divisive and confrontational means that does not solve problems but rather increases polarity and instability without justice and social development. This can be seen for example in the exclusive racist rhetoric of the Nationalist Party during apartheid that left deep and painful scars in the South African society.

Responsibility and accountability embrace justice but within the parameters of social, economic and political stability and sustainability. Justice that leads to a society that falls apart and self-destructs will benefit no-one. Therefore, the debate concerning redistribution of land without compensation must provide dignity to people who are landless and communities that have been deprived of economic development due to the devastation of apartheid legislation. At the land hearings of 2018 a participant said "The biggest humiliation you can visit upon an African is to take away his land. You can't separate us from the land. We are one with it" (Ledwaba 2019: 15). However, when land is returned without compensation and the process starts to undermine the basic principles of ownership of property (by individuals and/or communities the negative impact on economic stability in the country will be neither responsible nor accountable.

A further, obvious implication of redistribution of land is food security. It is clear that where the food security of the country is compromised the process of redistribution cannot be regarded as responsible and/or accountable. This can become a sensitive issue because tradition is embedded in people's existential and historical roots (See the South African Court Case of Nkosi v Buhrmann). A respondent at the land hearings states regarding sacred sites: "All these sacred sites are vulnerable to the greed of men. How do you destroy a whole ecosystem to build a hotel" (Ledwaba 2019: 15)? The tension between tradition and economics remains emotional and possibly divisive. The imperative of responsible and accountable sustainability highlights that a compromise must be sought for justice to prevail and economic growth that supports employment and the eradication of poverty. Building a hotel to create employment in an impoverished community may be regarded as a responsible development. Alternatively, developing a mine that may have environmental consequences could be viewed as ecologically irresponsible and unsustainable. The damage to the land that mining may cause could take centuries to recover therefore robbing future communities from accessing this scares resource.

The question of land redistribution cannot be understood in isolation. Southern Africa is part of the global market economy that will simply fail if ownership becomes contentious. At the same time the fact of globalisation does not mean that Southern Africa has to become a victim of multinational companies or international funding organisations (e.g. International Monetary Fund, IMF). Responsibility and accountability have to be considered as a critical ethic in terms of international relations for sustainability. In other words, to further delay redistribution of land for solely economic reasons would be catastrophic to the stability and development of the country. Critical ethics of land goes beyond ownership as an economic principle. It is not a market driven ethic; it is rather a people driven process for the flourishing of society. Anything less would be crude reductions that only privileges political elites and the greedy. A farmer from KwaZulu-Natal states during the land hearings "...We are people of this land. God made us to look like the soil of this land because we belong to it. We were born to farm on our land and trade livestock among ourselves. Money was never our thing as Africans" (Ledwaba 2019: 15). The notion of private ownership become sacral if the land owns the person. And at the same time it means that the person has the responsibility to use this gift to the advancement of the community and sustainability for future generations.

A hermeneutics of land envisions a flourishing Southern Africa by highlighting sustainability and the ethics of responsibility and accountability. This entails that pressing issue like poverty, unemployment and economic inequality within a global market system has to be dealt with and this has to happen in conjunction with community specific issues like tradition, the sacredness of land, ecology and cultural identity.

Conclusion

In this chapter we argue that culture and geographical location have an impact on the hermeneutics of land. This relationship is complex and dynamic. This was seen in the example of the Nongqawuse and the role that tradition played in the seemingly senseless destruction of livestock. At the same time this can be seen as an act of resistance to white oppression. The other example is Locke's functional understanding of land that may lead to ecological damage through technology. It is also a perspective that focusses on food security and economic sustainability. These examples highlight the necessity of a critical ethic of land that is responsible and accountable. In other words, issues of justice, redistribution of land, political and social stability, as well as economic growth should be dealt with in the context of poverty, unemployment and economic inequality in a manner that lead to a flourishing society in the global context.

References

Bosch, D.J. 1979. Currents and Crosscurrents in South African Black Theology. In *Black Theology: A Documentary History, 1966–1979*, ed. G.S. Wilmore and J.H. Cone. New York: Orbis Books. Maryknoll.

Braidotti, R. 2011. *Nomadic Subjects. Embodiment and Sexual Difference in Contemporary Feminist Theory*. New York: Columbia University Press.

Day, J.P. 1966. Locke on Property. *The Philosophical Quarterly* 16 (64): 207–220.

Diedericks, G. 2018. *A Re-evaluation of Locke's Theory of Property within the South African Context.* Dissertation submitted at the North-West University, Potchefstroom Campus.

Hendricks, F., L. Ntsebeza, and K. Helliker, eds. 2013. *The Promise of Land. Undoing a Century of Dispossession in South Africa.* Jacana: Pretoria.

Jacobs, J.U., ed. 2018. *Justify the Enemy. Becoming Human in South Africa: Zakes Mdla.* Pietermaritzburg: University of KwaZulu-Natal Press.

Ledwaba, L. 2019. The Land: SA's Unifying and Divisive Issue. *Mail & Guardian*, January 4 to 10, 2019.

Locke, J. 1823. The Works of John Locke. A New Edition, Corrected. In Ten Volumes (5). London: Printed for Thomas Tegg; W. Sharpe and Son; G. Offor; G. and J. Robinson; J. Evans and Co. Accessed 15 April 2019. https://www.yorku.ca/comninel/courses/3025pdf/Locke.pdf

Mautner, T. 1982. Locke on Original Appropriation. *American Philosophical Quarterly* 19 (3): 259–270.

Mda, Z. 2000. *The Heart of Redness.* Oxford: Oxford University Press.

———. 2018a. Interview: Zakes Md in conversation with Michele Betty. In *Justify the Enemy. Becoming Human in South Africa: Zakes Mdla*, ed. J.U. Jacobs, 95–99. Pietermaritzburg: University of KwaZulu-Natal Press.

———. 2018b. Justify the Enemy: Becoming Human in South Africa. In *Justify the Enemy. Becoming Human in South Africa: Zakes Mdla*, ed. J.U. Jacobs, 30–40. Pietermaritzburg: University of KwaZulu-Natal Press.

———. 2018c. The Pink Mountain. In *Justify the Enemy. Becoming Human in South Africa: Zakes Mdla*, ed. J.U. Jacobs, 41–53. Pietermaritzburg: University of KwaZulu-Natal Press.

———. 2018d. What it means to be an African: Shifting identities in the South African Context. In *Justify the Enemy. Becoming Human in South Africa*: Zakes Mda, ed. J.U. Jacobs, 205–215. Pietermaritzburg: University of KwaZulu-Natal Press.

Mignolo, W. 2007. Coloniality and Modernity/Rationality. *Cultural Studies* 21 (2–3): 155–167.

Rathbone, M., and A.H. Verhoef. 2012. Violence, Liberation and the Legacy of Modernity: Towards a Theology of Peace. *Scriptura: International Journal of Bible, Religion and Theology in Southern Africa* 109: 67–81.

———. 2015. The Collusive Power of Modernism and Reductionism: The Need for Alternative Ontologies of Land in the Context of South African Land Redistribution. *Journal of Theology of Southern Africa* 151: 149–161.

Saayman, W. 1991. *Christian Mission in South Africa: Political and Ecumenical.* Pretoria: University of South Africa.

Said, E.W. 1994. *Culture and imperialism.* London: Vintage.

———. 1995. Orientalism. In *The Post-Colonial Studies Reader*, ed. B. Ashcroft, G. Griffiths, and H. Tiffin. London and New York: Routledge.

Tomlinson, J. 1999. *Globalization and Culture.* Cambridge: Polity Press.

Verhoef, A.H., and M. Rathbone. 2013. Economic Justice and Prophetic Discourse in the South African Context—Towards a Dialogical Mode of Discourse. *Journal of Theology for Southern Africa* 145: 92–109.

———. 2015. A Theologically Informed Ontology of Land in the Context of South African Land Redistribution. *Journal of Theology for Southern Africa* 152 (July): 156–170.

15

What Can Ubuntu Do? A Reflection on African Moral Theory in Light of Post-colonial Challenges

Motsamai Molefe and Nolubabalo Lulu Magam

Introduction

The post-colonial-and-apartheid South Africa has been thought to be one that requires redemption and salvation. The ideas of *redemption* and *salvation* typically represent Western religious modes of conceptualising the process of spiritual restoration and healing, but we use these terms to signify that some form of human social rectification is a moral and political necessity if a just society is the ideal being pursued (Tabensky 2008). Politicians and academicians are wont and quick to invoke the moral idea

M. Molefe (✉)
Centre for Leadership Ethics in Africa, University of Fort Hare, Alice, South Africa
e-mail: mmolefe@ufh.ac.za

N. L. Magam
Department International and Public Affairs, University of Kwa-Zulu Natal, Durban, South Africa
e-mail: magamn@ukzn.ac.za

E. Masitera (ed.), *Philosophical Perspectives on Land Reform in Southern Africa*,
https://doi.org/10.1007/978-3-030-49705-7_15

of ubuntu as apropos and sufficient to the task of thinking about a just society insofar as they hold the belief that this moral idea can help in the restoration of an African identity and dignity in the new South Africa (Tutu 1999; Shutte 2001; Mbeki 2005; Zuma 2008, 2012).

Ubuntu tends to be invoked in many discourses because it is believed to be morally capacious to deliver a robust conception of a society, which would naturally encapsulate the urgent necessity to redress the scourges of colonisation and apartheid in (South) Africa. Ubuntu is attractive to its proponents because it is purported to have two features: on the one hand, it offers an African moral perspective on issues; and, on the other, more importantly, it is believed to offer an under-explored morally plausible vision of a good society (Ramose 1999; Shutte 2001; Metz 2007). What makes matters difficult, however, is that there are competing conceptions of ubuntu in the literature, and they all offer differing visions of what might count as a robust conception of a society.[1]

In this chapter, we reflect on these debates about ubuntu as a moral theory, specifically, with regards to what ubuntu might theoretically avail to resolve some of the post-colonial moral-political problems. For the sake of focus, we will consider these debates regarding ubuntu ethics and what it can offer in the post-colonial (South) Africa, by specifically considering the case of the Marikana massacre, where 34 miners were shot and killed by the South African Police Service (SAPS) in August 2012.

We focus on this specific case for two major reasons. Firstly, we do so because Thaddeus Metz, one of the leading scholars of ubuntu, has invoked ubuntu to evaluate the response of the South African state to the Marikana massacre. He offers a relational interpretation of ubuntu to evaluate the response of the state, and then he suggests how a state informed by the moral resources inherent in the discourse should have reacted, as a remedy, to the Marikana rigmarole. This kind of appeal to ubuntu as a moral theory provides an opportunity to reflect on discourses on ubuntu in light of their implications for political theory. It also allows for a meaningful moral-theoretical debate about what ubuntu can do. Hence, in this chapter, we engage in a critical conversation with Metz's

[1] In no particular order, we distinguish four salient interpretations of Ubuntu. (1) Ubuntu construed in terms of critical humanism (Praeg 2014); (2) ubuntu construed in terms of *strict cosmopolitanism* (Etieyibo 2017); (3) ubuntu construed in terms of *harmonious* relationships; and (4) ubuntu construed in terms of *self-realisation* (Ramose 1999; Shutte 2001; Van Niekerk 2007).

account regarding a plausible conception of ubuntu ala what is to count as a plausible response to the post-colonial world, particularly with regards to responding and redressing past injustices.

The second reason involves recognising that the Marikana massacre presents an opportunity to ponder on the present socio-economic injustices as, to a large extent, vestiges and extensions of colonial-apartheid injustices, without in anyway suggesting that the current inadequacies of the current government have not exacerbated matters. Put simply, the Marikana massacre provides an opportunity to evaluate how ubuntu, at the very minimum, might offer us an ethical-political response to historical injustices, or a way to remedy these historical injustices. Or stated differently, we will be theoretically exploring a view of restorative justice embodied in the discourse of ubuntu, at least in the light of interpretation of it proffered here. We pursue questions of historical injustices largely because scholars of ubuntu have not reflected on how ubuntu may moral-theoretically address them.[2]

On his part, Metz reaches the following conclusion regarding the performance of the state towards the Marikana massacre: 'I conclude that the government by and large did not act ethically' (Metz 2017, 1). That is, Metz informed by ubuntu ethics finds that the executive branch of the state failed to manifest ubuntu in the way it handled the aftermath of the massacre. Metz's (2017, 2) interpretation of ubuntu leads to the view that the best response by the state would have involved setting up a

> ...certain form of reconciliation that I argue follows from ubuntu, would have required the government to abandon a commission of enquiry in favour of something more like South Africa's Truth and Reconciliation Commission (TRC), which offered amnesty to offenders in exchange for full disclosure about their misdeeds.

[2] For example, Augustine Shutte (2001) in his analysis of Ubuntu totally ignores historical injustices. He simply elucidates on what ubuntu can contribute to the new South Africa. I am aware that in another place, Metz (2011) does touch on historical injustices in relation to ubuntu. It is important to note, however, the aim of the chapter is not dedicated to this theme, but he does so to indicate that his theory is robust enough to accommodate these considerations. We hold the view that Metz's theory of Ubuntu is implausible (Molefe 2017; Metz 2011).

In light of Metz's account of ubuntu, the best that was required in the aftermath of Marikana massacre was some form of ubuntu inspired reconciliation; hence, the last part of the title of his article reads—'Where is reconciliation?' The most concerning facet of Metz's evaluation of the Marikana situation is that it overlooks historical injustices, or so we read his analysis.

This chapter engages in a critical conversation with Metz's interpretation of ubuntu in light of his evaluation of the state using ubuntu. The crucial point to emerge from our analysis is that, we need an interpretation of ubuntu that balances the forward looking facet (like reconciliation as proposed by Metz) in light of backward looking consideration (redressing historical injustices). In other words, whereas Metz's call for reconciliation is a move in the right direction, such a move should be done in way that is rivetted on the demands of (historical) justice. A more plausible response to the Marikana massacre should demand a forward looking solution that does not sweep under the carpet crucial historical injustices that require remedy. We are not sure that reconciliation, in and of itself, is sufficient as a remedy in situations like that of Marikana. Reconciliation, therefore, would not be the first and only solution to historical injustices. A thoroughgoing remedy is required to make reconciliation meaningful and robust in the imagination of a new South Africa. Here, we propose the minimum conditions required in the direction of redressing historical injustices for reconciliation to be meaningful.

To make our case for a more plausible interpretation of ubuntu, we will take a different interpretation of it than that defended by Metz.[3] We will take a *self-realisation* approach to ubuntu as a moral theory, which Metz understands to be the '... dominant interpretation' in the literature; though he favours a relational interpretation of it (Metz 2007, 331). We will say more about the self-realisation account below, for now we roughly justify why we prefer it. First, we prefer it for the very reason that it is a salient interpretation of ubuntu in the literature, which might be an indi-

[3] Here, we advocate the self-realisation approach. We do not have space to consider all four salient approaches to ubuntu, and their nuances. It suffices that we inform the reader that we consider the views of ubuntu defended under the rubric of *critical humanism* and *strict cosmopolitanism* to be implausible.

cation that it is much closer to African moral cultures than other competing understandings of it (Magesa 1997; Mokgoro 1998; Ramose 1999; Bujo 2001; Shutte 2001). Second, we are convinced that the *relational* interpretation of ubuntu as proffered by Metz is implausible in several crucial regards. Elsewhere, we have offered reasons why we take the relational interpretation of ubuntu to be less than plausible (Molefe 2017). To base morality entirely in some interpersonal relationships strikes us as implausible since it exaggerates the importance of social relationships (Molefe 2017).

Finally, we prefer the self-realisation interpretation of ubuntu because it does accommodate a backward-looking moral logic, which we deem important to approximate a meaningful moral-political analysis that we will argue is crucial to respond adequately to the Marikana situation. Here, we have in mind issues related to addressing historical injustices, which cannot be ignored if our intention involves properly understanding the incident at Marikana. We believe a self-realisation interpretation of ubuntu can give us cues and clues as to what might be essential precursors to a meaningful discourse about reconciliation, something we suspect is missing in Metz's analysis. The aim of this critique is not to dismiss Metz's contribution that prescribes reconciliation, rather it is to reveal that ubuntu has got a lot more to offer than the sole emphasis on reconciliation as is typical among some of its advocates (Tutu 1999; Oelofsen 2015; Metz 2017). Ubuntu can also and should demand *justice* for victims of historical injustices and continued economic oppressions; and, it ought to do so. Metz's silence on the material needs that prompted the protests of the miners, in the first place, is worth noting.

The major limitation of this article is that it does not offer a full defence of the self-realisation approach, it simply indicates the promise of this interpretation of ubuntu.[4] We leave it for another occasion to show why this account of ubuntu is better than other interpretations of ubuntu. At best, this chapter does not aim to be exhaustive. It seeks merely to highlight some putative strengths characteristic of the self-realisation interpretation of ubuntu that have not been theoretically explored.

---

[4] For defence of the self-realisation approach to ubuntu ethics, see the following articles and book by one of us where the self-realisation interpretation of ubuntu (Molefe 2018a, b, 2019b).

To make our case for the moral-theoretical potency of ubuntu to offer a much more robust recommendation for what the state should have done in response to the Marikana massacre, we structure this analysis as follows. In the first section, we begin by providing our understanding of Metz's interpretation of ubuntu and the solution it recommends. Second, we discuss our understanding of ubuntu *qua* the self-realisation approach. Next, we explicate how this interpretation of ubuntu embodies a relationship between morality and politics, with the aim of specifying what basic conditions must be part of remedying past injustices. We show how the political ought to be primary in the discourse of ubuntu, specifically, we stipulate that the *political* is constituted by two conditions, namely: (1) the *humanity* and (2) *common good* conditions, which capture the essence of the basic conditions that are prior and necessary for the very possibility of morality. We conclude by making general comments derived from this analysis of ubuntu to the Marikana situation. Specifically, we strongly suggest that historical redress must inform our desires and efforts towards reconciliation.

Metz on Ubuntu and Reconciliation

Those familiar with Metz's moral theory should be aware that he offers two differing or even competing interpretations of it. The first interpretation of ubuntu takes some interpersonal relationships to be the highest good. The second interpretation takes some property or capacity of an individual to be the highest good (Metz 2007, 2010; Molefe 2017). Thus, one moral theory is relational and the other is individualistic. We will start with the individualistic approach to morality since it is not relevant in this analysis.

'Individualism' is the idea that morality is best understood in terms of some feature(s) intrinsic to a human person like a soul, pleasure, dignity and so on (Behrens 2011, 11; Metz 2012, 396; Molefe 2019a). On Metz's part, what captures his individualistic moral theory is the human *capacity* for friendship, which is tantamount to his conception of dignity (Metz 2010, 2012). On this individualistic interpretation of ubuntu, the aim of morality is merely that we respect persons for merely possessing this capacity, which is definitive of that which renders them as beings of superlative value of bearers of dignity (Metz 2010, 2011).

Crucial to note, however, is the fact that Metz in the article under scrutiny relies on a *relational* interpretation of ubuntu, which construes morality *qua* principle of right actions entirely in terms of some interpersonal relationships, specifically, those character-ised by 'love', broadly understood, or, more precisely, 'friendship' (Metz 2007, 337; Metz 2017, 3–4). On this understanding of ubuntu, morality is purely understood in terms of honouring certain relationships; and, moral failure is a function of disrespecting or disregarding them, by behaving in ways that are divisive and cause discord (ibid.). Right actions are those that are characteristically friendly and wrong ones are characterised by division and discord (ibid.).

At the heart of Metz's moral theory is the high prize attached to the value of friendship. This relationship defines the entire gamut of morality. Metz has a fairly precise understanding of what is to count as friendship. It is composed of two distinct relationships, namely: *identity* and *solidarity*. Roughly, 'identity' amounts to 'sharing a way of life', where one understands their personal identity in corporate terms of 'We', rather than I; it involves shared goals/projects/aims and collaboration/coordination of projects to achieve such shared goals (Metz 2007). 'Solidarity' refers to basic psychological/behavioural dispositions towards others characterised by sympathy, empathy and care, where the agent is committed to securing the well-being of others for their own sakes (ibid.). On Metz's account, right actions are those that prize relationships of identity and solidarity; and, wrong ones are characterised by division and ill-will.

Given Metz's (2017, 7) version of ubuntu that posits that 'communal relationships are the highest good', Metz proceeds to proffer a specific conception of reconciliation grounded on it. With regards to this version of reconciliation, he states:

> I proffer the following statement of what social reconciliation is, by the ethic of ubuntu: a con-dition consequent to serious social conflict in which former opponents interact on a largely voluntary, transparent and trustworthy basis for the sake of compossible ends largely oriented towards doing what will help one another and in which at least public institutions,

> if not also substantial numbers of the public and the wrongdoers themselves, disavow grave wrong-doing that had been a part of the conflict. (2017, 10)

So, according to Metz, instead of the state setting up the Farlam commission it should have pursued a commission that would have facilitated achieving reconciliation. Some of the things that would accompany such a process of reconciliation would be the state supporting families extensively economically and culturally (treating them in ways that respect their culture during the grieving process). The commission should have given full amnesty to those who would disclose the truth and this would have created an environment for transparency and truth, which is important to facilitate healing and reconciliation.

Below, we turn to discuss an alternative version of ubuntu, which we believe can supplement the kind of reconciliation imagined by Metz's interpretation of ubuntu. This interpretation of ubuntu will also seek to include other crucial facets that Metz's analysis does not consider in its response to the Marikana massacre. For example, Metz is completely silent on the question of the living wage (R12, 500) that was the primary cause of the unprotected and protracted strike in Marikana that ultimately led to the massacre.

The Self-Realisation Approach to Ubuntu

The self-realisation approach to ubuntu takes moral *individualism* as its moral point of departure. That is, this interpretation of ubuntu ultimately values individuals realising their own true humanity as the goal of morality. This way of understanding of ubuntu tends to be captured in terms of the normative idea of personhood in the literature.[5] This idea of *personhood* is taken from the maxim that captures the essence of ubuntu as a

[5] We advise the reader to note that there are scholars of African ethics, like Menkiti, Wiredu and Gyekye, who invoke the idea of personhood, but never use the term ubuntu. We assume that the idea of ubuntu and personhood have the same moral content at least as used by African scholars. We say so precisely because at the heart of the idea of ubuntu is the idea of personhood (Molefe 2019b).

moral theory—'a person is a *person* through others'. The first instance of a person, in this maxim, simply refers to a human being; and, the second one refers to what a human being can become morally speaking. In other words, the first instance of person-hood is ontological (human being); and, the second is normative capturing a morally excellent human being, which represents moral achievements of the agent.[6] Ubuntu understood in this self-realisation frame posits character development or perfection of some facets of human nature as the goal of morality (Gyekye 2010; Ikuenobe 2016). We believe Menkiti (1984, 172) had this way of thinking about ethics when he opined:

> For personhood is something which has to be achieved, and is not given simply because one is born of human seed. This is perhaps the burden of the distinction which Placide Tempels' native informants saw fit to emphasize to him—i.e., the distinction between a muntu mutupu (a man of middling importance) and *muntu mukulumpe* (a powerful man, a man with a great deal of force). Because the word "muntu" includes an idea of excellence.

Above, Menkiti draws a distinction between merely being human, being born of the human seed, and being a *person* (muntu), one characterised by moral excellence. In the same article, he talks of personhood as referring to a human being who has, by way of acquisition, 'inbuilt excellencies' or one that is 'marked by a widened ethical ... maturity' (1984, 173 and 176). This way of understanding of African ethics is endorsed by other influential African scholars. For example, Kwame Gyekye (2010), in an encyclopaedic article dedicated to 'African ethics', notes: 'African ethics is, thus, a character-based ethics that maintains that the quality of the individual's character is most fundamental in our moral life'. Kevin Behrens also equally interprets the idea of personhood to refer to a morally virtuous agent (2013, 114; see, Dzobo 1992; Gyekye 1992; Wiredu 1992, 2004, 2009; Shutte 2001; Ikuenobe 2006; Masolo 2010; Molefe 2017).

[6] This point corroborates footnote 4.

So, on this interpretation of ubuntu, morality is understood in terms of the agent realising ideals associated with nature [humanity], which is typically understood in terms of a virtuous character or the 'practice of virtue' (Gyekye 1992, 114). Different lists of virtues characteristic of ubuntu or personhood are mentioned by scholars of African ethical thought. Tutu (1999, 35), for example, mentions the following … 'Hey, so-and-so has ubuntu.' Then you are generous, you are hospitable, you are friendly and caring and com-passionate'. Mokgoro (1998, 3) claims: 'The meaning of the concept however, becomes much clearer when its social value is highlighted. Group solidarity, conformity, com-passion, respect, human dignity, humanistic orientation and collective unity have, among others been defined as key social values of ubuntu'. Gyekye (1997, 109) also makes the following remark: ' … ideal and moral virtues can be said to include generosity, kindness, compassion, benevolence, respect and concern for others'. One of the striking features of these virtues is that they are purely *relational*, i.e. they are those that throw one into relationships with others. In other words, these are virtues that construe African ethics, as, in some sense, envisaging an other-regarding morality.

The characterisation of this ethical theory as self-realising and, at the same time, as other-regarding might suggest a tension. To say ubuntu is a *self*-realising moral theory implies that its chief concern and goal is the self, or, it is primarily a self-regarding morality; but, then how is it also simultaneously touted as an *other*-regarding in its orientation. This seeming tension is defeasible by remembering the maxim that 'a person is a person *through other persons*'. In other words, concretely, this ubuntu maxim can be construed to mean that the person can only learn to be kind, loving, caring, friendly and so on—achieve a virtuous character—in the reality of being embedded in relationships where the person developing these virtues. It is in the lived reality with others that I can realise *my* true or genuine (moral) self (Metz 2010, 83). The insight here is that we need to draw a distinction between the *goal* posited by ubuntu, which is intrinsically intrapersonal insofar as it pertains to personal perfection; and, the means it prescribes which are communitarian, insofar as they posit some interpersonal relationships as decisive means to achieve this goal (Tshivhase 2013; Molefe 2017, 2019a).

The goal posited by ubuntu is for the agent to realise her true self, which is the self-regarding facet of this moral theory. The goal is agent-centred insofar as it concerns the agent achieving a sound character. The means, however, for achieving such a moral end requires the agent to engage with others in relationships. Shutte's (2001, 14) comment in this regard is informative:

> The moral life is seen as a process of personal growth ... Our deepest moral obligation is to become more fully human. And this means entering more and more deeply into community with others. So although the goal is personal fulfilment, selfishness is excluded.

The goal of morality is personal growth or to become fully human, i.e. to achieve a character characterised inter alia by kindness, friendliness, compassion and so on. To achieve personhood requires us to enter deeply into relationships with others in the community.[7] In other words, moral perfection requires a community of engagement and practice. It is in this community of engagement and practice that one can realise their true morality; and within this community, one recognises a truck of duties which she owes to others, which, whose fulfilment, is crucial for her moral development (Gyekye 2004). Put differently, the self-realisation approach to ubuntu is dialogical insofar as it marries the goal to self-perfect with our duties to others; hence, 'I am [self-regarding duty to perfect oneself] because we are [through other-regarding duties]' (Mbiti 1969).

Below, we proceed to consider the implications of the self-realisation interpretation of ubuntu concerning historical injustices, which, for convenience, we capture in terms of rectification justice, and will subsequently indicate how rectification justice figures into the Marikana issue.

[7] This way of understanding ubuntu suggests an egoistic reading, whereby the duty for personal perfection is entirely left in the hands of the agent.

Ubuntu, Politics and Morality

If ubuntu is to be a reality in the post-colonial-and-apartheid Africa then we must seriously reflect on the social-political conditions that are necessary for its realisation. In other words, it would be a moral-political disservice for ubuntu, as an ethical theory, to ignore crucial conditions it requires for a human life to be able to enter into the moral domain. Thus, it is one thing to talk of the values that ubuntu prescribes as the basis of a good life and a just society; and, quite another to go a step further to imagine the conditions ubuntu imagines as the basis for the very possibility of such a good life or a just society in the first place. The tendency in the literature is to focus on the values it espouses and prescribes, and to ignore the political conditions it requires for such values to take root and effect in individuals' lives.

Put more concretely, the self-realisation interpretation of ubuntu posits the achievement of a sound character as the goal of morality. It, therefore, becomes a necessity that we reflect on what (structural) conditions must prevail for this moral goal to be possible. The task becomes doubly heavy on us when we have to include historical injustices in our discussion of the requisite structural conditions for the possibility of ubuntu. If ubuntu is to be possible in the post-colonial South Africa, it is important, therefore, that we analyse how to deal with historical obstacles that made ubuntu almost impossible, and all this with the aim of specifying the conditions for the possibility of ubuntu. It is only when we have identified obstacles imposed by historical injustices and we have also specified the general conditions required for the possibility of ubuntu that the discourse on reconciliation will be meaningful. Below, we consider the relationship between ubuntu (personhood) and politics.

To judge someone to have achieved ubuntu (personhood) is to be engaged in a moral evaluation, which presupposes certain facts about history and politics. It is a 'moral' evaluation insofar as one is passing judgements about the quality of the character of the agent insofar as she manifests virtues like care, generosity and so on (Tutu 1999). This moral judgement, however, is rivetted in a particular engagement with the agent's *historical* conduct. The one morally evaluating the conduct of the agent must have access to the *history* of the agent for her to be able to reach the conclusions regarding whether they have achieved or failed at personhood [to have ubuntu]. Therefore, one must, to some extent, have the record of the performance of agent and in light of that record make the moral determination of moral triumph or failure.

The importance of the *historical record* of the *lived experience* of the agent is therefore crucial in the discourse of ubuntu. It is for this reason that Menkiti (2004, 326) speaks of morality in terms of a 'journey of the individual toward personhood'. Morality is conceived as a journey of the individual from merely being human to being a moral exemplar. The achievement of personhood is captured in terms of the analogy of a *journey* precisely because it takes time to develop a virtuous character (see, Wiredu 2009, 15). Menkiti (2004, 325, authors' emphasis) captures this facet of time required to achieve personhood: 'the thinking here is that in the normal process of growth and maturation, the heart does grow increasingly wiser, morally speaking. *But it all takes time,* and there are no short cuts … '.

In the same passage, Menkiti (2004, 325–326) also notes:

> The reason for this is that morality and the maturation of the human person are so intimately bound up that a still evolving specimen of the person, *lacking a full record in the area of lived experience*, would be hard-pressed to present the sort of personal history needed for an elevation into the status of a moral exemplar.

The point is that it takes time to achieve personhood. To say that one has achieved personhood, it is to make a judgement about how the agent in the unfolding of time and all its vicissitudes the agent has been able to consistently learn and practice virtue, which ultimately led to the acquisition of a sound character. In light of the above, it is crucial to note that the idea of personhood is one that tracks the agent's performance over the unfolding of time.

The significance of emphasising the dimension of history is to flag the point that personhood is not an event. Rather, it is a long process of moral practice where the agent is caught up in the activity of producing a rounded and sound character. The moral and historical facets of personhood also presuppose the *political*. The *political* refers to the prior basic conditions that must hold for ubuntu or talk of personhood to be possible. It is *political* insofar as it stipulates certain basic conditions of justice for the judgement that one is a person to be possible and plausible. Thus, if one was to create a world that would render the achievement of personhood impossible, it would be unjust and unfair to judge agents under such circumstances on the basis of ubuntu. Judgements rivetted on ubuntu are political in the first instance insofar as they require, for them to be meaningful and plausible, certain basic conditions to prevail (Praeg 2014). Two such political conditions tend to be associated with the discourse on ubuntu in the literature. The first condition involves issues pertaining to the very humanity of moral agents. The issue here is the *capacity* possessed by human beings, by which we can expect them to be able to practice virtue and produce virtuous characters. First, the ability/capacity that qualify every human being as a moral agent must never be brought to question or be tampered with. With regards to the first condition, Gyekye notes (1992, 113): 'Every individual is *capable* of becoming a person in as much as he has capacity for virtue—for performing morally right actions—and should be treated (at least potentially) as a morally responsible agent'.

For us, Gyekye captures the equal humanity condition. The equal humanity condition specifies ontological facts that qualify human beings as bearers of superlative value [dignity]. It is in virtue of possessing the capacity for virtue that each individual is regarded as equal to every other irrespective of their class or race. This talk of equal humanity condition is tantamount to Stephen Darwall's (1977) exposition of *recognition respect*, whereby the moral patient is respected merely because she possesses the relevant ontological features. This talk of equal humanity condition captured in terms of recognition respect, embodies a view of moral status or dignity suggested in the discourse of ubuntu, where we are required to respect all human beings merely because they have the ability to pursue and achieve ubuntu (Toscano 2011; Molefe 2018a). The equality of individuals is secured because they are respected because they possess the relevant ontological feature.

The second condition refers to the basket of basic needs that every human being requires to be able to lead an ordinary or even a flourishing human life.[8] Generally, this condition in Afro-communitarian moral-political thought is captured in terms of the notion of the common good (Gyekye 1992, 2004; Wiredu 1992). The idea of the *common good* is usually captured by appeal to the Siamese crocodile with two heads and one stomach. Gyekye (2010) comments thus on this moral imagery:

> The part of the motif relevant to moral thought is the single stomach … The common stomach … *indicates that at least the basic interests of all the members of the community are identical.* It can therefore be interpreted to be symbolizing … the good of all the individuals within a society.

The idea of the common good is predicated on the idea that humanity is a property shared in common by all human beings (see, Gyekye 2004, 2010). This idea of the common good presupposes that there are certain basic needs/goods that are necessary for a human life to be possible (Gyekye 2004). The idea of the common good insists that there are core interests whose fulfilment is the basic requirement for all humanity; otherwise, life would be handicapped or unfortunate. It is for this reason that in another place, Gyekye (1997, 67) refers to the common goods as 'human goods'. These basic goods cover material, social and economic conditions necessary for a human life to be possible. We call this the *common good* condition. This condition is crucial because it is reflective of the communitarian orientation of African ethics, which emphasises commonalities among human beings with regards to certain basic needs.

It is these two conditions that capture the basic political foundation that informs the possibility for moral agents to be able to self-realise or to achieve personhood. What is crucial to note about apartheid and colonisation is that they disrupted these very foundational political considerations for personhood to be possible. Both processes involved first, the denial of the humanity of African people and secondly, the removal of the common goods necessary for a human life to be possible. In a crucial way,

---

[8] I am here (content) merely to sign the blank cheque that there must a set of social and political conditions in place that are necessary for a possibility for a human (moral) life, i.e. certain basic conditions and goods are necessary for a human life. It is not necessary that to specify them to make an argument here. The point however here is to point out that colonisation and apartheid did not provide such basic conditions.

the great injustice committed against African people was their removal from the possibility of morality itself. To deny human beings these two conditions specified above is tantamount to deny or even remove them from the domain of morality. The possibility of the practice of morality depends on the robust political foundations. To disrupt the political conditions is to render the moral (almost) impossible, and to lay the foundation for rampant injustices against the possibility of a robust human life.

Here we anticipate the argument that one's moral development happens in *whatever* social circumstances one might be in. The force of this objection is that we cannot make morality to be dependent on certain favourable social circumstances. Well, we are sympathetic to this kind of argument insofar as it simply brings to our attention that we are living in the real world, which is far from ideal. It further challenges agents not to wait for favourable circumstances before they discharge their moral duties. A response to this kind of concern is that we buy into the idea of moral luck by Thomas Nagel (1979). Roughly, the idea of moral luck captures the intuition that moral conduct and responsibility can only be attributed or expected of individuals supposing that external circumstances are not so rough that they render morality impossible. It is (sometimes true) that people can make their lives what they want them to be in roughly almost any circumstance, but there are other circumstances like slavery/colonisation/apartheid that should be understood plainly in terms of moral (social) bad luck. For us, colonisation and apartheid amounts to such conditions of *bad luck*, at least for the majority of the people in such situation. It strikes as bizarre to expect Jewish people to be moral exemplars in circumstances like that of the holocaust.

To further clarify our response to this objection, consider the following example. In South Africa we tend to find students living in abject poverty and social deprivation, but some of them produce best academic results. This is truly impressive, but we should not learn the wrong lesson from this situation. The lesson is not that we must make life even more difficult so that we should get some of the best results. Rather, the lesson is how much more would be of benefit to society when these talented young people were given the opportunities they deserve, so they can best exemplify their talents. Further, we should equally bemoan the many that were so burdened by obnoxious circumstances that they could not make it academically, and they are many. The challenge is: a just society would want to level the playing field so that success is a possibility for all.

It is in light of these three facets, namely politics, history and morality, that the idea of (rectification) justice, becomes the plank over which issues of reconciliation gain their relevance. The violation of the humanity of African people must be corrected and the dignity of their humanity *qua* capacity for virtue must be respected. The removal of socio-political and economic conditions required for a human life to be possible must be corrected. Rectification justice matters, at the very least, because it is aiming at putting African people, among others, at the position they should be in if ubuntu is to be possible at all for them.

Hence, there must be a deep investigation into the past (injustices) so we can correct or even remove all socio-political technologies (obstacles) that were put in place to make a human life impossible for African peoples in the post-colonial world. The greatest challenge and goal of rectification justice is to re-insert African people into the realm of morality, where they can freely and fully exercise their humanity. So, central to the idea of personhood (the project of morality) with regards to rectification justice is a call to correct the past injustices (and their extensions into the post-colonial Africa) by putting in place the political conditions (the equal humanity and the common good conditions), which are absolutely crucial for the possibility of morality in the first place. It is for this reason that we strongly recommend that the Marikana massacre should be understood in light of historical injustices, and not just as a post-apartheid situation.

Personhood, Rectification Justice and Marikana

Whilst it makes sense why Metz would prize reconciliation as something that government should have done as the best response to the Marikana massacre, to offer reconciliation in and of itself does not address the deep historical injustices that create situations like Marikana in the post-apartheid South Africa. It is crucial to take note of the historical factors underpinning the Marikana situation. It is also important to remember that African peoples were first dispossessed of their lands, and were concentrated in limited and generally arid land. This dispossession of land laid an important foundation for economic injustices that have since characterised African peoples in South Africa.

Subsequent to the dispossession of land, African people were foisted into the money economy. By introducing hut taxes, black people were forced to go work so they can pay the newly imposed economic burdens to run a home. The new mining industry required high volumes of cheap labour, and the mines made huge profits. The central source of these profits were based on the fact that black people were suppliers of cheap labour (Ramose 2003). The Marikana strike for a living wage of R12,500 in the new South Africa, makes sense when understood in the backdrop of this rough/short history of exploitation of black miners. The mining industry has a long history of labour exploitation in South Africa.

At the heart of the strike that led to the massacre at Marikana is this underpinning economic injustice that begun in the colonial period and continued both under the apartheid regime and the so-called *new* South Africa. The legally unprotected strike in Marikana emerges as an outcry for a living wage by the workers of the mine. This strike could be understood as an attempt to interrupt the economic injustices of cheap black labour that have continued to be a feature of the post-apartheid South Africa. These miners were also raising issues pertaining to their housing conditions in the mine. Their housing was not humane at all. Put simply, the cry of the miners was one that cannot be read as simply a phenomena of post-apartheid, but a continued legacy of erstwhile injustices. It represents the continued struggle of the African people, largely, for emancipation in the economic front. We should also keep in mind that the oppression of colonisation and that of apartheid was a totalising one, which also encompassed economic exclusions of black people. So, the emergence of Marikana massacre requires that we truly look into how we can address the historical injustices meted to miners in places like Marikana, and many others, where the legacies of cheap labour are still continuing.

In this light, Metz's assertion that 'I do not consider what precisely happened at Mari-kana, or what caused those events' is unfortunate because it does not correctly locate Marikana as part of the continued historical extensions of the socio-economic oppressions that Marikana should be understood within. These economic issues, in our understanding of ubuntu, have serious implications for the very possibility of realising a true humanity. If we are correct that Marikana should be understood in light of these social, economic and material injustices, then it occurs to us that the first responsibility of the state may not be to effect reconciliation particularly if it is interested in a genuine reconciliation.

We do not mean to deny the importance of reconciliation, we are just not convinced by Metz's suggestion that it should be the solution for resolving the Marikana issue. In the very first instance, it appears to me the state should think seriously and broadly about creating socio-political-and-economic conditions conducive for human life to be possible for miners and the families of the killed victims of the police. The serious and broad moral responsibility to create, on the part of the state, real possibilities for humanity ought to involve addressing the historical injustices that create situations like Marikana. The phenomena of cheap black labour violates the equal humanity and the common good conditions of ubuntu *qua* the self-realisation theory. Meaningful employment must affirm the humanity of the workers, and not exploit them. The conditions of employment must be characteristically decent and humane, and the remuneration must be such that it makes life possible, and not pauperise workers.

We are not blind to the fact that addressing historical injustices is a complex issue, but that should not give us a license to wish away historical injustices by a hasty call for 'recon-ciliation'. Ubuntu would be rendered unjust if it will push for reconciliation by avoiding to redress past injustices. The illusion that has characterised those who advocate for recon-ciliation, and we are not suggesting that Metz is part of this group, is to forget that what alienated, oppressed and marginalised people in South Africa was not just the ideology of racism, but the ideology of apartheid had massively negative social and economic implications for the lives of Africans. One of the failures of the post-apartheid state has been to imagine a robust society that enables human beings *en toto* to self-realise, by extending the provisions of the two conditions suggested above. It is not convinced that reconciliation in and of itself can deliver this required environment for agents to be able to self-realise.

At the heart of this submission, as a prerequisite to a meaningful talk of reconciliation, is the demand for equalising socio-economic conditions both for the victims and perpetrators that at the point of reconciliation we have equals dialoguing about forgiveness, healing, peace and a better future for all. How do we make sure that the humanity of the workers at Marikana (and everywhere else) is truly and fully recognised and respected? How do we make sure that the government itself can be trusted as a stakeholder interested in creating conditions for freedom, equality, dignity and rights? Therefore, we submit that we should expect much from the government if ubuntu, as we understand it, is to be true. The government must set itself to task of creating a world where humanity is possible, a process that will require rectification justice and reconstruction. Specifically with regards to Marikana, the practice of cheap labour as a feature of our economic practices must be systematically extirpated. Only when we have somewhat addressed these socio-economic injustices can we talk of reconciliation among social equals.

Conclusion

We believe that it is crucial that we imagine a discourse of ubuntu that is not placated by the status quo and the dominant ideologies of neoliberalism. If ubuntu is to serve as a robust and plausible moral theory then it must critically position itself as an emancipatory discourse in the search for freedom and dignity of peoples below the Sahara, and world over (Praeg2014). The position advocated here re-imagines the moral in light of the political. It stipulates the political as primary if the moral is to be possible at all. This means, the political embodies the minimum standards of justice if ubuntu is to be a plausible project at all for individuals. These basic political conditions, captured in terms of the equal humanity and common good conditions, are to be a precursor to a meaningful talk of reconciliation.

We leave it for another occasion to elaborate on some of what is to count as the content of the common good conditions. It suffices for now to note that some basket of basic needs is necessary for humanity to be possible. The task of the post-colonial state is the avail these conditions to all South Africans.

References

Behrens, K. (2011). African Philosophy, Thought and Practice and Their Contribution to Environmental Ethics. Johannesburg: University of Johannesburg.

Behrens, K. (2013). Two 'Normative' Conceptions of Personhood. Quest, 25, 103–119.

Bujo, B. 2001. *Foundations of an African Ethic: Beyond the Universal Claims of Western Morality*. New York: The Crossroad Publishing Company.

Darwall, S. 1977. Two Kinds of Respect. *Ethics* 88 (1): 36–49. https://doi.org/10.1086/292054.

Dzobo, K. 1992. Values in a Changing Society: Man, Ancestors and God. In *Person and Community: Ghanaian Philosophical Studies*, ed. K. Gyekye and K. Wiredu, vol. 1, 223–242. Washington, DC: Council for Research in Values and Philosophy.

Etieyibo, E. 2017. Ubuntu, Cosmopolitanism, and Distribution of Natural Resources. *Philosophical Papers* 46 (1): 139–162.

Gyekye, K. 1992. Person and Community in African Thought. In *Person and Community: Ghanaian Philosophical Studies*, ed. K. Gyekye and K. Wiredu, vol. 1, 101–122. Washington, DC: Council for Research in Values and Philosophy.

———. 1997. *Tradition and Modernity: Philosophical Reflections on the African Experience*. New York: Oxford University Press.

———. 2004. Beyond Cultures: Perceiving a Common Humanity. *Ghanaian Philosophical Studies. Accra: The Ghana Academy of Arts and Sciences.*

———. 2010. African Ethics. In *The Stanford Encyclopaedia of Philosophy*, ed. N.E. Zalta. Accessed 16 January 2013. http://plato.stanford.edu/archives/fall2011/entries/african-ethics.

Ikuenobe, P. 2006. The Idea of Personhood in Chinua Achebe's 'Things Fall Apart'. *Philosophia Africana* 9: 117–131.

———. 2016. Good and Beautiful: A Moral-Aesthetic View of Personhood in African Communal Traditions. *Essays in Philosophy* 17 (1): 125–163. https://doi.org/10.7710/1526-0569.1546.

Magesa, L. 1997. *African Religion: The Moral Traditions of Abundant Life*. New York: Orbis Books.

Masolo, D. 2010. *Self and Community in a Changing World*. Indianapolis: Indiana University Press.

Mbeki, T. 2005. Address of the President of South Africa, Thabo Mbeki, on the Occasion of the Heritage Day Celebrations, Taung, North West Province. September 24. Accessed 23 January 2016. http://www.thepresidency.gov.za/pebble.asp?relid=3157.

Mbiti, J. 1969. *African Religions and Philosophy*. New York: Doubleday.

Menkiti, I. 1984. Person and Community in African Traditional Thought. In *African Philosophy: An Introduction*, ed. R.A. Wright, 171–181. Lanham: University Press of America.

———. 2004. On the Normative Conception of a Person. In *Companion to African Philosophy*, ed. K. Wiredu, 324–331. Oxford: Blackwell Publishing.

Metz, T. 2007. Ubuntu as a Moral Theory: Reply to Four Critics. *South African Journal of Philosophy* 26: 369–387.

———. 2010. Human Dignity, Capital Punishment and an African Moral Theory: Toward a New Philosophy of Human Rights. *Journal of Human Rights* 9: 81–99.

———. 2011. Ubuntu as a Moral Theory and Human Rights in South Africa. *African Human Rights Law Journal* 11: 532–559.

———. 2012. An African Theory of Moral Status: A Relational Alternative to Individualism and Holism. *Ethical Theory and Moral Practice: An International Forum* 15: 387–402.

———. 2017. An Ubuntu-Based Evaluation of the South African State's Responses to Marikana: Where's the Reconciliation? *Politikon: South African Journal of Political Studies* 44 (2): 287–303.

Mokgoro, Y. 1998. Ubuntu and the Law in South Africa. *Potchefstroom Electronic Law Journal* 1: 1–11.

Molefe, M. 2017. Relational Ethics and Partiality: A Critique of Thad Metz's. *Towards an African Moral Theory* 64: 53–76.

———. 2018a. Personhood and Rights in an African Tradition. *Politikon* 45: 217–231.

———. 2018b. Personhood and Partialism in African Philosophy. *African Studies* 78 (3): 309–323.

———. 2019a. Solving the Conundrum of African Philosophy Through Personhood: The Individual or Community? *Journal of Value Inquiry*. https://doi.org/10.1007/s10790-019-09683-8.

———. 2019b. *An African Philosophy of Personhood, Morality and Politics*. New York: Palgrave Macmillan.

Nagel, T. 1979. Moral Luck. In *Thomas Nagel, Mortal Questions*, 24–38. Cambridge: Cambridge University Press.

Oelofsen, R. 2015. Afro-communitarian Forgiveness and the Concept of Reconciliation. *South African Journal of Philosophy* 34 (3): 368–378.

Praeg, L. 2014. *A Report on Ubuntu*. Pietermaritzburg: University of KwaZulu of Press.

Ramose, M. 1999. *African Philosophy Through Ubuntu*. Harare: Mond Books.

Ramose, M.B. 2003. I Doubt, Therefore African Philosophy Exists. *South African Journal of Philosophy* 22 (2): 113–127.

Shutte, A. 2001. *Ubuntu: An Ethic for a New South Africa*. Pietermaritzburg: Cluster Publications.

Tabensky, P.A. 2008. The Postcolonial Heart of African Philosophy. *South African Journal of Philosophy* 27: 285–295.

Toscano, M. 2011. Human Dignity as High Moral Status. *The Ethics Forum* 6: 4–25.

Tshivhase, M. 2013. Personhood: Social Approval or a Unique Identity? *Quest: An African Journal of Philosophy* 25: 119–140.

Tutu, D. 1999. *No Future without Forgiveness*. New York: Random House.

Van Niekerk, J. 2007. In Defence of an Autocentric Account of Ubuntu. *South African Journal of Philosophy* 26: 364–368.

Wiredu, K. 1992. Moral Foundations of an African Culture. In *Person and Community: Ghanaian Philosophical Studies*, ed. K. Wiredu and K. Gyekye, vol. 1, 192–206. Washington, DC: The Council for Research in Values and Philosophy.

———. 2004. Introduction: African Philosophy in our Time (pp. 1–27). Companion to African Philosophy. Oxford: Blackwell.

———. 2009. An Oral Philosophy of Personhood: Comments on Philosophy and Orality. *Research in African Literatures* 40: 8–18.

Zuma, J. 2008. Address by ANC President Jacob Zuma to the ANC Presidential Religious Summit. November 27. Accessed 23 January 2016. http://www.anc.org.za/show.php?id=3790.

———. 2012. Message by President Jacob Zuma on Reconciliation Day. December 16. Accessed 23 January 2016. http://www.sabc.co.za/news/a/6cbbc5804dd3e958b190bbb7074a8d3f/Use-national-daysto-embrace-ubuntu:-Zuma-20121612.

16

Appraising Zimbabwe's Land Reform Programme in the Context of *Unhu/Ubuntu*: Towards an Appropriate Ethical-Moral Ideology on Land Distribution in Sub-Saharan Africa

Rodwell Kumbirai Wuta

Introduction

The discourse on land distribution-redistribution in Zimbabwe spans from the onset of colonialism to the present. The Occidental colonialists occasioned a land distribution pattern which was skewed in their favour. Such an arrangement could be expected of the colonialists since they were racists of a Hegelian making whose philosophy of life was quite antithetical to that of *Unhu/Ubuntu*. Thus, through land expropriation and apportionment in colonial Zimbabwe, Africans were dispossessed of their ancestral land which was and still is the fountain of all hopes that make life worth living. Africans were consequently marginalised socially, politically and economically. Hence, the advent of Zimbabwe's political independence in 1980 begot optimism for a fairer distribution of land consistent with the

R. K. Wuta (✉)
Department of Educational Foundations, Great Zimbabwe University, Masvingo, Zimbabwe

E. Masitera (ed.), *Philosophical Perspectives on Land Reform in Southern Africa*,
https://doi.org/10.1007/978-3-030-49705-7_16

philosophy of *Unhu/Ubuntu* and the loud-mouthed policy of reconciliation. However, this did not materialise as anticipated. Therefore, it is against this background that the topical discourse on Zimbabwe's land redistribution regime is undertaken, perpetuated and immortalised.

Problematising Land Redistribution in Zimbabwe in the Context of *Unhu/Ubuntu*

The problem engaged in this reflection is the absence of a sustainable solution to the capricious atmosphere surrounding land distribution-redistribution in Zimbabwe. This volatile situation is evidenced by persistent contestations and petitioning by the dispossessed former European settler farmers against the Government of Zimbabwe. Thus:

> There are some farmers who still contest the legitimacy of the government takeover of 'their' farms. There are pending cases within the Zimbabwean High Court and even with the Southern Africa tribunal. (Masitera 2017: 271)

Here, particular reference is made to the Mike Campbell et al versus Republic of Zimbabwe case of 2007 (Masitera 2017: 271). A scenario of this nature demonstrates that Zimbabwe's land reform was undertaken haphazardly. Hence, the entire land redistribution regime created politico-socio-economic challenges for Zimbabwe. This calls for a further philosophical reflection with a view to coming up with an ethical-moral ideology deemed appropriate to address the volatile situation observably surrounding Zimbabwe's land distribution and ownership today. The ethical-moral ideology referred to in the foregoing should be able to properly guide any future land reform in Sub-Saharan Africa. Thus, the above-referred moral thought should be that which is capable of fostering the concept of peace-building which happens to suffuse the conceptual framework within which this chapter is grounded.

Conceptual Framework

This chapter is conceptualised within the framework of 'reconciliation in the context of land distribution and possession' because the land question is fundamentally perceived to be the genesis of disharmony in postcolonial Sub-Saharan Africa in general and Zimbabwe in particular. According to Hapanyengwi-Chemhuru (2013), land reform in postcolonial Zimbabwe was consistent with the dispossession of European settlers without redress because, in the eyes of the Africans, the European settler farmers had unjustly acquired the land during colonial subjugation. Yet, these European settler farmers claim that they owned the land by right of conquest. This state of affairs precipitated adversarial relations between the affected former European settler farmers and the Africans whom these former European settler farmers perceive to have had unlawfully grabbed 'their' land. It is this *status quo* which calls for peace building through reconciliation (Okoro 2010: 141), an ideal endorsed by Hapanyengwi-Chemhuru and Shizha (2012) where they underscore that the concept of reconciliation is in close propinquity with peace building.

The character of land reform in any African country where it is undertaken could be a potential source of conflict and war. Hence, "peace building addresses the root cause of conflict to stave off a notion of war" (Okoro 2010: 140). In the context of this chapter, the potential root cause of conflict to be staved off is Zimbabwe's land reform exercise, which, from a Eurocentric perspective, is perceived to be retributive. The process of peace building is, therefore, "with the aim of laying the basis for sustainable peace in conflict torn societies" (Okoro 2010: 141). Thus, the Zimbabwean society is no exception to the above as it witnesses conflict which revolves around land distribution-redistribution. Hence, the exigency of conflict resolution, reconciliation and peace building is of paramountcy.

According to Hapanyengwi-Chemhuru and Shizha (2012: 17), reconciliation refers to "a process that re-establishes love and understanding between two or more estranged parties … Reconciliation is an overarching process that includes the key instruments of justice, truth, healing, and reparation for moving from a divided past to a shared future." This accentuates a drift from a fractured society to an integrated one. Thus, in the context of land reform, reconciliation duly holds that the wrongs of the past need to be righted. It is further argued in Hapanyengwi-Chemhuru (2013: 81) that, "if reconciliation is to occur, what is important is that the initial cause of conflict must be honestly and earnestly reappraised with a view to finding a genuine solution." Hence, reconciliation should be premised on the truth. Thus, the truth which surrounds the land question in Zimbabwe should be unearthed first. Correspondingly, Hapanyengwi-Chemhuru and Shizha (2012: 17) underline that, "reconciliation involves self-appraisal, negotiation and compromise," connoting that both the conflicting parties require self-introspection, self-evaluation and preparedness to accommodate others' plight. "It [reconciliation] involves getting used to living with each other" (Hapanyengwi-Chemhuru 2013: 81). Thus, reconciliation champions communalism as regards land distribution and ownership meaning that everyone should own land regardless of race, colour, sex or creed.

Hapanyengwi-Chemhuru (2013: 81) concludes that, "Reconciliation therefore seeks to reconnect, to re-establish the harmony disturbed or destroyed by the conflict through arriving at a common understanding." Thus, reconciliation should be restorative as it should seek to restore good human relations. In the context of the current reflection, this restitution should be through a just land redistribution process. "Reconciliation requires cooperation of the parties involved in the creation of a new dispensation acceptable to all" (Hapanyengwi-Chemhuru 2013: 82).

This concurs with Hapanyengwi-Chemhuru and Shizha (2012: 18) where they profess that reconciliation "implies the adoption of a shared vision for a collective destiny." It is, thus, argued that genuine reconciliation is always mutual.

Reconciliation in the context of the land question should be grounded in social justice, truth, empathy and integration-inclusivity and should, therefore, be consistent with the philosophy of *Unhu/Ubuntu*. Hence, Hapanyengwi-Chemhuru and Shizha (2012: 18) decisively highlight that for genuine reconciliation, "there is need for openness about the cause of conflict, clarity about what is at stake and a willingness to work for the benefit of all."

Above all, this reflection is cognisant of the radical sentiments that are dismissive of the reconciliation thesis and the *Unhu/Ubuntu* philosophy—ideals which some myopic and bigoted minds may tend to consider as irrelevant to Zimbabwe's land question. However, the writer undertakes to consistently embrace this moderate conciliatory-reconciliatory stance so that the chapter approaches the issue of land with an open mind which is necessary for achieving a non-prejudiced and dispassionate erudition.

A Historical Perspective

This section stretches from 1894—the year which marks the genesis of land grabbing put into motion by the colonialists as epitomised by the creation of the Gwaai and Shangaan Reserves in Matabeleland, which was consequent upon the Ndebele defeat in the 1893–1894 War of Dispossession. The first phase covers the period 1894–1979, the second phase being the period 1980–1999 and the third phase stretching from 2000 onwards. The term 'land redistribution' is contextually used to refer to "re-arranging or changing land distribution and ownership in Zimbabwe" (Masitera 2016: 4). Thus, it reposes within land reform.

Reporting on the first phase, Masaka (2011: 336) submits that upon the failure of mining fortunes in Zimbabwe, white settlers turned their focus "to agriculture, thereby occasioning serious land alienation as large tracts of land were confiscated from the indigenous black people." This was blatant marginalisation of Africans by colonialists, who, by history, were not the rightful owners of the land between Zambezi and Limpopo. Masaka's submission in the foregoing is endorsed by Masitera (2016: 4) where he states that, "during the colonial period, the Rhodesian agricultural land was divided along racial lines with the white farmers being awarded large tracts of land in arable, high rainfall areas" (Masitera 2016: 4), a distribution of land which was severely and brazenly skewed in favour of the colonialists.

"The Land Tenure Acts of 1930, 1951 and 1969, to mention a few, promoted the division of land along racial lines and the confining of blacks to Tribal Trust Lands" [TTLs] (Masitera 2016: 5). The TTLs were relatively dry, tsetse-ridden, sandy, at times rocky and virtually unproductive. The preceding quote is endorsed by Masitera (2017: 269) where he submits that, "the real intention was to separate and segregate races with the net effect that the settlers or white race get to occupy the best land in areas that also had good rainfall patterns while the other races occupy poor areas." Thus, racism of a Hegelian making was the colonialist's watchword in propagating injustice.

Masitera (2016: 5) also observes that the redistribution of Rhodesian land involved the use of armed force and violence in removing the indigenes from the areas they occupied. The Acts [tenure acts of 1930, 1951 and 1969] in other words supported the abrogation of blacks' rights to land. The use of armed force and violence as well as the violation of Africans' rights were, in themselves, acts and/or practices that were destitute of moral rectitude. Correspondingly, Masitera (2017: 269) writes:

> The colonial government in turn justified the violent land takeovers by issuing title deeds to the settlers. In order to disempower the indigenous people, the colonial government promulgated laws that limited the indigenes' herds of livestock [5 beasts at most] per family.

This is particularly true of the Native Land Husbandry Act of 1951, which compounded the injustice that had already been perpetrated against Africans. This whole business of wanton European land grabbing-acquisition, distribution and ownership was premised on the belief that the land between Zambezi and Limpopo belonged to the British South Africa Company and settlers by right of conquest. This is opposed to the African belief that the land belongs to Zimbabweans as bequeathed to them by their African indigenes and history.

Thus, the outbreak of the Second Chimurenga was not a surprise as Africans sought to "end years of white political and economic subjugation" (Masaka 2011: 336), that is, to end the 'uncouth white settler practices' like land and cattle expropriation, taxation and forced labour.

> The Lancaster House Agreement that ended the war was crafted in such a way that the redistribution of land, the main cause of the war could only effectively take place after ten years of independence. Before then, land could only be secured on a willing seller willing buyer principle. (Hapanyengwi-Chemhuru and Shizha 2012: 18)

The willing buyer/willing seller principle "stipulated that the buyer has to pay full compensation for the farm that was bought" (Masaka 2011: 343).

In view of such a strict legal framework, the writer concludes that the injustice in the distribution of land in Zimbabwe was not addressed at Lancaster. This is endorsed by Masaka (2011: 340) where he submits that the Lancaster House Agreement-Constitution enshrined a lot of sacrifices on the part of the nationalist movements as they were cornered to accept the willing-buyer and willing-seller clause which prevented the independence Government of Zimbabwe to implement a meaningful land reform programme.

Moreover, Masaka (2011: 340) submits that Britain allegedly "failed to respect her commitment as contained in the Lancaster House Constitution to bankroll Zimbabwe's land reform programme" whereas Dzimbanhete (2014: 309) states that it is "the USA which promised to establish a fund that would help Zimbabwe bear the economic burden of compensation for land." The mere fact that neither of the two materialised, thus, denotes that Britain and the USA acted with insincerity. In 1980, the new independence government of Zimbabwe, therefore, inherited some land resource distribution disequilibria. Hence, Hapanyengwi-Chemhuru (2013: 20) argue that, "In Zimbabwe, the land appropriated from the Africans remained with those who had unjustly acquired it during colonial subjugation."

Recounting the second phase, Masitera (2016: 6) submits that, "at the time of independence the Zimbabwean government was committed to the policy of 'reconciliation' and 'economic growth with equity through planned change." This would correspondingly translate to reconciliation in terms of conflict over the land, land distribution and ownership. According to Masitera (2016: 6), between 1980 and 1999 land redistribution was a slow process. Hence, Masaka (2011: 342) argues that the process was dampened by the inception of ESAP which seemed inclined "to predicate land transfers on the willing seller/willing buyer principle." This angered the ordinary Africans, who, in response, championed the sporadic 1997–1999 land invasions which were a precursor to, "the 2000 accelerated land invasions that were championed and led by war veterans" (Masitera 2016: 6). The chapter, thus, argues that this was in a quest for reform and redress on the part of Africans.

The foregoing signals the failure of the policy of reconciliation in Zimbabwe. Correspondingly, Hapanyengwi-Chemhuru and Shizha (2012: 20) argue that in Zimbabwe, Namibia and South Africa it was reconciliation without justice because the policies "prevented an assault on inequality in wealth and income." Justice and *Unhu/Ubuntu* are in close propinquity, hence, the failure of reconciliation in the above-said countries was as a result of the absence of *Unhu/Ubuntu*. Hapanyengwi-Chemhuru and Shizha (2012: 20), thus, argue that, "justice in Zimbabwe required a radical redistribution of land to the previously dispossessed, if reconciliation was to succeed." However, in the writer's opinion, being 'radical' could be outside the framework of the *Unhu/Ubuntu* philosophy.

The sporadic 1997–1999 land invasions preceded the third phase which was characterised by the accelerated people-driven white farm invasions which were later termed the Fast-Track Land Redistribution (Masitera 2016: 7) or the Third Chimurenga (Hapanyengwi-Chemhuru and Shizha 2012: 20). In agreement with Masaka (2011), Masitera (2016: 7) submits that, "the programme was also led by war veterans and then the ZANU PF-led Government supported the initiative." In the writer's opinion, chances are high that the Government had an ulterior motive in hastily supporting the above initiative. Masitera (2016: 7) adds that, "in turn the ZANU PF Government hijacked the programme." This is endorsed by Scoones et al. (2011: 9) where they state that, "Once the official Fast Track Land Reform Programme was launched, officials from the government arrived and imposed an official plan," for development. "Closely linked to this was the fact that the government took this as an opportunity to punish the white farmers who had been supporting the newly formed MDC party" (Masitera 2016: 9).

"The Zimbabwean government, thus, used armed force to confiscate lands [violence and bloodshed ensued] from white farmers by targeting 5–10 million hectares by 2001" (Masitera 2016: 7). The affected farmers were displaced together with their farm workers. Scoones et al. (2011: 6) add that, "farm workers were displaced in large numbers, often ending up destitute, living in camps on the farms. After the invasions, the Constitutional Amendment Act No. 16 of 2000 and Constitutional Amendment No. 17 of 2005 were promulgated to legalise the takeover of these farms" (Masitera 2016: 7).

In the same vein, Masitera (2016: 8) writes:

> Both Zimbabwean courts of law and regional [SADC] tribunals were approached in order to obtain redress and regain possession of redistributed farms. The SADC tribunal judgements were passed in favour of the

farmers as it was found that the programme had violated the rule of law. However, the Zimbabwean government ignored the judgements.

This is contempt of law on the part of the government, which has negative moral implications in the context of *Unhu/Ubuntu*. "The Zimbabwean courts generally considered the resettlements above board since they were done within the parameters of constitutional Amendment Acts Number 16 and 17" (Masitera 2016: 7). It should, however, be considered that the foregoing pieces of legislation were promulgated well after the commencement of the Fast Track Land Reform Programme. Thus they were *ad hoc* edicts decreed in a ploy to legitimise the perceivably unprocedural land grabbing process.

Masaka (2011: 343) submits that, "among the major issues that the GNU is expected to address is the highly contentious land resource distribution disequilibria between the white community and the indigenous people of Zimbabwe." This implies that all the political parties that constituted the GNU were agreed on the irreversibility of land reform and redistribution. However, they were not agreed on the *modus operandi* and to make matters worse "Zimbabwe's land reform still lacks international acceptance … primarily because of its lawless nature and its affront of human and property rights" (Masaka 2011: 344). Thus, reflections bent on coming up with an appropriate ethical-moral ideology become exigent not optional.

In terms of redress, an option which the Government of Zimbabwe had initially put on the table is to have beneficiaries of the controversial land reform programme to pay compensation to the displaced white farmers. To this effect, the Lands and Agriculture Minister Perrance Shiri pronounced that the state would not been burdened with paying compensation, as it was individual resettled farmers that benefitted (Bulawayo24 2018). Should the contents of the foregoing, which are in line with the willing buyer willing seller clause, be implemented then the government would be acting in direct contravention of a commitment that it made earlier—a commitment to compensate the affected former White settler farmers.

Mthuli Ncube, the Finance Minister of Zimbabwe later on fleshed out a compensation plan for the former White settler farmers. According to Bulawayo24 (2019), the Government of Zimbabwe owes USD 9 billion and was now offering RTGS 53 million for the compensation cause.

Though unreasonable a figure, this was a gesture purportedly in the right direction, but it could be interpreted as having been in a desperate hope for the eventual lifting of the economic sanctions imposed by the West on Zimbabwe.

The Philosophy of *Unhu/Ubuntu*: Definition and Derivation of the Term

Hapanyengwi-Chemhuru and Makuvaza (2014: 8) confirm Gelfand's the cardinal virtues of life as the hallmarks of *Unhu/Ubuntu* and these include, "respect for human life, respect for others, human dignity, compassion, an awareness of the needs of others, kindness, courtesy, consideration and friendliness in the relationship between people, a code of behaviour, an appreciative attitude to other people and to life." These principal virtues are, thus, a desideratum for humanness and social cohesion in the Southern African context.

Samkange and Samkange (1980) bring to the fore the word 'personhood' as a befitting synonym of *Unhu/Ubuntu*. To Samkange and Samkange (1980), *Unhu/Ubuntu* is "a philosophy that sets a premium on human relations." Thus, *Unhu/Ubuntu* is a communocentric African epistemology premised on the aphorism, *kunzi munhu vanhu* or *umuntu ngumuntu ngabantu* translated, "a person is a person through other persons" (Hapanyengwi-Chemhuru and Makuvaza 2014: 6). This concurs with Mbiti's (1987: 106) adage, "I am because we are, since we are, therefore I am." Mbiti's adage, thus, mirrors Samkange and Samkange's (1980: 6–7) exaltation of the fundamental Ubuntuist principle of interdependence and mutuality.

Furthermore, Samkange and Samkange (1980) submit that the *Unhu/Ubuntu* philosophy views a human person as more than just a biological being, he/she is a biological being plus something else and that something else is the *soul* [*Unhu/Ubuntu*] which is indefinable yet identifiable. Although Makuvaza (1996) avows that there is no adequate English translation for the term *Unhu/Ubuntu* yet, Ramose (1999) defines *Unhu/Ubuntu* with the use of alternative English words 'humanness' and 'being'. To Ramose (1999: 49), *Unhu/Ubuntu* "is the root of African philosophy ... Ubuntu ... is the wellspring flowing with African ontology and epistemology." The foregoing quote, thus, explains why *Unhu/Ubuntu* is concisely referred to as the African philosophy of life.

Nziramasanga (1999: 62) also proffers that *Unhu/Ubuntu* is a concept that denotes a good human being, well behaved and morally upright person, characterised by qualities such as responsibility, honesty, justice, trustworthiness, hardwork, integrity, a co-operative spirit, solidarity, hospitality, devotion to family and the welfare of the community. This conceptualisation of *Unhu/Ubuntu* concurs with Gelfand's cardinal virtues of life that seem to define humanness from an African perspective. Correspondingly, Venter (2004: 156) submits that, "Ubuntu is a concrete manifestation of the inter-connectedness of human beings—it is the embodiment of African culture and lifestyle." Thus, *Unhu/Ubuntu* is a philosophy which promotes the common good of society, communitarianism, Africanness, humanness and altruism.

Manda (2009) argues that the term *Unhu/Ubuntu* is a hyphenated word [U+nhu/Ubu+ntu] not an 'ism' [*Hunhuism/Ubuntuism*] as Samkange and Samkange (1980) purport. Okoro (2010) also submits that the word *Ubuntu* was coined by Paul Kagame of Rwanda, whilst the term is also thought to have originated from among the Nguni, particularly the Zulu and the Xhosa (Tirivangana 2013). Among the Shona, the word *Ubuntu* is pronounced as *Unhu*. To Hapanyengwi (2011: 19), in U+nhu/Ubu+ntu, U/Ubu serves a qualitative or quantitative denotation whilst nhu/ntu evokes the idea of 'being' in general.

According to Hapanyengwi-Chemhuru and Shizha (2012: 22), "the philosophy of *Hunhu/Ubuntu* is attractive for the values it extols such as love for one another, respect for each other, brotherhood, and respect for the sacredness of human life." This philosophy, thus, cherishes the virtues, values and humane attributes that are of global relevance. To Hapanyengwi-Chemhuru and Makuvaza (2014: 8), *Unhu/Ubuntu* is the enshrinement of ethics and morality, *inter-alia*, in the Southern African context.

Tirivangana (2013) opts to define *Unhu/Ubuntu* as the cornerstone of African values and humanism. This is endorsed by Hapanyengwi-Chemhuru et al. (2016: 106) where they state that "the development of the self involves that assimilation of the values and norms which result in the acquisition of *hunhu*." Thus, as a humanistic school of thought, *Unhu/Ubuntu* is against all forms of inhumane and wayward behaviour. According to Samkange and Samkange (1980), it is this *Unhu/Ubuntu* which makes the Shona upon seeing an African and a Westerner walking together comment '*munhu ari kufamba nemurungu*', literally meaning 'a human being is walking side by side with a Westerner'. This depicts the fact that the Westerner does not possess *Unhu/Ubuntu*, does not subscribe to the philosophy of *Unhu/Ubuntu* and hence cannot be described as '*munhu*'. *Unhu/Ubuntu*, thus, "reflects a fuller realisation of being" (Hapanyengwi-Chemhuru et al. 2016: 106), in the Southern African context, of course.

Above all, "*Unhu/Ubuntu* forces us to come to terms with the fact that whether we are African, European, or Shona or Ndebele … we are all human beings]. We all need to live together" (Hapanyengwi-Chemhuru and Shizha 2012: 22). *Unhu/Ubuntu* is, thus, a philosophy whichvehemently detests ethnic-racial prejudice and discrimination.

Unhu/Ubuntu with a Religious Dimension

"Ubuntu usually has a strong religious meaning" (Manda 2009: para. 9). This religious dimension is amplified by Hapanyengwi-Chemhuru et al. (2016: 106) where they describe *Unhu/Ubuntu* as "a unifying vision or worldview which serves as the spiritual foundation of African societies." *Unhu/Ubuntu* is, thus, a philosophy which has a strong moral-religious grounding, hence, it should inform land reform in Sub-Saharan Africa, where being human should be conceived of as a God-given status. Therefore, in the context of *Unhu/Ubuntu*, every human being should benefit from the land resource regardless of race, colour, sex or creed.

Unhu/Ubuntu with an Epistemological Dimension

Venter (2004: 156) expresses this epistemological facet of *Unhu/Ubuntu* as follows, "in an African context, it is very important to gain knowledge by listening to your fellow human beings." *Unhu/Ubuntu*, thus, calls upon individuals to render to each other a listening ear because receptiveness and good neighbourness are a recipe for progress in the society. In the context of this chapter, the Government of Zimbabwe must have paid heed to the SADC Tribunal ruling that the Fast Track Land Reform programme had violated the rule of law, despite the fact that this ruling was in favour of the former White farmers.

Unhu/Ubuntu with a Political Dimension

Unhu/Ubuntu stresses unity, reconciliation [for instance, between Africans and former Western colonisers in Sub-Saharan Africa], democracy, citizenship, partnership, equity and inter-sectorial collaboration (Manda 2009; Nabudere 2005), which are largely political concepts. Hence, this chapter has vested interest in *Unhu/Ubuntu* as a philosophy which stresses reconciliation especially in the context of addressing the land resource distribution disequilibria. Correspondingly, Waghid (2013: 431) proclaims that, "as a politico-ideological concept, *Unhu/Ubuntu* is a practice of communal sharing encouraged by peace, social harmony and socio-political consensus." *Unhu/Ubuntu*, thus, accentuates communal sharing of the land resource which constitutes the substratum of the political economy of Africa South of Sahara.

Unhu/Ubuntu with a Social Dimension

This dimension seeks to revolutionise the concept of 'individuality'. Hence, the Cartesian [coined after Rene Descartes] mind's conception of individuality has to transform "from solitary to solidarity, from independence to interdependence, from individuality *vis-à-vis* community to individuality *à la* community" (Manda 2009: para. 29). *Unhu/Ubuntu*, thus, places emphasis on the individual in solidarity rather than the individual in solitary. Implicit here is the fact that an individual should live and work for his/her own good and for the good of the community. This is endorsed by Hapanyengwi-Chemhuru et al. (2016: 109) where they argue that, "the focus of *hunhu* is on the welfare of the community and the person as an organic component of the community. Indeed, this emphasis on groupness, sameness and commonality is characteristic of many African communities."

The foregoing concurs with Sibanda (2014: 27) where he proclaims that the philosophy of *Unhu/Ubuntu* is conceived and comprehended in communalistic terms. The communal-orientedness of the philosophy in question is affirmed by Hapanyengwi-Chemhuru and Makuvaza (2014: 8) where they submit that, "*Hunhu* emphasizes dialogue among people for the edification of the community." Emphasis on dialogue, thus, implicitly stresses the amicable addressing of the land resource distribution disequilibria for the benefit of all people regardless of race, colour, sex or creed.

Critiquing the Philosophy of *Unhu/Ubuntu*: The Debates

At a continental level, Nabudere (2005: 1) argues that, "it does not follow that all the African people propagate or are even consciously aware of the philosophy [of *Ubuntu*] as such." This implies that *Unhu/Ubuntu* is not a philosophy of continent-wide recognition. "Indeed, some of those who are aware of it sometimes dismiss it as a post-colonial 'Utopia' invention and/or a 'prophetic' illusion crafted by the African political elites in the age of globalisation" (Nabudere 2005: 1). Thus, other African societies question the authenticity and genuineness of the *Unhu/Ubuntu* philosophy.

Hence, Nabudere (2005: 1) submits that, "some of the cynics even question the philosophy on the grounds that, at best, it is a 'Bantu' philosophy not related to the ways of life and outlook of other 'tribal' groupings of Africa." Implicit here is the notion that *Unhu/Ubuntu* is peculiarly a Southern [Bantu] African philosophy. On the contrary, Professor Cheick Anta Diop of Senegal, cited in Nabudere (2005: 2):

> has traced the generic term for man or *ntu*, to be the same on other African languages with similar term *nit* in Wolf, *nti* in Egyptian, *neddo* in Peul. He argues that the designation of a people by a generic term meaning man has been general throughout Black Africa, starting with Egypt.

This, thus, suggests that the *Unhu/Ubuntu* philosophy is of continental relevance and applicability.

At a regional level, the philosophy of *Unhu/Ubuntu* is also under severe criticism for its failure to abate upheavals in Sub-Saharan Africa where this philosophy is claimed to be the torchlight of life. According to Manda (2009), this finds testimony, for instance, in Rwanda where there are people who are relatively conversant with the philosophy of *Unhu/Ubuntu* yet they allowed the genocide to occur. Therefore, *Unhu/Ubuntu* may not be a panacea to the socio-political challenges vexing Sub-Saharan Africa. However, the outbreak of the above-referred Rwandan Genocide was not solely consequent upon the shortcomings of *Unhu/Ubuntu* as a philosophy. The carnage is also blamed on the foreign hand since the Belgians, the World Bank and the French are, for their respective reasons, known to have had a hand in igniting the genocide in 1994 (Monnier 2010).

At a local level, Hapanyengwi-Chemhuru and Makuvaza (2014: 8) cite Louw where he argues that *Unhu/Ubuntu* "has a potential dark side in terms of which it demands an oppressive conformity and loyalty to the group." However, Hapanyengwi-Chemhuru and Makuvaza (2014: 8) declare that this line of argument is mendacious because tolerance is a virtue cherished in *Unhu/Ubuntu*, hence, they submit that, "*Unhu/Ubuntu* enjoins us to have respect for particularity, individuality and historicality which goes against oppressive conformity." This is endorsed by Shutte, cited in Hapanyengwi-Chemhuru and Makuvaza (2014: 7), where she argues that, "in *hunhu*, the community is not opposed to the individual, nor does it simply swallow the individual up, it enables each individual to become a unique centre of shared life."

While the concept of *Unhu/Ubuntu* "sounds easily attainable at surface level, its identificability and definability may not be as easy. This is due to lack of laid down standards or parameters for its enculturation" (Sibanda 2014: 27). Hence, the concept of *Unhu/Ubuntu* has remained a paradox to the younger generations (Sibanda 2014: 27). Sibanda (2014: 27) also "complains of the vagueness and mystification of traditional African belief representations." This alleged vagueness renders *Unhu/Ubuntu* a mystery if not a fictitious philosophy especially to the youths of today.

Correspondingly, Sibanda (2014: 27) argues that *Unhu/Ubuntu* is difficult to measure because of the obscurities that surround its definition.

However, the foregoing deliberations do not suggest denial of the centrality as well as credibility of *Unhu/Ubuntu* to the cultural philosophy of Zimbabwe. This is because *Unhu/Ubuntu* remains the African philosophy of life and the cornerstone of African values, which, in itself, is an edification of the ethical-moral ideology deemed appropriate to properly guide land distribution and ownership in Sub-Saharan Africa in general and Zimbabwe in particular.

Zimbabwe's Land Reform in Conformity with the Principles of *Unhu/Ubuntu*

The nationalist ideological thesis—the school of thought which consistently glorifies the underlying ethos of the liberation struggle—holds that Zimbabwe's land redistribution regime unfolded in accordance with the principles of the *Unhu/Ubuntu* philosophy. This is because the nationalist ideological argument magnifies and amplifies the assertion that during colonialism the Europeans unjustly grabbed land in Zimbabwe which the Africans had rightfully owned since great antiquity.

According to John Stuart Mill, cited in Masaka (2011: 335), the philosophy of utilitarianism submits that, "actions are right in proportion as they tend to promote happiness, wrong as they tend to produce the reverse of happiness." This is happiness to the majority of people affected by the given action. Hence, from a utilitarian perspective, "Zimbabwe's land reform programme can be rationalized as ethically appropriate because of its utility to the generality of Zimbabwe, who, by historical misfortune, find themselves crowded in inhabitable and agriculturally unproductive parts of Zimbabwe" (Masaka 2011: 335). Zimbabwe's land reform programme can, thus, be viewed as having had been utilitarian and in conformity with the dictates of the humanistic *Unhu/Ubuntu* philosophy because the programme is being claimed to have had been in the interests of the 'landless' majority of Zimbabweans.

In an attempt to answer the question: Who got the land and what is the profile of new settlers? Scoones et al. (2011: 6) mention that, "the majority of new settlers are ordinary people; from both surrounding communal areas and urban areas." The same source adds that some are civil servants [teachers, agricultural extension workers and local government workers], security service personnel and former farm workers. "Across all these categories are war veterans" (Scoones et al. 2011: 6). It can, thus, be argued that a redistribution of this nature which cuts across the population strata is perceivably equitable and inclusive.

According to Msila (2009), equity and fairness are social justice principles which are in close propinquity with the philosophy of *Unhu/Ubuntu*. Inclusivity, as a measure to take on board the marginalised, is an ideal which is also in congruency with the humanistic-communalistic principles of *Unhu/Ubuntu*. It could, therefore, be argued that Zimbabwe's land redistribution process was undertaken within the ethical confines of the philosophy of *Unhu/Ubuntu*.

Zimbabwe's Land Reform in Violation of the Principles of *Unhu/Ubuntu*

From a primeval and pristine ethno-philosophical viewpoint, Zimbabwe's land reform programme is perceived as having been undertaken in flagrant contravention of *Unhu/Ubuntu* as conceptualised in its prehistoric sense. Hence, Masaka (2011: 334) writes:

> The forcible recovery of land ... was ... also a retributive stance towards a group of people that had earlier dispossessed Africans of their land resource in a violent and insensitive manner.

Thus, if an act is said to be 'retributive' and 'forcible' it means it is incompatible with the dictates of *Unhu/Ubuntu* because this African philosophy of life extols restoration-restitution and dialogue not the use of force which is usually accompanied with violence. Although the European settlers are said to have had initially taken African land by force, in the context of *Unhu/Ubuntu* a sin should not be addressed by another sin

[*Hatidzoreri chivi nechivi*]. The retributive stance taken by the indigenous people of Zimbabwe, as articulated above, is at divergence with restorative-restitutive justice which is accentuated by the pristine *Unhu/Ubuntu* philosophy.

Considering the tone in which the Fast Track Land Reform Programme codenamed the Third Chimurenga was executed as from 2000, one would note that it was dehumanisation and brutalisation of European settler farmers. This is because there was untold suffering for the evicted European settler farmers whose property was destroyed or impounded. This is human rights infringement which is inconsistent with the *Unhu/Ubuntu* philosophy. Moreover, European settler formers were given unreasonably short notices, for instance, 48 hours to vacate the farms, which was by any standards a tall order. To make matters worse, it was eviction without compensation. According to Masaka (2011: 344), former European settlers need to be adequately compensated for their land that would have been taken away for redistribution "because not all white farmers in Zimbabwe were inheritors of stolen land. Quite a number of white farmers bought these farms using their personal savings." Hence, it becomes an indictment of the Government of Zimbabwe "to ignore the need to fully compensate those farmers who invested their monies in the Zimbabwe's farmlands, who have no traceable colonial connections" (Masaka 2011: 344). Acts of violence perpetrated largely by war veterans in connivance with the ruling party characterised the entire land redistribution process. All this constitutes retributive not restorative justice and hence it is inconsistent with the dictates of *Unhu/Ubuntu*.

Commenting on the resettled new farmers, Scoones et al. (2011: 5) exclaim that, "as has been widely reported, there are some who made it only through patronage. These are the so-called 'cronies' of the party, well connected to the machinery of the state and able to gain advantage." Scoones et al. (2011: 6) add that, it is recurrently reported that, "all the land went to 'Mugabe's' cronies; those with access to elite connections and benefitting from political patronage." Notwithstanding the fact that the use of the word 'all' sounds polemic, the claim that land went to Mugabe's cronies seems to be sound, strong and logical. Scoones et al. (2011: 6) testify this viewpoint where they state that, "this did, of course, happen, and continues to do so." This brazen partisanship is sheer manifestation of corruption which is abhorred by the *Unhu/Ubuntu* philosophy. Politics of patronage which subsumes partisan favouritism, therefore, constitutes corruption at a party-government level, a situation, which, in itself, is antithetical to the principles of *Unhu/Ubuntu*.

As has been hinted earlier, the Government of Zimbabwe led by ZANU PF seems to have highjacked the land redistribution initiative with an ulterior motive, that of seeking to punish the White farmers who had been supporting the newly formed MDC party (Masitera 2016: 9). This, in itself, is vivid manifestation of retributive justice which is vividly adversative to the *Unhu/Ubuntu* philosophy because this philosophy exalts restorative-restitutive justice. Furthermore, punishing a certain group of people for having supported a political party of their choice is, in itself, being very undemocratic. This, again, is in sharp conflict with the democratic principles of *Unhu/Ubuntu*. Zimbabwe's land redistribution, thus, seems to have offered itself for favouritism whereby the ruling ZANU PF party sought to harness it in order to obtain other political benefits like votes. This is affirmed by Masaka (2011: 342) where he argues that "ZANU PF used it as a political tool to bolster its waning fortunes during and after the 2000 plebiscites." Hence, Zimbabwe's land reform programme got derailed as it got bedevilled by favouritism and vote-buying which turn out to be direct manifestations of wrongdoing, vice and unfairness—phenomena highly abhorred by the pristine *Unhu/Ubuntu* philosophy.

In critiquing the utilitarian thesis advanced earlier, Masaka (2011: 335) argues that:

> Even though Zimbabwe's land reform programme has, in the short run, proved to be a panacea to arable and productive land hunger among the generality of Black Zimbabweans, in the long-run, it has brought less utility to the greatest number of people affected by it primarily because it has caused lawlessness in Zimbabwe's body politic ... and heightened state fragility.

This lawlessness is perceived in the violent and haphazard invasions of European settler farms characteristic of the Fast Track Land Redistribution regime. The haphazardness of this exercise is confirmed by Masaka (2011: 336) where he states that, "a chaotic land redistribution exercise took place," as from year 2000. Masaka (2011: 338) even refers to the Fast Track Land Redistribution regime as, "the chaotic agrarian reforms in Zimbabwe." Furthermore, the Government acted irresponsibly by blessing such lawlessness, a *status quo* which is incompatible with *Unhu/Ubuntu*—a philosophy which exalts responsibility and obedience to the laws of the land [citizenship].

Masaka (2011: 340) further argues in the context of the Third Chimurenga that, "although redressing land imbalances in Zimbabwe was morally justified, the means of executing it … took a racial dimension." Hence, it is this racial dimension which renders the Fast Track Land Redistribution programme discordant with the philosophical principles of *Unhu/Ubuntu*. This is because *Unhu/Ubuntu* is a communalistic-humanistic philosophy which apotheosises the oneness and happiness of humanity, connoting that it detests racial discrimination.

Masaka (2011: 341) also observes that through this chaotic Fast Track Land Redistribution programme:

> There has been an increase in cases of political interferences in local environmental government, invasion of protected forests and state lands that have severely undermined the otherwise successful natural resource management initiatives like CAMPFIRE.

The above *status quo* whereby individuals—masquerading as representatives of the central government—undermine or usurp the powers vested in the local government constitutes brazen totalitarianism which militates against democratic principles. This translates to militancy against *Unhu/Ubuntu*, a philosophy, which, in itself, exalts democracy. Protected forests and state lands are communal property which is not individually owned. Hence, communal property should be under good stewardship by the local community, an arrangement which is in line with the *Unhu/Ubuntu* philosophy. Thus, the invasion of protected forests and state lands for individual benefit was and still is adversative to *Unhu/Ubuntu*.

"Those who led the land invasions were often able to secure land in the A1 self-contained plots, but many were side-lined in the allocation of larger A2 farms" (Scoones et al. 2011: 7). This is manifestation of greed and egoistic tendencies on the part of the senior party and government officials who presided over the allocation of farms. The above is substantiated by Scoones et al. (2011: 7) where they argue that, "some senior officials often linked to the security services, were able to gain access to land, often by influencing allocations following the land invasions." This made it possible for some gluttonous individuals to grab numerous farms which they were and still are not even able to put to full utility. Such a scenario where a clique benefits at the expense of the rest is quite antithetical to the communalistic-communitarian principle of equitable sharing as enshrined in the philosophy of *Unhu/Ubuntu*. The undue influence by the officials in question boils down to corruption, a phenomenon which *Unhu/Ubuntu* strongly detests. Moreover, the fact that the land redistribution process manifested in the form of 'land invasions' automatically follows that it was unlawful, a dispensation which is also incompatible with the philosophy of *Unhu/Ubuntu*.

Scoones et al. (2011: 7) also write, "Land was allocated unevenly to men and women. In most cases it is men whose names appear on the offer letters by the government ... Across our sample only 12% of households had a woman named as the landholder on the permit." This is flagrant violation of gender equity, a topical social justice theory which suffuses national and international discourse today. Although it is a contemporary social justice theory, gender equity is also entrenched in *Unhu/Ubuntu*, a philosophy which is against gender inequity and insensitivity (Eklund 2008: 21). Thus, by infringing gender equity, land redistribution deviated from the philosophical principles of *Unhu/Ubuntu* in Zimbabwe.

Considering the epistemological position of the *Unhu/Ubuntu* philosophy, it could be noted that the Government of Zimbabwe acted in discordance with the dictates of *Unhu/Ubuntu* because it ignored the SADC Tribunal judgement which had ruled in favour of the former White farmers after this Tribunal had discovered that the Fast Track Land Reform programme had violated the rule of law. Even though this SADC Tribunal judgement was in favour of the former White farmers, the Government of Zimbabwe was supposed to pay heed to it.

An Appropriate Ethical-Moral Ideology

Within the discourse towards proffering the ethical-moral thought deemed appropriate for future land reform in the region in question, Waghid (2013: 431) submits that:

> As a politico-ideological concept, *Unhu/Ubuntu* seems to be the only option capable of resolving the political and social problems on the African continent because the practice does not favour one ethnic community [micro-nation] over another, but rather advocates that sharing power and resources more equitably can produce lasting peace and the opportunity to utilise resources [specifically oil, land and water] for the benefit of all Africans. It is *Unhu/Ubuntu* that Africans need to draw upon to enable diverse ethnic communities to reconcile.

The foregoing quote, therefore, stresses the envisaged centrality of *Unhu/Ubuntu* as a philosophy informing peace-building and reconciliation within the context of land redistribution. *Unhu/Ubuntu*, thus, exalts the equitable and peaceful redistribution of land in the Sub-Saharan region.

"Predicated on the Afrocentric theory and utilitarianism," Masaka's (2011: 344) paper "argued a case for an orderly redistribution of Zimbabwe's land resource in order to effect sustainable development of Zimbabwe's agricultural sector." This chapter, consequently, advocates for organised land reform programmes in Sub-Saharan countries premised on true reconciliation, which, in itself, is based on truth and justice. According to Hapanyengwi-Chemhuru (2013: 97), reconciliation "has to be informed by the philosophy of *Hunhu/Ubuntu* which has the potential to foster humane relations among Zimbabweans," and even among all peoples in Sub-Saharan Africa. This will, in the long-run, build sustainable peace in Sub-Saharan Africa.

Regional and national deliberations to achieve restorative justice in the context of land distribution and ownership should be embarked on with a view to restoring fairness, equality and equity in a non-punitive fashion since these are the ideals that are constitutive of the philosophy of *Unhu/Ubuntu*. Thus, the spirit of reconciliation as embedded in *Unhu/Ubuntu* should be the torchlight of land reform in Sub-Saharan Africa.

"A focus on rights needs not emphasise only individual private property rights, while an advocacy of redistribution must also accept appropriate compensation for those who lost out" (Scoones et al. 2011: 17). The first part of the foregoing quote calls on the human rights agenda to also focus on land as communal public property whilst the latter part emphasises the notion of being restorative-restitutive rather than being retributive. The foregoing, thus, lays emphasis on communalism and reconciliation, ideals embedded in the philosophy of *Unhu/Ubuntu* as well. Thus, everyone regardless of race should equitably benefit from land and emphasis should be placed on the need for redress where it is due.

Masitera (2017: 281) proffers the communal approach to land redistribution, proposes fresh land reform, stresses dialogue and advocates that all should benefit and that land redistribution be guided by views of the people. This is consistent with the communalistic-communitarian and democratic orientations of *Unhu/Ubuntu*, a humanistic philosophy which extols the oneness and happiness of humanity.

The 'notion of dialogue' as proclaimed by Masitera (2017), thus, calls for the court system which he also refers to as *Indaba/Matare*. Hence, Masitera (2017: 282) impresses upon the understanding that through the *Indaba/Matare* system, "the therapeutic and corrective aspect of *Unhu* philosophy becomes apparent." This court system, thus, has underpinnings from the philosophy of *Unhu/Ubuntu*. The court system lays great emphasis on "discussions that focus on settling ownership and compensation contentions" (Masitera 2017). Thus, the *Indaba/Matare* system exalts dialogue rather than the use of violence and armed force in addressing land redistribution concerns. This court system could, therefore, be instrumental in reconciling the contesting parties, ironing out inequalities, correcting injustices and compensating those who deserve so that there is a new beginning. Above all, Masitera (2017) stresses participation by all in the *Indaba/Matare* system of discussions to ensure transparency and genuine reconciliation.

Unhu/Ubuntu, as the suggested ethical-moral ideology, concurs with Hapanyengwi-Chemhuru and Shizha's (2012: 22) proclamation that, "we must promote the transition from a culture of imposition, force, violence and war to a culture of dialogue, conciliation, alliance, understanding and peace in human relations." Thus, emphasis should be placed on land reform practices that foster the oneness of humanity as enshrined in *Unhu/Ubuntu*.

Conclusion

The foregoing reflection largely demonstrates that land reform in Zimbabwe, though initially a worthwhile initiative, offered itself for favouritism whereby it got unduly and unscrupulously harnessed by other individuals and political parties for political expediency. Thus, it principally got derailed by politics of patronage and gluttonous elements bent on profiteering. This chapter, therefore, rationalises that *Unhu/ Ubuntu* is the most viable option for adoption as the ethical-moral ideology deemed germane framework to guide any future land reform in Sub-Saharan Africa since this philosophy is in close propinquity with the ideals of reconciliation and peace-building.

References

Bulawayo News24 Online Community. 2018. Zimbabwe Has No Capacity to Compensate Displaced White Farmers. Accessed November 27, 2018. https://bulawayo24.com.

———. 2019. Mthuli Ncube to Flesh Out Compensation Plan for White Farmers Ahead of US Trip. Accessed April 6, 2019. https://bulawayo24.com.

Dzimbanhete, J.A. 2014. *Zimbabwe's Fight for Independence: Aspects of ZANLA's Guerrilla War*. Gweru: Booklove Publishers.

Eklund, H. 2008. *Ubuntu: An Analysis of the Political Rhetoric of a Traditional Concept in Contemporary South Africa*, School of Culture and Media, Hogskolan Dalarna.

Hapanyengwi, O. 2011. Benefactors or Collaborators: An African Perspective of Missionary Provision of Education in Zimbabwe, Unpublished Doctoral Thesis. Harare: University of Zimbabwe.

Hapanyengwi-Chemhuru, S. 2013. Reconciliation, Conciliation, Integration and National Healing: Possibilities and Challenges in Zimbabwe. *African Journal on Conflict Resolution* 13 (1): 79–99.

Hapanyengwi-Chemhuru, O., and N. Makuvaza. 2014. *Hunhu*: In Search of an Indigenous Philosophy for the Zimbabwean Education System. *Journal of Indigenous Social Development* 3 (1): 1–15.

Hapanyengwi-Chemhuru, O., and E. Shizha. 2012. *Unhu/Ubuntu* and Education for Reconciliation in Zimbabwe. *Journal of Contemporary Issues in Education* 7 (2): 16–27.

Hapanyengwi-Chemhuru, O., N. Makuvaza, and J. Mutasa. 2016. *Hunhu*: Making Human Rights Education Discourse Relevant. *Africology: The Journal of Pan-African Studies* 9 (2), 100–115.

Makuvaza, N. 1996. Educatedness in an African Context: The Case for Education Hunhuism /Ubuntuism in Zimbabwe. *The Bulletin of Teacher Education* 4 (3): 89–100.

Manda, D.S. 2009. Ubuntu Philosophy as an African Philosophy for Peace. Accessed April 15, 2016. www.africafiles.org/article/asp?ID=20359.

Masaka, D. 2011. Zimbabwe's Land Contestations and Her Politico-Economic Crises: A Philosophical Dialogue. *Journal of Sustainable Development in Africa* 13 (1): 331–347.

Masitera, E. 2016. *A Critical Analysis of Distributive Justice in Zimbabwe Land Redistribution: Making Use of the Capability Approach and Entitlement Theory to Formulate a Land Based Compromise*. Unpublished Doctoral Thesis, University of Pretoria, Pretoria.

———. 2017. Dilemmas and Controversies Surrounding the Land Debacle in Zimbabwe: Appropriating Some Ideas from the Shona Unhu [Ubuntu] Justice. In *The African Conundrum: Rethinking the Trajectories of Historical, Cultural, Philosophical and Developmental Experiences of Africa*, ed. M. Mawere, T.R. Mubaya, and J. Mukusha, 267–286. Bamenda: RPCIG.

Mbiti, J. S. 1987. *African Religions and Philosophy*. 2nd ed. London: Heinemann.

Monnier, C. 2010. Globalising Cultures: The Question of Cultural Diversity. Accessed https://globalsociology.pbworks.com/w/page/14711190.

Msila, V. 2009. Africanisation of Education and the Search for Relevance and Context. *Educational Research and Review 4* (6): 310–315.

Nabudere, D. 2005. *Ubuntu Philosophy: Memory and Reconciliation*. Texas: Texas Scholarworks.

Nziramasanga, C.T. 1999. *Report of the Presidential Commission of Inquiry into Education and Training*. Harare: Government Printers.

Okoro, K. 2010. African Traditional Education: A Viable Alternative for Peace Building Process in Modern Africa. *Journal of Alternative Perspectives in the Social Sciences* 2 (1): 136–159.

Ramose, M.B. 1999. *African Philosophy through Ubuntu*. Harare: Mond Books.

Samkange, T.M., and S. Samkange. 1980. *Hunhuism or Ubuntuism: A Zimbabwean Indigenous Political Philosophy*. Salisbury: Graham Publishing.

Scoones, I., N. Marongwe, B. Mavedzenge, F. Murimbarimba, J. Mahenehene, and C. Sukume. 2011. *Zimbabwe's Land Reform: A Summary of Findings*. Brighton: IDS.

Sibanda, P. 2014. The Dimensions of 'Hunhu/Ubuntu' (Humanism in the African Sense): The Zimbabwean Conception. *IOSR Journal of Engineering (IOSRJEN) 4* (1): 26–29.

Tirivangana, A.M. 2013. Hunhu/Ubuntu as the Cornerstone of African Education. *The Patriot*. Accessed April 15, 2016. www.thepatriot.co.zw/old_posts/hunhuubuntu-as-the-cornerstone-of-african-education.

Venter, E. 2004. The Notion of *Ubuntu* and Communalism in African Educational Discourse. *Studies in Philosophy and Education* (23), 149–160.

Waghid, Y. 2013. African Philosophy of Education. In *Education Studies: History, Sociology and Philosophy*, ed. K. Horsthemke, P. Siyakwazi, E. Walton, and C. Wolhuter. Oxford: University Press Southern Africa.

Index

E. Masitera (ed.), *Philosophical Perspectives on Land Reform in Southern Africa*,
https://doi.org/10.1007/978-3-030-49705-7

N

O

P

R

V

W

Z

The manufacturer's authorised representative in the EU is Springer Nature Customer Service Centre GmbH, Europaplatz 3, 69115 Heidelberg, Germany. If you have any concerns regarding our products, please contact ProductSafety@springernature.com

Printed and bound by CPI Group (UK) Ltd, Croydon, CR0 4YY
05/10/2026
02228125-0012